Introduction to Go Programming

Maxwell Vector

Contents

2

Chapter 1

Package Declaration and File Structure

Structural Overview of a Go Source File

A Go source file represents the fundamental unit in the construction of programs within the Go language. The intrinsic design of such a file is dictated by a strict ordering of elements that enforces clarity and modularity. At the very forefront of this structure lies the declaration of the package to which the file belongs. This opening declaration is not a mere formality but a precise syntactic and semantic assertion that binds all subsequent definitions under a common namespace. Embedded within the file is an implicit commitment to a design philosophy where each file contributes to a larger, cohesive system of modules.

Package Declaration

The package declaration occupies a position of primacy at the beginning of every Go source file. Its placement and form are critical to the integrity of the program's compilation process, as it demarcates the scope in which the various identifiers are defined and later referenced.

1 Formal Syntax and Structural Position

The package clause is consistently the first construct encountered in a source file. This declaration establishes the identity of the collection of source files that are compiled together. It is embedded within the formal grammar of the language, ensuring that every file adheres to a uniform structure. The declaration acts as a header, immediately informing the compiler of the logical boundaries of the code contained within the file. Such precision in placement underscores the deterministic nature of package composition, where the order of declarations is integral to maintaining the semantic integrity of the codebase.

2 Taxonomical Role in Code Organization

Beyond its syntactic necessity, the package declaration serves as a taxonomical tool that groups related code elements into a coherent unit. By assigning a distinct package name, a source file is effectively categorized, thus enabling a structured approach to code reuse and namespace management. This grouping mechanism fosters a disciplined approach to software construction where components are encapsulated within a well-defined scope. The package serves as a repository for types, functions, and variables that share a common purpose, and it facilitates a clear demarcation between public and private identifiers based on the rules of exportation. The hierarchical nature of packages reflects an underlying commitment to modular design and promotes an architecture that is both scalable and maintainable.

Organizational Principles of Go Packages

The organization of Go code into packages is a central tenet of the language's design, emphasizing both logical cohesion and physical file system structure. This paradigm influences how multiple source files interrelate and how code is aggregated into distributable and reusable units.

1 Directory Structure and File Cohesion

In Go, the physical organization of source files is intertwined with the logical compartmentalization provided by packages. Each directory in the file system conventionally corresponds to a single package, thereby aligning physical storage with conceptual grouping. This correspondence ensures that all files declared to belong to a particular package are isolated within a common directory, enhancing coherence and easing navigation of the project structure. Such an arrangement reinforces the principle that related functionalities should reside together, thereby simplifying the management of dependencies and the overall build process.

2   Encapsulation and Modularity

The organizational model adopted by Go is predicated on the notions of encapsulation and modularity. By partitioning code into discrete packages, the language enforces boundaries that limit the exposure of internal implementation details. This compartmentalization allows each package to serve as a self-contained unit that can be developed, tested, and maintained independently. The segregation of internal and external identifiers through controlled export mechanisms contributes to a robust system of abstraction. In this way, the package structure not only organizes the code but also instills a disciplined approach to software engineering that mitigates the complexity inherent in large-scale systems.

Go Code Snippet

```
package main

import (
        "bufio"
        "flag"
        "fmt"
        "log"
        "os"
        "path/filepath"
        "strings"
)

// getPackageName scans a Go source file to extract its package
↪   declaration.
// It returns the package name if found, otherwise an error.
func getPackageName(filePath string) (string, error) {
        file, err := os.Open(filePath)
        if err != nil {
                return "", err
        }
        defer file.Close()
```

```go
        scanner := bufio.NewScanner(file)
        for scanner.Scan() {
                line := strings.TrimSpace(scanner.Text())
                // Ignore empty lines and single-line comments
                if line == "" || strings.HasPrefix(line, "//") {
                        continue
                }
                // Check if the line starts with the "package"
                ↪   keyword
                if strings.HasPrefix(line, "package ") {
                        parts := strings.Fields(line)
                        if len(parts) >= 2 {
                                return parts[1], nil
                        }
                }
        }
        if err := scanner.Err(); err != nil {
                return "", err
        }
        return "", fmt.Errorf("package declaration not found in
        ↪   file: %s", filePath)
}

// main traverses the file system from a given directory and prints
↪   the package
// declaration of every Go source file. This demonstrates how Go
↪   source files
// are organized into packages based on their file structure.
func main() {
        // Define and parse the directory flag (default is the
        ↪   current directory)
        dirPtr := flag.String("dir", ".", "Directory to scan for Go
        ↪   source files")
        flag.Parse()

        // Walk through the directory structure recursively
        err := filepath.Walk(*dirPtr, func(path string, info
        ↪   os.FileInfo, err error) error {
                if err != nil {
                        return err
                }
                // Process only files with .go extension
                if !info.IsDir() && filepath.Ext(path) == ".go" {
                        pkg, err := getPackageName(path)
                        if err != nil {
                                log.Printf("Error processing %s:
                                ↪   %v\n", path, err)
                                return nil
                        }
                        fmt.Printf("File: %s => Package: %s\n",
                        ↪   path, pkg)
                }
```

17

```go
            return nil
    })
    if err != nil {
            log.Fatalf("Error scanning directory: %v", err)
    }
}
```

Chapter 2

Importing Packages in Go

Import Statement Fundamentals

The import mechanism in the Go programming language constitutes a fundamental syntactic construct that enables the integration of independently developed code modules. Central to this mechanism is the import statement, which explicitly declares dependencies on external packages. This directive is formulated with a strict syntactic format that allows a source file to incorporate one or more packages either in a singular ungrouped form or as a consolidated group within a pair of parentheses. Such structural flexibility not only enhances code readability but also reinforces the language's emphasis on modularity and explicit dependency management. The import process is intrinsically tied to the discipline of static analysis, ensuring that all external references are determinable at compile time and that unused or spurious dependencies are detected with precision.

Integration of Standard Library Packages

The standard library furnished with Go comprises a diverse collection of packages that address a broad spectrum of computational needs, spanning from elementary input/output operations to sophisticated network communications. When a package from the

19

standard library is imported, its suite of types, functions, and variables becomes immediately available for utilization within the program's namespace. The semantic consistency of these packages is upheld by a rigorous naming convention and a well-defined hierarchy of exported identifiers. Due to the inherent organization of Go's file system—where each directory conventionally corresponds to a unique package—the inclusion of a standard library package also implies adherence to a predetermined physical structure. This alignment between logical modules and their physical manifestation underpins a deterministic model whereby all referenced identifiers are unambiguously resolved, thereby facilitating both static validation and runtime optimization.

Incorporation of Third-Party Packages

The expansion of a program's functional repertoire beyond the confines of the standard library is achieved through the incorporation of third-party packages. Such packages are developed independently and distributed through repositories that comply with established versioning and dependency management protocols. The import statement, when applied to a third-party package, serves as a declarative means of integrating externally maintained code. This integration process necessitates a sophisticated dependency resolution system that not only retrieves the requisite modules but also ensures compatibility with the existing codebase through precise version control. In contexts where naming conflicts or ambiguities might arise, secondary mechanisms such as aliasing provide additional layers of clarity. The careful orchestration of third-party package imports reinforces an extensible architectural design that is capable of accommodating a broad range of functionalities while maintaining consistency in identifier scope and semantic integrity.

Go Code Snippet

```
package main

import (
        "errors"
        "fmt"
        "math"

        // Example of aliasing a third-party package:
```

20

```go
        // c "github.com/fatih/color"
)

// solveQuadratic computes the roots of the quadratic equation:
//     a*x^2 + b*x + c = 0
// It returns an error if a is zero or if the discriminant is
// ↪   negative.
// The roots are calculated using the well-known formula:
//     x = (-b ± (b^2 - 4ac)) / (2a)
func solveQuadratic(a, b, c float64) (float64, float64, error) {
        if a == 0 {
                return 0, 0, errors.New("coefficient a cannot be
                ↪   zero in a quadratic equation")
        }
        discriminant := b*b - 4*a*c
        if discriminant < 0 {
                return 0, 0, errors.New("discriminant is negative,
                ↪   complex roots not supported")
        }
        sqrtDisc := math.Sqrt(discriminant)
        root1 := (-b + sqrtDisc) / (2 * a)
        root2 := (-b - sqrtDisc) / (2 * a)
        return root1, root2, nil
}

// arithmeticSum calculates the sum of integers from 1 to n using
// ↪   two methods:
// 1. The closed-form arithmetic series formula: n*(n+1)/2.
// 2. An iterative algorithm that accumulates the sum in a loop.
func arithmeticSum(n int) (int, int) {
        formulaSum := n * (n + 1) / 2

        iterativeSum := 0
        for i := 1; i <= n; i++ {
                iterativeSum += i
        }
        return formulaSum, iterativeSum
}

func main() {
        // Demonstration of the quadratic equation solver.
        fmt.Println("Quadratic Equation Solver for equation: 2x^2 +
        ↪   5x - 3 = 0")
        x1, x2, err := solveQuadratic(2, 5, -3)
        if err != nil {
                fmt.Printf("Error: %v\n", err)
        } else {
                fmt.Printf("The roots are: x1 = %.2f, x2 = %.2f\n",
                ↪   x1, x2)
        }

        // Demonstration of the arithmetic sum calculation.
        n := 10
```

21

```go
    formulaSum, iterativeSum := arithmeticSum(n)
    fmt.Printf("\nArithmetic Sum of numbers from 1 to %d:\n", n)
    fmt.Printf("Using formula: %d\n", formulaSum)
    fmt.Printf("Using iteration: %d\n", iterativeSum)

    // Example usage of the math package: computing sine of 90°.
    degrees := 90.0
    radians := degrees * math.Pi / 180
    fmt.Printf("\nSine(%.0f°) = %.2f\n", degrees,
    ↪    math.Sin(radians))

    // Example of integrating a third-party package using
    ↪    aliasing.
    // Uncomment the next line if the package is installed.
    // c.Red("This output would be colored using a third-party
    ↪    package!\n")
}
```

Chapter 3

Comments and Documentation Conventions

Single-Line Comments

The Go programming language provides a succinct mechanism for incorporating annotations into source files through single-line comments. Such comments are introduced by the symbol //, which designates that all text following this token on the same line is to be treated as non-executable. This syntactic construct facilitates brief clarifications, temporary annotations, and inline remarks that isolate specific code segments without interfering with the program's logic. The use of single-line comments is integral to maintaining code legibility and segregating meta-information from operational code, thereby contributing to a clearer understanding of computational intent and structure.

Multi-Line Comments

Complementing the single-line comment construct, Go supports multi-line comments, which are enclosed between the delimiters /* and */. This block-comment mechanism allows for extended expository content that spans several lines, providing a granular level of detail that is impractical to convey in a single-line format. Multi-line comments are particularly effective for annotating complex algorithmic procedures, elucidating design rationales, and temporarily disabling segments of code during analysis or debugging phases. The structural integrity offered by these delimiters ensures that the commentary is isolated from executable code, thus preserving the syntactic hygiene of the source file.

Documentation Conventions

A critical aspect of code quality in the Go ecosystem is the systematic documentation practice embedded within the commenting framework. Documentation serves not only as an auxiliary narrative detailing the logical underpinnings of functions and packages but also as a foundational element in the automated generation of reference materials. In the Go convention, comments that directly precede declarations are utilized to encapsulate comprehensive explanations, including descriptions of functional behavior, parameter semantics, and return value definitions. This approach leverages concise yet descriptive commentary, wherein every annotation is expected to adhere to a standard of clarity and precision. The conventions mandate that commentary should employ consistent grammatical structures, proper sentence construction, and unambiguous phrasing so that the resulting documentation accurately reflects the intended computational model. The self-contained nature of these annotations ensures that the codebase functions as an intelligible document, wherein the embedded documentation is both a resource for static analysis and an aid to long-term maintainability.

Go Code Snippet

```
package main

import (
    "errors"
    "fmt"
    "math"
)

/*
    The following function calculates the roots of a quadratic
    ↪   equation
    using the quadratic formula:
```

```go
        x = (-b ± sqrt(b² - 4ac)) / (2a)
    It demonstrates both error handling for degenerate cases and the
    ↪  use of
    single-line and multi-line comments for clarity.
*/

// CalculateQuadraticRoots calculates and returns the two real roots
↪  of the
// quadratic equation represented by ax² + bx + c = 0. It returns an
↪  error if
// the equation is degenerate (i.e., a == 0) or if the discriminant
↪  is negative,
// which indicates complex roots not handled in this implementation.
func CalculateQuadraticRoots(a, b, c float64) (float64, float64,
↪  error) {
    // Validate that the coefficient 'a' is non-zero for a proper
    ↪  quadratic equation.
    if a == 0 {
        return 0, 0, errors.New("coefficient a cannot be zero; not a
            ↪  quadratic equation")
    }

    // Compute the discriminant as b² - 4ac.
    discriminant := b*b - 4*a*c

    // Check if the discriminant is negative. A negative
    ↪  discriminant means the roots are complex.
    if discriminant < 0 {
        return 0, 0, errors.New("discriminant is negative; the
            ↪  equation has complex roots")
    }

    // Calculate the square root of the discriminant.
    rootDiscriminant := math.Sqrt(discriminant)

    // Compute both roots using the quadratic formula.
    root1 := (-b + rootDiscriminant) / (2 * a) // Positive branch
    ↪  calculation.
    root2 := (-b - rootDiscriminant) / (2 * a) // Negative branch
    ↪  calculation.

    return root1, root2, nil
}

// Factorial calculates the factorial of a non-negative integer n
↪  using recursion.
// It returns 1 for n equal to 0 (the base case), and for any n > 0,
↪  it returns n multiplied
// by the factorial of (n - 1).
func Factorial(n int) int {
    // Base case: the factorial of 0 is defined as 1.
    if n == 0 {
        return 1
```

```go
	}
	// Recursive call to calculate factorial of n.
	return n * Factorial(n-1)
}

func main() {
	// Demonstration of Quadratic Roots Calculation.
	a, b, c := 1.0, -3.0, 2.0
	fmt.Printf("Quadratic Equation: %.1fx² + %.1fx + %.1f = 0\n", a,
	↪ b, c)

	// Calculate the roots of the quadratic equation.
	root1, root2, err := CalculateQuadraticRoots(a, b, c)
	if err != nil {
		// Print error if the roots cannot be calculated.
		fmt.Println("Error:", err)
	} else {
		fmt.Printf("The roots are: %.2f and %.2f\n", root1, root2)
	}

	// Demonstration of Factorial Calculation.
	number := 5
	fact := Factorial(number)
	/*
		The following output displays the factorial of 'number'.
		For instance, 5! is calculated as 5 * 4 * 3 * 2 * 1.
	*/
	fmt.Printf("Factorial of %d is %d\n", number, fact)
}
```

Chapter 4

Basic Data Types Overview

Integer Types

Within the landscape of numerical computation, integer types embody the discrete values fundamental to a multitude of algorithms and data representations. The language encompasses both signed and unsigned integer constructs, each characterized by a fixed bit-width that dictates the range of representable values. Signed integers, implemented via two's complement arithmetic, permit the expression of both negative and positive quantities, while unsigned integers are confined to nonnegative values. These types are parameterized by common bit-widths such as 8-bit, 16-bit, 32-bit, and 64-bit, each ensuring a balance between memory footprint and the granularity of numerical expression. The theoretical underpinnings of these types, derived from number theory and computer architecture, serve as the basis for robust arithmetic operations and form the substrate upon which more complex computational structures are built.

Floating-Point Types

Floating-point types extend the domain of representation to encompass real numbers, introducing a mechanism for approximating continuous values. Their implementation adheres to the IEEE 754 standard, which specifies critical aspects such as precision, rounding methodologies, and the handling of special values including Not-a-Number (NaN) and infinities (∞). The dual precision modes typically available facilitate both high-performance calculations and applications requiring enhanced precision. Inherent challenges such as rounding errors and precision loss are central to the theoretical exploration of floating-point arithmetic, and these phenomena underscore the importance of judicious application in numerical algorithms. The detailed specification of these types provides a rigorous framework for understanding the limitations and strengths of mathematical approximations in computer-based environments.

Boolean Types

Boolean types represent the simplest form of data, embodying the binary states that support logical and relational operations integral to programmatic control structures. This type is restricted to two distinct values, typically denoted as true and false, which serve as the foundational elements in the construction of conditional expressions and decision-making protocols. The binary nature of Boolean logic is rooted in classical logic and set theory, and its implementation in the language ensures unambiguous evaluation of logical expressions. These operations, while ostensibly straightforward, entail significant formal properties that impact both compiler optimizations and the overall correctness of algorithms.

String Types

Strings constitute an ordered sequence of characters drawn from a defined character set, most commonly encoded using the UTF-8 standard. This encoding facilitates a comprehensive representation of text, accommodating a diverse array of linguistic and symbolic elements. In this paradigm, strings are treated as immutable sequences, ensuring that once instantiated, the character sequence remains invariant throughout its lifetime. This immutability enforces a level of consistency and safety, particularly in concurrent execution environments where shared data integrity is paramount. The conceptual model of strings aligns with theoretical constructs in formal language theory and automata, providing a rich foundation for text manipulation, pattern matching, and data encoding operations.

Go Code Snippet

```go
// Comprehensive Go code snippet demonstrating equations, formulas,
↪   and algorithms
// related to the basic data types explored in this chapter.

package main

import (
        "fmt"
        "math"
        "strings"
)

func main() {
        fmt.Println("== Integer Types Demo ==")
        integerDemo()

        fmt.Println("\n== Floating-Point Types Demo ==")
        floatingPointDemo()

        fmt.Println("\n== Boolean Types Demo ==")
        booleanDemo()

        fmt.Println("\n== String Types Demo ==")
        stringDemo()

        fmt.Println("\n== Arithmetic Series Calculation Demo ==")
        arithmeticSeriesDemo(10)

        fmt.Println("\n== Newton's Method for Square Root Demo ==")
        sqrtValue := newtonSqrt(25.0, 1e-10, 100)
        fmt.Printf("Square root of 25 using Newton's method: %f\n",
        ↪   sqrtValue)
}

// integerDemo demonstrates integer operations including displaying
↪   the limits
// of int8 and the two's complement overflow behavior.
func integerDemo() {
        var a int8 = 127   // Maximum positive value for int8
        var b int8 = -128  // Minimum negative value for int8
        fmt.Printf("int8 maximum: %d, int8 minimum: %d\n", a, b)

        // Demonstrate overflow in two's complement arithmetic.
        overflow := int8(a + 1)
        fmt.Printf("Overflow result (127 + 1): %d\n", overflow)
}

// floatingPointDemo illustrates floating-point types, their
↪   precision, and use of special
// IEEE754 values such as NaN and Infinity.
```

29

```go
func floatingPointDemo() {
        var f1 float32 = 3.1415926
        var f2 float64 = 3.141592653589793
        fmt.Printf("float32 value: %.7f\n", f1)
        fmt.Printf("float64 value: %.15f\n", f2)

        // Using math package to demonstrate special floating-point
        ↪   values.
        nanValue := math.NaN()
        infValue := math.Inf(1)
        fmt.Printf("NaN value: %f, is NaN? %t\n", nanValue,
        ↪   math.IsNaN(nanValue))
        fmt.Printf("Infinity value: %f, is Inf? %t\n", infValue,
        ↪   math.IsInf(infValue, 1))
}

// booleanDemo demonstrates the use of boolean types and logical
↪   operators to build
// conditional statements and decision-making expressions.
func booleanDemo() {
        flagTrue := true
        flagFalse := false

        fmt.Printf("Boolean flagTrue: %v, flagFalse: %v\n",
        ↪   flagTrue, flagFalse)
        fmt.Printf("flagTrue AND flagFalse: %v\n", flagTrue &&
        ↪   flagFalse)
        fmt.Printf("flagTrue OR flagFalse: %v\n", flagTrue ||
        ↪   flagFalse)
        fmt.Printf("NOT flagTrue: %v\n", !flagTrue)
}

// stringDemo highlights string manipulation in Go. It shows that
↪   strings are immutable,
// how to perform case conversion, and the correct way to slice
↪   strings.
func stringDemo() {
        original := "hello, "
        fmt.Printf("Original string: %s\n", original)

        // Convert to upper case. Since strings are immutable, a new
        ↪   string is created.
        upperCase := strings.ToUpper(original)
        fmt.Printf("Upper case string: %s\n", upperCase)

        // Extract a substring (slicing may differ for multi-byte
        ↪   characters; here we use a byte slice).
        if len(original) >= 5 {
                substring := original[:5]
                fmt.Printf("Substring (first 5 bytes): %s\n",
                ↪   substring)
        }
}
```

```go
// arithmeticSeriesDemo calculates the sum of the first n natural
↪    numbers using the formula:
// Sum = n(n+1)/2
func arithmeticSeriesDemo(n int) {
        formulaSum := n * (n + 1) / 2

        // Calculate the sum using an iterative loop for
        ↪    verification.
        sumLoop := 0
        for i := 1; i <= n; i++ {
                sumLoop += i
        }

        fmt.Printf("Arithmetic series sum using formula for n=%d:
        ↪    %d\n", n, formulaSum)
        fmt.Printf("Arithmetic series sum using loop for n=%d:
        ↪    %d\n", n, sumLoop)
}

// newtonSqrt computes the square root of a number x using Newton's
↪    method.
// It iterates until the difference between successive
↪    approximations is less than the
// provided tolerance or until the maximum number of iterations is
↪    reached.
func newtonSqrt(x float64, tolerance float64, maxIterations int)
↪    float64 {
        guess := x / 2.0 // Initial guess for the square root.
        for i := 0; i < maxIterations; i++ {
                prevGuess := guess
                guess = (guess + x/guess) / 2.0
                if math.Abs(guess-prevGuess) < tolerance {
                        break
                }
        }
        return guess
}
```

Chapter 5

Variables: Declaration and Initialization

Declaration Using the var Keyword

The explicit declaration of variables in the language is fundamentally achieved through the use of the var keyword. This construct establishes a binding between an identifier and a specific memory location, simultaneously enforcing the declaration of an associated type. When a variable is declared with the var keyword, an explicit type annotation may be provided. In cases where an initializer expression accompanies the declaration, the identifier is immediately associated with a computed value; however, in the absence of such an expression, the variable is automatically assigned a well-defined zero value corresponding to its declared type. This behavior, derived from the formal underpinnings of the type system, guarantees that every variable exists in a state of defined initialization prior to any subsequent manipulation. Furthermore, the syntactic structure supporting the declaration of several variables in a single statement underscores the language's emphasis on precision and clarity in both the developmental and analytical phases of program construction.

The semantics associated with the var keyword are deeply rooted in type theory and static analysis techniques, ensuring that any declared variable adheres to a specific domain of admissible values. Such rigor not only facilitates early detection of type mismatches during compilation but also provides a robust framework for reasoning about variable scope and lifetime. The mechanism for default initialization, which systematically assigns a zero-equivalent value to any variable that is not explicitly initialized, is instrumental in avoiding undefined behavior, thereby serving as a cornerstone for safe and predictable software design.

Shorthand Variable Declarations

An alternative to the explicit declaration via the var keyword is provided by the shorthand syntax. This form of variable declaration, characterized by the operator $:=$, encapsulates both the declaration and initialization processes within a single syntactic construct. In this concise form, the identifier is dynamically bound to the result of an expression, and the compiler deduces the type from the corresponding value. Such type inference is governed by well-defined rules that ensure the deduced type conforms to expectations derived from the expression's context, thereby maintaining strict type safety without the verbosity of explicit type annotations.

This approach to variable declaration is particularly prevalent in situations where clarity and brevity are paramount. The inherent expressiveness of the shorthand notation not only streamlines code but also minimizes the potential for redundancy by obviating the need for reiteration of type information that is already implicit within the initializer. Notably, the application of this notation is confined to local scopes, a restriction that reflects its design as a tool for enhancing readability and reducing extraneous syntax in function bodies and similar localized regions of imperative code.

Initialization Guidelines

The process of initialization occupies an essential role in the lifecycle of a variable as it transitions from a mere declaration to participating in computational logic. Adherence to rigorous initialization guidelines is critical for ensuring that variables embody a consistent and well-defined state from the moment of their creation. The default zero values, as automatically assigned in the absence of an explicit initializer, are defined by the intrinsic characteristics of the variable's type. Such default behavior provides an assurance against uninitialized memory access and contributes to the overall stability and predictability of program execution.

Best practices in variable initialization advocate for the explicit setting of values when the logical requirements of the program demand a state other than the default. This practice not only enhances the semantic clarity of the code but also facilitates the process of formal verification and static analysis by narrowing the range of possible states that a variable may assume at runtime. The choice between utilizing explicit initialization via the var keyword and adopting the shorthand declaration method is influenced by considerations of readability, scope, and the immediacy of the initialization value. In contexts where emphasis on the intrinsic default state is insufficient for program correctness, the deliberate assignment of an initial value serves as a safety net that reinforces the robustness of the subsequent computational processes.

Moreover, the temporal relationship between declaration and initialization is a subject of theoretical interest in the realm of programming language semantics. The guarantee that a variable's value is well-defined immediately after its declaration—either through explicit assignment or automatic defaulting—contributes to a disciplined model of state transitions within a program. This model underlies various compiler optimizations and formal reasoning methods, thereby playing a pivotal role in both the performance and reliability of software systems.

Go Code Snippet

```go
package main

import (
        "fmt"
        "math"
)

func main() {
        // Declaration Using the var Keyword: Explicit declaration
        ↪  with a type annotation.
        // The variable 'explicitInt' is initialized with a value.
        var explicitInt int = 10

        // Declaration without initialization: The variable
        ↪  'explicitFloat'
        // is automatically assigned the zero value for its type
        ↪  (0.0 for float64).
        var explicitFloat float64
```

```go
	fmt.Println("Explicitly declared integer with
	↪   initialization:", explicitInt)
	fmt.Println("Explicitly declared float without
	↪   initialization (zero value):", explicitFloat)

	// Shorthand Variable Declarations: Using := to declare and
	↪   initialize variables.
	// Type inference is applied so that explicit type
	↪   annotation is unnecessary.
	shorthandStr := "Go Programming"
	shorthandFloat := 25.5

	fmt.Println("Shorthand declared string:", shorthandStr)
	fmt.Println("Shorthand declared float:", shorthandFloat)

	// Important Equation: Quadratic Formula
	// Given a quadratic equation in the form: ax² + bx + c = 0,
	// the solutions are computed using the formula:
	// x = (-b ± sqrt(b² - 4ac)) / (2a)
	// Here we demonstrate the algorithm to compute the roots.
	a, b, c := 1.0, -3.0, 2.0
	fmt.Printf("Solving quadratic equation: %vx² + %vx + %v =
	↪   0\n", a, b, c)

	x1, x2, err := solveQuadratic(a, b, c)
	if err != nil {
		fmt.Println("Error:", err)
	} else {
		fmt.Printf("The solutions are: x1 = %v, x2 = %v\n",
		↪   x1, x2)
	}
}

// solveQuadratic calculates the roots of a quadratic equation given
↪   coefficients a, b, and c.
// It returns an error if 'a' is zero or if the discriminant is
↪   negative (i.e., no real solutions).
func solveQuadratic(a, b, c float64) (float64, float64, error) {
	// Ensure coefficient 'a' is not zero to avoid division by
	↪   zero.
	if a == 0 {
		return 0, 0, fmt.Errorf("coefficient 'a' cannot be
		↪   zero")
	}

	// Calculate the discriminant: b² - 4ac.
	discriminant := b*b - 4*a*c

	// If the discriminant is negative, the equation has no real
	↪   solutions.
	if discriminant < 0 {
		return 0, 0, fmt.Errorf("no real solutions
		↪   (discriminant is negative: %v)", discriminant)
```

```go
    }

    // Compute the square root of the discriminant.
    sqrtDiscriminant := math.Sqrt(discriminant)

    // Compute the two solutions using the quadratic formula.
    x1 := (-b + sqrtDiscriminant) / (2 * a)
    x2 := (-b - sqrtDiscriminant) / (2 * a)

    return x1, x2, nil
}
```

Chapter 6

Variable Scope and Shadowing

Lexical Scoping in Go

Within the Go programming language, the concept of variable scope is established by the principles of lexical scoping. Each variable, once declared using constructs such as *var*, is bound to a specific region of the source code that delineates its visibility and lifetime. The boundaries of these regions are determined by the syntactic structure of the program, where compound statements and block delimiters define hierarchical levels of scope. In such a structured environment, every identifier assumes a place in a well-organized symbol table that the compiler consults during static analysis. This approach permits a precise mapping between identifiers and their associated memory locations, thereby ensuring type safety and preventing ambiguities during the evaluation of expressions.

The lexical determination of scope implies that an identifier's binding is resolved based strictly on the location of its declaration. Consequently, the static context in which a variable is introduced governs every subsequent usage of that identifier. This rigorous alignment between declaration and reference not only supports a robust method for formal reasoning about program semantics but also simplifies the task of verifying that a variable always possesses a well-defined value at every point in the program.

Shadowing in Nested Blocks

The phenomenon of shadowing arises when an inner block contains a declaration of an identifier that is identical to one declared in an outer block. In such cases, the inner declaration introduces a new binding that locally obscures the outer declaration within its own lexical region. As a result, all references to the identifier in the inner block are resolved to the locally defined variable, while the binding in the outer block remains intact but temporarily masked. This mechanism is an explicit feature of the language's design, allowing distinct variable instances to coexist in different regions of code even if the same name is re-used.

The implementation of shadowing conforms to the strict rules of lexical scoping. The new binding established in a nested block is active solely within that block and any blocks nested within it. Upon exit from the inner block, the outer binding once again becomes visible. The systematic treatment of shadowing is indispensable for preventing unintended interactions among variables and facilitates a disciplined approach to reusing common identifier names in different contexts. Such shadowing, when employed judiciously, contributes to localizing variable behavior and supports modular reasoning about program segments.

Static Analysis and Formal Considerations

The static analysis of variable scope and shadowing in Go is conducted via the construction of comprehensive symbol tables that reflect the hierarchy of lexical environments present in the source code. Each variable declaration contributes a node to an abstract syntax tree that encapsulates critical semantic information, including type, binding time, and the specific points in the code where the variable is active. When an identifier is re-declared in a subordinate block, the compiler registers a new binding that overrides the existing one in that localized context, an effect that is rigorously governed by the standard rules of lexical scoping.

From a formal perspective, the resolution of identifiers in the presence of shadowing adheres to the substitution model of computation in which the most immediate binding in the lexical chain is substituted during expression evaluation. This ensures that each occurrence of an identifier corresponds unambiguously to a particular declaration. The deployment of such precise substitution rules not only augments the reliability of the language's type-checking process but also enhances the overall consistency of its operational semantics. The interplay between variable scope and shadowing constitutes a critical aspect of Go's semantic framework, underscoring the balance between allowing flexible identifier reuse and maintaining strict control over variable lifetimes.

Go Code Snippet

```go
package main

import (
        "fmt"
)

// Scope represents a lexical scope with a mapping of identifiers to
↪   their integer values.
// Each scope may have a parent scope representing its outer lexical
↪   context.
type Scope struct {
        parent  *Scope
        symbols map[string]int
}

// NewScope creates a new scope, optionally linked to a parent
↪   scope.
func NewScope(parent *Scope) *Scope {
        return &Scope{
                parent:  parent,
                symbols: make(map[string]int),
        }
}

// Define adds a new binding in the current scope for an identifier.
func (s *Scope) Define(name string, value int) {
        s.symbols[name] = value
}

// Resolve searches for an identifier in the current scope.
// If not found, it recursively checks parent scopes, which
↪   simulates the substitution
// model of lexical scoping: the innermost binding is used,
↪   shadowing any outer ones.
func (s *Scope) Resolve(name string) (int, bool) {
        if value, ok := s.symbols[name]; ok {
                return value, true
        }
        if s.parent != nil {
                return s.parent.Resolve(name)
```

```go
        }
        return 0, false
}

// printScope recursively prints the symbols in the given scope and
// ↪  all enclosing scopes.
func printScope(s *Scope, level int) {
        indent := ""
        for i := 0; i < level; i++ {
                indent += "  "
        }
        fmt.Println(indent, "Scope Level", level, "Symbols:",
        ↪  s.symbols)
        if s.parent != nil {
                printScope(s.parent, level+1)
        }
}

func main() {
        // Global (outermost) scope creation.
        globalScope := NewScope(nil)
        globalScope.Define("x", 10) // Global variable 'x' defined
        ↪  as 10.
        fmt.Println("Global scope - x:", globalScope.symbols["x"])

        // Entering first nested block to demonstrate shadowing.
        fmt.Println("\n-- Entering first nested scope --")
        firstScope := NewScope(globalScope)
        firstScope.Define("x", 20) // Shadows global 'x' with a new
        ↪  local binding.
        firstScope.Define("y", 30) // Local variable 'y' defined as
        ↪  30.

        // Resolving identifiers in the first nested scope.
        if value, ok := firstScope.Resolve("x"); ok {
                fmt.Println("First scope - x (shadowed):", value)
        }
        fmt.Println("First scope - y:", firstScope.symbols["y"])

        // Entering a deeper nested block.
        fmt.Println("\n-- Entering second nested scope --")
        secondScope := NewScope(firstScope)
        secondScope.Define("z", 40) // Variable 'z' defined in
        ↪  second nested scope.
        secondScope.Define("y", 50) // Shadows 'y' from the first
        ↪  scope with a new local binding.

        // Demonstrate the resolution of variables in the second
        ↪  nested scope.
        if value, ok := secondScope.Resolve("x"); ok {
                // 'x' is not redefined here, so it resolves to the
                ↪  one in firstScope.
                fmt.Println("Second scope - x (inherited):", value)
```

40

```go
    }
    if value, ok := secondScope.Resolve("y"); ok {
        // 'y' is locally defined and shadows the outer 'y'.
        fmt.Println("Second scope - y (shadowed):", value)
    }
    fmt.Println("Second scope - z:", secondScope.symbols["z"])

    // Exiting second nested scope to illustrate scope
    ↳  boundaries.
    fmt.Println("\n-- Exiting second nested scope, back to first
    ↳  scope --")
    // In firstScope, 'y' remains bound to its original value.
    if value, ok := firstScope.Resolve("y"); ok {
        fmt.Println("First scope - y (after exiting second
        ↳  scope):", value)
    }

    // Simulating static analysis by printing the symbol table
    ↳  hierarchy.
    fmt.Println("\nSimulated Symbol Table (from current scope
    ↳  upward):")
    printScope(firstScope, 0)

    // Demonstration of the substitution model in expression
    ↳  evaluation:
    // For instance, in firstScope, where 'x' is 20, evaluating
    ↳  the expression "x + 5"
    // substitutes 'x' with 20, resulting in 25.
    if xVal, ok := firstScope.Resolve("x"); ok {
        result := xVal + 5 // Expression evaluation:
        ↳  substitute the value of x then add 5.
        fmt.Println("\nEvaluation of 'x + 5' in first scope
        ↳  where x =", xVal, "results in:", result)
    }

    // This complete example illustrates:
    // 1. Lexical scoping, as each scope inherits from its
    ↳  parent.
    // 2. Shadowing, where inner bindings override outer ones
    ↳  without deleting them.
    // 3. A simple simulation of static analysis via recursive
    ↳  symbol table printing.
}
```

Chapter 7

Constants and Enumerated Values

Declaration of Constants

Constant declarations in the language establish immutable associations between identifiers and their corresponding unchanging values. These declarations serve as fixed binders, often introduced by a dedicated keyword such that, once established, the designated value cannot be altered throughout the lifetime of the program. The semantic role of such constant bindings is to provide invariants that facilitate static analysis, eliminate unintended side effects, and support compile-time optimizations. In the formal framework of the language, a constant declaration is treated as a substitution in the operational semantics, whereby every instance of the identifier is replaced with its literal value. This substitution model ensures that the properties associated with the bound value remain preserved and guarantees that the behavior of the program is free from the ambiguities inherent to mutable state.

Furthermore, constants contribute to the rigorous reasoning about program invariants and type soundness. Once bound, they are incorporated into the language's symbol table with a binding time that coincides with the compilation phase. This early resolution allows the compiler to propagate constant values in expressions, thereby reducing overhead during runtime. The immutable nature of constants also serves as a safeguard in the development of critical systems, where the assurance that certain values remain fixed is of paramount importance. In theoretical terms, such declarations can be compared to fixed points in a mathematical structure, where the constant acts as an invariant marker that assists in proving properties about the system as a whole.

Enumerated Values with the *iota* Identifier

The language offers a concise and elegant mechanism for generating sequences of related constant values through the use of a special predeclared identifier known as *iota*. This identifier functions as an implicit counter that is automatically incremented for each successive constant within a contiguous declaration group. The *iota* mechanism streamlines the creation of enumerated values, obviating the need for explicit assignments for each individual constant and thereby reducing the risk of human error. In a formal setting, *iota* can be viewed as a generator that produces a sequence isomorphic to the set of natural numbers, providing a clear and predictable mapping between the position of a declaration and the associated value.

The automatic incrementation property of *iota* significantly enhances code readability and succinctness in contexts where a series of constants represent distinct states, categories, or enumerated types. By leveraging *iota*, the sequence of constants is inherently linked by their defined order, which contributes to a more self-documenting style of code. This implicit association aids in semantic clarity, making it evident that the values are part of an ordered set and are to be interpreted collectively rather than as isolated numerical literals. The reliance on *iota* not only simplifies the syntactic burden placed on programmers but also facilitates the maintenance of large codebases, where the explicit management of sequential values would otherwise necessitate greater vigilance against inconsistencies.

Go Code Snippet

```go
package main

import (
    "fmt"
)
```

```go
// Constants: Immutable associations used in formulas and throughout
↪   the program.
const (
    // Mathematical constants for common formulas.
    Pi = 3.141592653589793  // , used in circle area calculations.
    E  = 2.718281828459045  // Base of the natural logarithm, useful
    ↪   in exponential growth.
)

// Enumerated constants using iota for representing system states.
const (
    StateInitialized = iota  // 0: System has been initialized.
    StateProcessing          // 1: System is processing data.
    StateCompleted           // 2: Processing has completed.
    StateFailed              // 3: An error occurred during
    ↪   processing.
)

// Additional example constant.
const GoldenRatio = 1.61803398875  // A fixed mathematical constant.

// circleArea computes the area of a circle using the formula: A =
↪   * r^2.
func circleArea(radius float64) float64 {
    return Pi * radius * radius
}

// expGrowth calculates exponential growth by multiplying the
↪   initial value by E repeatedly.
// This simplistic loop-based approach multiplies the initial value
↪   'exponent' times.
func expGrowth(initial float64, exponent float64) float64 {
    result := initial
    for i := 0; i < int(exponent); i++ {
        result *= E
    }
    return result
}

// printState outputs a message based on the system state enumerated
↪   constant.
func printState(state int) {
    switch state {
    case StateInitialized:
        fmt.Println("System State: Initialized")
    case StateProcessing:
        fmt.Println("System State: Processing")
    case StateCompleted:
        fmt.Println("System State: Completed")
    case StateFailed:
        fmt.Println("System State: Failed")
    default:
```

44

```go
        fmt.Println("System State: Unknown")
    }
}

func main() {
    // Demonstrate the use of constant expressions by calculating
    ↪   the area of a circle.
    radius := 5.0
    area := circleArea(radius)
    fmt.Printf("Circle with radius %.2f has an area of %.2f\n",
    ↪   radius, area)

    // Demonstrate exponential growth using the constant E.
    initialValue := 100.0
    exponent := 3.0
    growthValue := expGrowth(initialValue, exponent)
    fmt.Printf("Exponential growth: Starting with %.2f and applying
    ↪   exponent %.0f yields %.2f\n", initialValue, exponent,
    ↪   growthValue)

    // Demonstrate the usage of enumerated constants with iota in
    ↪   simulating system state transitions.
    fmt.Println("System state transitions:")
    printState(StateInitialized)
    printState(StateProcessing)
    printState(StateCompleted)
    printState(StateFailed)
}
```

45

Chapter 8

Arithmetic Operators and Expressions

Basic Arithmetic Operators

Arithmetic operators constitute the fundamental apparatus for performing numerical computations within the language. The operator + is designated for addition, facilitating the summation of numerical values, whereas the operator − is employed for subtraction, thereby calculating the difference between operands. The multiplication operator, symbolized by *, and the division operator, represented by /, enable the determination of products and quotients respectively. Moreover, the modulus operator, typically denoted by %, computes the remainder following an integer division. In addition, a unary minus may be applied to invert the sign of its operand. Within the formal framework of the language, these operators are defined as either binary or unary functions that map one or more numeric inputs to a unique numerical output in accordance with traditional arithmetical laws. The precise definition and treatment of these operators is critical to ensuring that the semantics of expression evaluation mirror those found in classical mathematics.

Operator Precedence

The evaluation of compound arithmetic expressions is governed by a rigorously defined hierarchy known as operator precedence. In the absence of explicit grouping symbols, the operators $*$, $/$, and % are accorded higher precedence relative to the lower-precedence operators $+$ and $-$. Consequently, an expression such as $a+b*c$ is invariably resolved by first evaluating the multiplication $b*c$, with the sum $a + (b * c)$ computed subsequently. This predetermined hierarchy guarantees an unambiguous interpretation of nested expressions. Furthermore, the language specifies associativity rules for operators that possess identical precedence levels. For instance, binary operators such as $+$ and $-$ are typically evaluated from left to right, thus providing a clear procedural framework for their sequential application. Parentheses, denoted by (), are available as mechanisms for overriding the default precedence, thereby permitting the explicit specification of the intended grouping within expressions. The underlying grammar of the language is meticulously designed to enforce these precedence and associativity relations during the syntactic analysis phase.

Construction of Numerical Expressions

Numerical expressions are constructed by systematically combining constant values, variables, and arithmetic operators into well-formed constructs that adhere to the syntactic rules of the language. The construction process is inherently recursive; an expression may consist either of a solitary operand or of a composite formed by the application of an operator to one or more subexpressions. In the formal language definition, production rules are utilized to capture this recursive structure, thus ensuring that every valid expression can be unambiguously parsed into a corresponding abstract syntax tree. Semantically, each composite expression is interpreted as a functional mapping that applies an arithmetic operator to a set of operands, yielding a resultant numerical value. The evaluation of such expressions is executed in strict compliance with the prescribed operator precedence and associativity, ensuring consistency between the syntactic representation and its mathematical interpretation. Parenthesized subexpressions play a pivotal role by explicitly delineating alternative evaluation orders, thereby mitigating potential ambiguity. The formalism underlying the construction and evaluation of numerical expressions not only guarantees precise computational results but also facilitates compile-time optimizations, such as constant folding, by enabling the early resolution of invariant subexpressions.

Go Code Snippet

```go
package main

import (
        "fmt"
)

func main() {
        // Initialization of variables for demonstration
        var a, b, c int = 10, 3, 4

        // Basic Arithmetic Operations:
        // Addition and Subtraction
        sum  := a + b      // 10 + 3 = 13
        diff := a - b      // 10 - 3 = 7

        // Multiplication, Division, and Modulus
        product  := a * b  // 10 * 3 = 30
        quotient := a / b  // Integer division: 10 / 3 = 3
        remainder := a % b // 10 % 3 = 1

        // Unary minus: Inverting sign of 'a'
        negA := -a         // -10

        // Operator Precedence Examples:
        // Without parentheses, multiplication is performed before
        ↪     addition.
        // Expression: a + b * c  => 10 + (3 * 4) = 10 + 12 = 22
        expr1 := a + b * c

        // Using parentheses to override default precedence.
        // Expression: (a + b) * c => (10 + 3) * 4 = 13 * 4 = 52
        expr2 := (a + b) * c

        // Associativity Review:
        // Left-to-right evaluation in subtraction:
        // Expression: a - b - c => ((10 - 3) - 4) = 3
        expr3 := a - b - c

        // Left-to-right evaluation in division:
        // Expression: 100 / 5 / 2 => ((100 / 5) / 2) = (20 / 2) =
        ↪    10
        expr4 := 100 / 5 / 2

        // Construction of a Complex Numerical Expression:
        // Expression: -a + (b * c) - (a / b) + (a % b)
        // Calculation: -10 + (3 * 4) - (10 / 3) + (10 % 3)
        //                  => -10 + 12 - 3 + 1 = 0
        complexExpr := -a + (b * c) - (a / b) + (a % b)

        // Output the computed results to the console
```

```go
    fmt.Println("Basic Arithmetic Operations:")
    fmt.Printf("a = %d, b = %d, c = %d\n", a, b, c)
    fmt.Printf("Sum: %d + %d = %d\n", a, b, sum)
    fmt.Printf("Difference: %d - %d = %d\n", a, b, diff)
    fmt.Printf("Product: %d * %d = %d\n", a, b, product)
    fmt.Printf("Quotient: %d / %d = %d\n", a, b, quotient)
    fmt.Printf("Remainder: %d %% %d = %d\n", a, b, remainder)
    fmt.Printf("Unary Minus: -%d = %d\n", a, negA)

    fmt.Println("\nOperator Precedence Examples:")
    fmt.Printf("Expression a + b * c (default precedence):
    ↪  %d\n", expr1)
    fmt.Printf("Expression (a + b) * c (with parentheses):
    ↪  %d\n", expr2)
    fmt.Printf("Subtraction associativity (a - b - c): %d\n",
    ↪  expr3)
    fmt.Printf("Division associativity (100 / 5 / 2): %d\n",
    ↪  expr4)

    fmt.Println("\nComplex Numerical Expression:")
    fmt.Printf("Expression (-a + (b * c) - (a / b) + (a %% b)):
    ↪  %d\n", complexExpr)

    // Additional Demonstrations:
    // Evaluating a multi-step arithmetic operation to reflect
    ↪  syntactic structure.
    // For instance, computing an expression that involves
    ↪  nested operations and explicit grouping.
    firstPart := (a + b) * c       // (10 + 3) * 4 = 52
    secondPart := a - (a / b)      // 10 - (10 / 3) = 10 - 3 = 7
    finalResult := firstPart + secondPart + remainder
    // finalResult should be: 52 + 7 + 1 = 60

    fmt.Println("\nAdditional Complex Calculation:")
    fmt.Printf("First Part (a + b) * c: %d\n", firstPart)
    fmt.Printf("Second Part a - (a / b): %d\n", secondPart)
    fmt.Printf("Added Remainder: %d\n", remainder)
    fmt.Printf("Final Result: %d\n", finalResult)
}
```

Chapter 9

Relational and Logical Operators

Relational Operators

1 Formal Definitions and Properties

Relational operators establish binary predicates that compare two operands to yield a boolean outcome. The operator $==$ is employed to assert equality between operands, while the operator $\neq$ denotes inequality. In addition, the operators $<$, $>$, $\leq$, and $\geq$ impose an order on elements drawn from domains that possess a natural ordering, such as numerical or lexically comparable sets. These operators are defined in a manner analogous to mathematical relations on well-structured sets where properties such as reflexivity, antisymmetry, and transitivity are applicable. The resulting boolean values, often conceptualized as either *true* or *false*, provide the foundational components for the construction of conditional expressions in computational logic.

2 Semantic Considerations

Within a formal system, the evaluation of relational expressions adheres to deterministic rules ensuring that given operands of compatible types, the computed outcome is both unique and unambiguous. These operations are interpreted as maps from pairs of elements from the underlying set to the Boolean domain. The semantic structures that govern these operators are rooted in classical logic and set theory, thereby providing a rigorous framework for the comparison of values. When employed in expressions, relational operators are evaluated in such a way that the intrinsic mathematical properties of ordering and equivalence are preserved, lending predictability and consistency to decision-making processes in code evaluation.

Logical Operators

1   Fundamentals of Boolean Connectives

Logical operators, which form the cornerstone of Boolean algebra, are used to compose and manipulate truth values obtained from simpler relational comparisons. The primary logical operators include the conjunction operator $\land$, which yields *true* only when both operands are *true*; the disjunction operator $\lor$, which produces *true* if at least one operand is *true*; and the negation operator $\neg$, which inverts the truth value of its operand. These operators are defined by a set of axioms ensuring that their behavior aligns with the principles of Boolean logic. Their formalized definitions facilitate the systematic construction of complex logical expressions that encapsulate decision criteria within higher-level computational constructs.

2   Evaluation Strategies and Operator Precedence

Logical expressions can become intricate when multiple operators are used in combination. The evaluation strategy often incorporates the concept of short-circuit evaluation, where the ordering of operands determines whether subsequent operators require evaluation. Precedence rules are rigorously defined to resolve potential ambiguities in compound expressions. Typically, relational operators are resolved prior to the application of logical connectives. The associativity and distributivity inherent in the operators $\land$ and $\lor$ further refine the structure of logical expressions, ensuring that the grouping of operands—either by default evaluation or through explicit parenthesizing using ()—leads to a coherent and deterministically evaluated outcome.

Interplay in Decision-Making Constructs

The synthesis of relational and logical operators enables the formation of precise conditions that drive decision-making processes in computational systems. Initially, relational operators compare individual operands to produce intermediate Boolean values. Subsequently, logical operators amalgamate these boolean results to articulate compound conditions with intricate logical dependencies. Such composite expressions are integral to control structures, where the final boolean outcome governs the selection of execution paths. The formal semantics of these operators guarantee that, regardless of the complexity of the conditional expression, the evaluation conforms to well-established principles of mathematics and logic. This interplay is fundamental to the implementation of robust, verifiable, and predictable decision-making mechanisms in modern programming languages.

Go Code Snippet

```go
package main

import (
        "fmt"
)

// compareNumbers demonstrates the use of relational operators.
// It checks if three integers are in strict ascending order.
func compareNumbers(a, b, c int) bool {
        // Using relational operators: < checks the natural
        ↪   ordering.
        return (a < b) && (b < c)
}

// validateInput demonstrates short-circuit evaluation with logical
↪   operators.
// It returns true if the input is positive and even, otherwise
↪   false.
func validateInput(x int) bool {
        // The && operator ensures that if x > 0 is false, the
        ↪   second condition is not evaluated.
        return (x > 0) && (x%2 == 0)
}

// determineCategory uses relational and logical operators to
↪   classify weather conditions.
// It categorizes based on temperature and humidity values.
```

```go
func determineCategory(temperature float64, humidity float64) string
↪ {
    // Check if the weather is "Hot and Humid"
    if (temperature >= 30) && (humidity > 0.7) {
        return "Hot and Humid"
    } else if (temperature >= 30) && (humidity <= 0.7) {
        // Weather is "Hot and Dry"
        return "Hot and Dry"
    } else if (temperature >= 15) && (temperature < 30) &&
    ↪ (humidity >= 0.4) && (humidity <= 0.7) {
        // Weather is "Mild"
        return "Mild"
    } else if temperature < 15 {
        // Weather is "Cold"
        return "Cold"
    }
    // Fallback category if none of the above apply
    return "Unknown"
}


// main demonstrates the interplay of relational and logical
↪ operators in Go.
func main() {
    // Example demonstrating relational operators.
    a, b, c := 10, 20, 30
    fmt.Println("Comparing numbers:", a, b, c)
    if compareNumbers(a, b, c) {
        fmt.Println("The numbers are in ascending order.")
    } else {
        fmt.Println("The numbers are not in ascending
        ↪ order.")
    }

    // Demonstrate short-circuit evaluation using logical
    ↪ operators.
    testValues := []int{-2, 0, 4, 7}
    for _, val := range testValues {
        if validateInput(val) {
            fmt.Printf("Input %d is positive and
            ↪ even.\n", val)
        } else {
            fmt.Printf("Input %d does not meet the
            ↪ criteria (positive and even).\n", val)
        }
    }

    // Demonstrate decision-making using relational and logical
    ↪ operators
    // in a real-world context: weather classification.
    temperatures := []float64{32.5, 31.0, 22.0, 10.0}
    humidities := []float64{0.75, 0.65, 0.5, 0.3}
    for i := 0; i < len(temperatures); i++ {
```

53

```
        category := determineCategory(temperatures[i],
        ↪  humidities[i])
        fmt.Printf("At temperature %.1f°C and humidity %.2f,
        ↪  the weather is: %s\n",
             temperatures[i], humidities[i], category)
    }

    // Illustrate operator precedence in a composite boolean
    ↪  expression.
    // In the expression: a < b || a == b && c > b
    // The && operator is evaluated before the || operator.
    condition := (a < b) || ((a == b) && (c > b))
    fmt.Println("The evaluated condition for (a < b) || ((a ==
    ↪  b) && (c > b)) is:", condition)

    // Demonstrate the logical negation operator: it reverses
    ↪  the truth value.
    // Here we invert the result of compareNumbers with reversed
    ↪  order.
    isNotAscending := !(compareNumbers(c, b, a))
    fmt.Println("The negation of the comparison (c, b, a) is:",
    ↪  isNotAscending)
}
```

Chapter 10

Control Flow: if Statements Basics

Syntactic Structure and Formal Notation

The fundamental construct that governs conditional execution in Go is the if statement. In its simplest form, an if statement comprises a condition expressed as a Boolean-valued expression and a block of statements that executes only if the condition yields the logical value *true*. The condition, which must evaluate strictly to either *true* or *false*, adheres to a formal grammar that excludes the use of extraneous syntactic delimiters such as parentheses. This minimalist syntactic design underscores a commitment to clarity and conciseness. The underlying rule can be expressed as a mapping

$$\text{if} : \text{Expression} \rightarrow \{true, false\},$$

where the expression is evaluated once, and if the result is *true*, the subsequent block is executed. This control construct does not inherently necessitate an alternative branch, and thus the absence of an else clause is both syntactically correct and semantically complete for cases requiring only monolithic conditional execution.

Semantic Evaluation and Deterministic Execution

The semantic interpretation of the if statement is rooted in the deterministic evaluation of Boolean expressions. When an if statement is encountered, the embedded condition is evaluated in a strict left-to-right order according to the language's evaluation rules. The determinism is guaranteed by the well-defined operational semantics of Go, wherein each basic computation in the Boolean expression is executed with clearly specified outcomes that conform to Boolean algebra. The evaluation process may be formally described by a function

$$E : \text{Expression} \rightarrow \{true, false\},$$

which ensures that every subexpression is reduced to a Boolean constant. Only upon the evaluation resulting in $true$ does the control flow transition into the block of statements nested within the if construct. This guarantees that the execution state is altered exclusively in cases that satisfy the predetermined condition, thereby establishing a clear and unambiguous branch in the computational process.

Conditional Execution in Control Flow Constructs

The if statement plays a critical role in directing the program's execution by delineating a pathway for conditionally executing segments of code. This conditional mechanism acts as a bifurcation point, whereby the program's state is altered based upon the outcome of the Boolean condition. The act of conditional execution may be understood as a selective operation, in which the computational process is partitioned into mutually exclusive segments based on the evaluation outcome. In formal terms, if the condition is denoted as C, and the subsequent block is represented by a transformation function T, then the overall operational behavior is modeled as

$$\text{ControlFlow}(C, T) = \begin{cases} T(s), & \text{if } C(s) = true, \\ s, & \text{if } C(s) = false, \end{cases}$$

where s represents the state of the program prior to the evaluation. This mechanism ensures that the domain of application for the block of statements is precisely determined by the Boolean nature of the condition. The structural simplicity of the if statement not only enhances the readability of the code but also facilitates formal reasoning about control flow, particularly in proofs of program correctness and invariance properties within the context of temporal logic and state transitions.

Go Code Snippet

```go
package main

import "fmt"

// ControlFlow simulates the if statement's conditional execution as
//    described in the chapter.
// It accepts an initial state 's', a condition function 'C' that
//    evaluates to a bool,
// and a transformation function 'T' that modifies the state.
// Formally, it models:
//     ControlFlow(C, T) = { T(s), if C(s)==true; s, if C(s)==false
//    }.
func ControlFlow(s int, C func(int) bool, T func(int) int) int {
    // The condition is evaluated strictly according to Go's
    //    left-to-right evaluation.
    if C(s) {
        return T(s)
    }
    return s
}

func main() {
    // Demonstration of a basic if statement in Go without
    //    extraneous parentheses.
    // Here, we check if a value is even.
    value := 10
    if value % 2 == 0 { // The Boolean expression evaluates to true
    //    or false.
        fmt.Println("Value is even.")
    }

    // The following is a more elaborate demonstration integrating
    //    the concepts from the chapter.
    // It illustrates the mapping:
    //     E : Expression -> {true, false} where E(s) is the
    //    evaluation function.
    //     And the control flow operation is defined as:
    //         ControlFlow(C, T) =
```

```go
//          T(s), if C(s)==true,
//          s,    if C(s)==false.
initialState := 7
fmt.Println("Initial state:", initialState)

// Define a condition function 'C' which checks if the state is
// ↪ positive and odd.
condition := func(s int) bool {
    // E(s) = (s > 0 && s % 2 != 0)
    return s > 0 && s % 2 != 0
}

// Define a transformation function 'T' that modifies the state.
// For example, we add 5 to the state.
transform := func(s int) int {
    return s + 5
}

// Apply the custom ControlFlow function to simulate the
// ↪ if-statement execution.
newState := ControlFlow(initialState, condition, transform)
fmt.Println("New state after ControlFlow:", newState)

// This example demonstrates deterministic evaluation:
// - The state is transformed only when the condition holds
// ↪ true.
// - Otherwise, the state remains unchanged.
}
```

Chapter 11

Control Flow: if-else Chains

Syntactic Structure and Formal Definition

The if-else chain represents a fundamental control construct designed to facilitate multiple conditional branches within a program's execution sequence. This structure is formally characterized by an initial if clause followed by a series of else-if clauses and a terminal else clause. In abstract notation, the general form can be rendered as

$$\text{if } C_1 \text{ then } S_1 \quad \text{else if } C_2 \text{ then } S_2 \quad \ldots \quad \text{else } S_n,$$

where each C_i is a Boolean expression that deterministically yields either *true* or *false*, and each S_i is a block of statements effecting a transformation on the program state. The semantics of this structure ensure that upon the evaluation of these conditions in a left-to-right manner, the first condition C_i that evaluates to *true* triggers the exclusive execution of the corresponding statement block S_i, precluding the evaluation of any subsequent conditions. This mutually exclusive nature of the branches lays the groundwork for rigorous formal reasoning regarding control flow and computational state transitions.

Operational Semantics and Deterministic Evaluation

The evaluation of an if-else chain is governed by deterministic operational semantics that enforce a sequential and exclusive decision process. Denote an arbitrary program state by s and consider that each conditional block S_i induces a state transformation $S_i(s)$. The evaluation function for the if-else chain, denoted by CH, can be formally defined as

$$
\text{CH}(s) = \begin{cases}
S_1(s), & \text{if } C_1(s) = true, \\
S_2(s), & \text{if } C_1(s) = false \text{ and } C_2(s) = true, \\
\vdots & \\
S_n(s), & \text{if } C_1(s) = false, \ C_2(s) = false, \ \ldots, \ C_{n-1}(s) = false.
\end{cases}
$$

This formulation encapsulates a left-to-right evaluation strategy in which each condition C_i is inspected sequentially. The operational semantics necessitate that once a condition returns $true$, the corresponding block is executed as the unique mapping of the initial state s to its subsequent state. In scenarios where none of the initial conditions are met, the final default block S_n is executed, ensuring that the control flow mechanism is complete and deterministic. The explicit ordering of evaluations safeguards against ambiguity and fosters a rigorous understanding of state transitions within the computational model.

Decision Paradigms and Best Practices

The precise formulation of if-else chains imposes a structured paradigm for delineating multiple decision branches, which is essential for both theoretical analysis and practical implementation. In designing such chains, the conditions $C_1, C_2, \ldots, C_{n-1}$ should be ordered to reflect their relative computational cost and the anticipated likelihood of their satisfaction. This ordering aids in minimizing unnecessary evaluations and ensures that the most probable conditions are tested at the earliest juncture.

A well-organized if-else chain delineates a clear partitioning of the input space, thereby enabling a one-to-one correspondence between potential input states and the resultant state transformations

$S_i(s)$. The clarity gained from such a structure enhances formal verification efforts by allowing each branch to be considered independently while still contributing to the overall system behavior. Furthermore, the encapsulation of decision logic into discrete, non-overlapping segments reinforces the invariance properties that may be exploited in proofs of program correctness, particularly within contexts that necessitate rigorous state transition analysis.

Adherence to these best practices in the formulation of if-else chains is paramount. The systematic arrangement of alternative branches reduces cognitive load during analysis and supports scalability in complex systems. The deliberate design of these constructs—emphasizing mutual exclusivity, sequential evaluation, and deterministic mapping—ensures that the program's decision-making process remains robust, verifiable, and amenable to formal scrutiny.

Go Code Snippet

```go
package main

import (
        "fmt"
)

// evaluateChain applies a series of state transformations based on
↪    an if-else chain.
// It mirrors the formal operational semantics discussed in the
↪    chapter:
//
// The abstract form of the if-else chain is defined as:
//    CH(s) = S1(s),   if C1(s) == true
//            S2(s),   if C1(s) == false and C2(s) == true
//            S3(s),   if C1(s) == false, C2(s) == false, and C3(s) ==
↪    true
//            S4(s),   otherwise
//
// In this implementation:
//    - Condition C1: if the state s is greater than 100, then S1(s)
↪    applies (s + 10)
//    - Condition C2: if s is not > 100 but greater than 50, then
↪    S2(s) applies (s * 2)
//    - Condition C3: if s is not > 100 nor > 50 but greater than 0,
↪    then S3(s) applies (s - 5)
//    - Default: if none of the above conditions hold, then S4(s)
↪    applies (s remains unchanged)
//
// The function returns the transformed state along with a
↪    descriptive string.
```

```go
func evaluateChain(s int) (int, string) {
        if s > 100 {
                // C1(s) is true: apply S1(s) = s + 10
                return s + 10, "Branch 1: s > 100; Applied S1: s +
                ↪   10"
        } else if s > 50 {
                // C1(s) is false and C2(s) is true: apply S2(s) = s
                ↪   * 2
                return s * 2, "Branch 2: 50 < s <= 100; Applied S2:
                ↪   s * 2"
        } else if s > 0 {
                // C1(s) and C2(s) are false, C3(s) is true: apply
                ↪   S3(s) = s - 5
                return s - 5, "Branch 3: 0 < s <= 50; Applied S3: s
                ↪   - 5"
        } else {
                // None of the conditions met: default branch S4(s)
                ↪   with no transformation
                return s, "Default Branch: s <= 0; Applied S4: s (no
                ↪   transformation)"
        }
}

func main() {
        // Define an array of sample states to simulate different
        ↪   execution paths.
        testStates := []int{150, 75, 30, -20}

        fmt.Println("Demonstrating if-else chain evaluation based on
        ↪   operational semantics:")
        for _, state := range testStates {
                newState, branchInfo := evaluateChain(state)
                fmt.Printf("Initial State: %d, New State: %d ->
                ↪   %s\n", state, newState, branchInfo)
        }
}
```

Chapter 12

Control Flow: Switch Statements Fundamentals

Syntactic Structure

The switch statement synthesizes a compact form of multi-branch decision-making that contrasts with the verbosity of chained if-else constructs. Structurally, the switch statement begins with an expression E, whose evaluated value is later matched against a series of case labels. Formally, consider an expression E that yields a value x. The syntax may be abstractly represented as

$$\texttt{switch } E \, \{\, \texttt{case } v_1 : S_1; \quad \texttt{case } v_2 : S_2; \quad \ldots; \quad \texttt{default} : S_n \,\},$$

where each v_i represents a discrete, comparable constant, and each S_i denotes a block of statements associated with the corresponding case. The default clause serves as the terminal branch, ensuring that a well-defined path exists even if none of the explicit case labels match the evaluated value x.

Operational Semantics

The operational semantics of the switch statement prescribe a deterministic evaluation and execution model. Upon evaluation of the expression E, its value x is compared sequentially against the case labels $v_1, v_2, \ldots$. Define a state transition function T such that, if $x = v_i$ for some index i, then the program state transforms according to $T(S_i)$. In formal terms, the evaluation of a switch statement can be encapsulated by the function

$$\text{SW}(x) = \begin{cases} T(S_1), & \text{if } x = v_1, \\ T(S_2), & \text{if } x = v_2, \\ \vdots \\ T(S_n), & \text{if } x \neq v_i \quad \forall\, i \text{ (default case)}. \end{cases}$$

This precise sequential inspection of case labels ensures that the first matching branch exclusively determines the subsequent state, thereby precluding any ambiguity in program behavior. The absence of an implicit fallthrough mechanism, unless explicitly enabled, reinforces the univocal nature of the mapping from the evaluated value to its corresponding execution block.

Utility and Use Cases

The switch statement is employed as an efficient alternative to extensive if-else chains in scenarios where a single expression is subjected to a multitude of potential comparisons. Such constructs are prevalent in the control logic of state dispatch mechanisms, pattern selection, and event-driven programming, where the clarity and brevity of code are paramount. By consolidating multiple conditional checks into a single structured form, the switch statement enhances the readability and maintainability of control flow decisions.

Moreover, the intrinsic organization of case labels in the switch construct admits formal reasoning about program correctness and scalability of decision logic. The compact syntax facilitates a more straightforward mapping from a theoretical model of decision branches to an actual implementation. In mathematical terms, the correspondence between the evaluated value x and the set of predetermined constants $\{v_1, v_2, \ldots\}$ yields a partitioning of the input domain that is both exhaustive and mutually exclusive. This property underpins rigorous analyses of control flow, ensuring that any state transformation is both predictable and systematically derived from the underlying expression E.

Go Code Snippet

```go
package main

import "fmt"

// evaluateSwitch simulates the operational semantics of the switch
↪   statement.
// It mirrors the theoretical function SW(x) as described in the
↪   chapter:
// For a given input x, it returns a transformed state based on
↪   matching cases.
func evaluateSwitch(x int) string {
    switch x {
    case 10:
        // T(S1): Transformation when x equals 10.
        return "State Transformation: Action S1 executed for x = 10"
    case 20:
        // T(S2): Transformation when x equals 20.
        return "State Transformation: Action S2 executed for x = 20"
    case 30:
        // T(S3): Transformation when x equals 30.
        return "State Transformation: Action S3 executed for x = 30"
    default:
        // Default branch: executed if x does not equal any defined
        ↪   case value.
        return "State Transformation: Default action executed as no
        ↪   case matched"
    }
}

func main() {
    // Demonstrate evaluateSwitch with various sample inputs.
    testValues := []int{10, 20, 30, 40}
    fmt.Println("Demonstrating the switch operational semantics:")
    for _, value := range testValues {
        outcome := evaluateSwitch(value)
        fmt.Printf("For x = %d: %s\n", value, outcome)
    }

    // Additional example: Using a switch statement to evaluate the
    ↪   day of the week.
    day := 3 // Assuming a numerical representation: 1=Monday,
    ↪   2=Tuesday, etc.
    fmt.Println("\nDay evaluation using switch:")
    switch day {
    case 1:
        fmt.Println("Monday: Kickstart the week!")
    case 2:
        fmt.Println("Tuesday: Keep the momentum!")
    case 3:
        fmt.Println("Wednesday: Midweek check-in.")
```

65

```go
case 4:
    fmt.Println("Thursday: Almost there!")
case 5:
    fmt.Println("Friday: Wrap up the week.")
default:
    fmt.Println("Weekend: Enjoy your time off!")
}

// Example demonstrating a switch without an expression,
// where each case is a boolean condition.
age := 16
fmt.Println("\nAge evaluation using condition-based switch:")
switch {
case age < 13:
    fmt.Println("Child: Enjoy your youthful years!")
case age >= 13 && age < 20:
    fmt.Println("Teenager: Embrace this phase of growth.")
    // Note: No implicit fallthrough in Go; 'fallthrough' must
    ↪   be explicit if desired.
case age >= 20:
    fmt.Println("Adult: Welcome to the realm of
    ↪   responsibility.")
default:
    fmt.Println("Age not specified.")
}
}
```

Chapter 13

Control Flow: Type Switch Mechanism

Syntactic Structure

The type switch mechanism is a control construct designed to facilitate decision-making based on the dynamic type of an interface variable. Unlike conventional value-based switch statements, the type switch operates on type assertions and is expressed syntactically as

switch v.(type) { case T_1 : S_1; case T_2 : S_2; ...; default : S_d },

where v is an interface variable and each T_i denotes a concrete type. In this formulation, the case labels are not arbitrary values but explicit type identifiers against which the dynamic type of v is compared. Each statement block S_i is associated with the condition that the dynamic type of v equals T_i. The structural definition enforces that the cases represent mutually exclusive partitions of the domain of dynamic types available to the variable. The default clause, represented by the block S_d, is executed when none of the explicitly listed types match the dynamic type of v, thereby ensuring that the construct maintains exhaustiveness over the possible types.

Operational Semantics

The operational semantics of the type switch mechanism are predicated upon the evaluation of the interface variable's dynamic type at runtime. Upon entering the switch construct, the system introspects the value of v to extract its concrete type, here denoted as τ. For each case branch specified as case $T_i : S_i$, a runtime comparison is executed; if $\tau = T_i$, the state is transformed by executing the corresponding block S_i. This process can be formally captured by the mapping

$$
\mathcal{S}(\tau) = \begin{cases} T(S_1), & \tau = T_1, \\ T(S_2), & \tau = T_2, \\ \vdots \\ T(S_d), & \tau \notin \{T_1, T_2, \dots\}, \end{cases}
$$

where the function $T(\cdot)$ represents the state transition effected by the statements within each block. The evaluation occurs sequentially, with the execution of the first matching branch precluding further comparisons. The semantics ensure that no implicit fallthrough occurs between branches unless explicitly indicated, thereby preserving a one-to-one correspondence between the dynamic type of v and the executing statement block.

Conceptual Underpinnings

At its core, the type switch is an embodiment of runtime polymorphism and reflective type analysis. The mechanism capitalizes on the inherent ability of interface variables to encapsulate values of disparate types. By enabling the switch to inspect these types dynamically, the construct circumvents the limitations imposed by static type assertions. Consider the set D of all types that satisfy the interface contract of v. The type switch partitions D into disjoint subsets, each corresponding to one of the explicit type cases $\{T_1, T_2, \dots, T_n\}$. This partitioning guarantees that if the dynamic type τ of v is an element of one such subset, then the associated control path is uniquely determined. The rigorous formulation of this concept draws upon principles from type theory, wherein the safety of type assertions is fundamental. The mechanism thereby ensures that decisions based on τ are both deterministic and verifiable within a formal framework.

Use Cases in Type-Dependent Control Flow

The applicability of the type switch mechanism is most apparent in systems that manage heterogeneous collections of interface variables or when precise behavioral differentiation is required based on concrete types. In scenarios such as dynamic dispatch, visitor pattern implementations, or reflective computations, the ability to distinguish between types at runtime enables the execution of type-specific routines that enhance modularity and maintainability. By aligning control flow with the inherent properties of the dynamic type, the type switch construct optimizes decision-making processes and streamlines the implementation of polymorphic behavior. The formal structure of the mechanism also permits rigorous analysis with respect to the completeness and exclusivity of the case partitions, ensuring that every conceivable dynamic type scenario is accounted for in the control strategy.

Go Code Snippet

```
package main

import (
        "fmt"
)

// processValue demonstrates the type switch mechanism using a
↪   control structure
// based on the dynamic type of an interface{} variable. The
↪   algorithm corresponds
// to the mapping as described in the chapter:
//
//  S() = {
//      T(S1)  if  == int     --> perform integer-specific
↪   operation,
//      T(S2)  if  == float64 --> perform float-specific operation,
//      T(S3)  if  == string  --> perform string-specific
↪   operation,
//      T(Sd) else            --> default case for unsupported
↪   types,
//  }
//
// Each case represents an exclusive branch that processes the
↪   variable according
// to its dynamic type without fallthrough.
func processValue(v interface{}) {
        fmt.Println("Processing value:", v)
```

```go
switch val := v.(type) {
case int:
        // T(S1): For a dynamic type int, perform an
        ↪ operation specific to integers.
        // Example: Multiply the integer by 2.
        fmt.Printf("Type is int; after processing: %d\n",
        ↪ val*2)
case float64:
        // T(S2): For a dynamic type float64, perform an
        ↪ operation specific to floats.
        // Example: Square the float value.
        fmt.Printf("Type is float64; after processing:
        ↪ %f\n", val*val)
case string:
        // T(S3): For a dynamic type string, perform an
        ↪ operation specific to strings.
        // Example: Append additional text to indicate
        ↪ processing.
        fmt.Printf("Type is string; after processing: %s\n",
        ↪ val+" - processed")
default:
        // T(Sd): Default branch when none of the above
        ↪ types match.
        // This ensures exhaustiveness in the type switch.
        fmt.Println("Unsupported type encountered; no
        ↪ operation performed.")
    }
}


// evaluateValue applies a transformation algorithm based on the
↪ dynamic type of v.
// It mirrors the operational semantics wherein the state
↪ transformation T(·) is applied
// to v depending on its concrete type.
func evaluateValue(v interface{}) interface{} {
        switch val := v.(type) {
        case int:
                // If the dynamic type is int, double the value.
                return val * 2
        case float64:
                // If the dynamic type is float64, return its
                ↪ square.
                return val * val
        case string:
                // If the dynamic type is string, append a custom
                ↪ suffix.
                return val + " [evaluated]"
        default:
                // For unsupported types, return nil to indicate the
                ↪ absence of a valid transformation.
                return nil
        }
}
```

```go
// main function demonstrates the usage of processValue and
↪   evaluateValue functions
// with diverse types such as int, float64, string, and a slice
↪   (unsupported type).
func main() {
        // Define a slice of interface{} holding different dynamic
        ↪   types.
        values := []interface{}{42, 3.14, "GoLang", []int{1, 2, 3}}

        fmt.Println("=== Processing Values using processValue ===")
        for _, v := range values {
                processValue(v)
                fmt.Println("-----------------------------------")
        }

        fmt.Println("\n=== Evaluating Values using evaluateValue
        ↪   ===")
        for _, v := range values {
                result := evaluateValue(v)
                if result != nil {
                        fmt.Printf("Original: %v, Evaluated: %v\n",
                        ↪   v, result)
                } else {
                        fmt.Printf("Original: %v, Evaluated:
                        ↪   Unsupported type\n", v)
                }
        }
}
```

Chapter 14

Looping Constructs: Basic For Loops

Syntactic Structure

The fundamental syntactic design of the for loop in Go is encapsulated in a singular, yet highly expressive, iterative construct. This construct is defined by three principal components: an initialization clause, a loop control condition, and an update expression. In its canonical form, the for loop can be denoted as

$$\text{for } I; \ C; \ U \ \{ \ S \ \},$$

where I represents the initialization statement executed once prior to the commencement of iteration, C is a boolean expression evaluated before each execution of the loop body, and U is the update expression that is performed subsequent to each full cycle through the body S. The deliberate use of semicolons to separate these components not only facilitates a clear structural delineation but also aids formal static analysis by partitioning the loop into its constituent operational phases. Moreover, this syntactic formulation is sufficiently malleable to accommodate the omission of any of its three components in order to reproduce alternative iterative idioms, all underpinned by the same structural principles.

Operational Semantics

The operational semantics of the for loop are governed by a deterministic evaluation process that initiates with the execution of the initialization clause I. Upon completion of I, the conditional expression C is evaluated; a truth value of `true` prompts the execution of the loop body S, whereas a `false` outcome terminates the loop. Immediately following each execution of S, the update expression U is executed, thereby effecting a state change that is immediately visible in the next evaluation of C. Formally, if the state of the loop variables is captured by s, and the update function is denoted by $U(s)$, then the progression of the loop may be abstractly modeled by the iterative mapping

$$s_{n+1} = U(s_n),$$

with the continuation condition given as $C(s_n) = $ `true`. This guarantees that the loop executes its body for every state s_n satisfying the condition, and it ceases execution once there exists an n for which $C(s_n) = $ `false`. Such an evaluation paradigm ensures that each iteration is discrete and that the state transitions adhere to deterministic computation, providing a well-defined operational framework for repetitive execution.

Conceptual Underpinnings

The conceptual foundation of Go's for loop is rooted in the abstraction of iterative computation as a process of repeated application of a state transition function under a governing predicate. By consolidating the notions of initialization, condition evaluation, and state update into a single syntactic entity, the for loop eliminates redundancies inherent in multiple distinct looping constructs. This unification is not only a design simplification but also an invitation to formal reasoning: if the state at loop entry is denoted by s_0, and after each iteration the state is updated as

$$s_{n+1} = U(s_n),$$

then the series of states $\{s_0, s_1, s_2, \ldots\}$ constitutes a sequence generated by successive applications of U, with the continuation of this process strictly contingent upon the invariant that $C(s_n)$ remains `true`. Such a formulation parallels mathematical induction, where the base case is established by the initialization and the inductive step by the update mechanism. This intimate correspondence with principles of mathematical rigor ensures that the for loop can be analyzed in terms of loop invariants and termination conditions, thus providing a robust framework for verification and reasoning in the realm of repetitive task execution.

Go Code Snippet

```go
package main

import (
        "fmt"
)

// updateState applies the state transition function U(s).
// In this example, U(s) doubles the current state, which can be
// formally represented as:
//     s = U(s) = s * 2
// This function encapsulates that operation.
func updateState(s int) int {
        return s * 2
}

// main demonstrates the canonical structure of the Go for loop,
// which follows the format:
//     for Initialization; Condition; Update {
//         Statements (Loop Body)
//     }
// It models an iterative process where the state evolves according
//     to:
//     s = U(s)
// The loop continues as long as the condition C(s) holds true.
func main() {
        // Example 1: Iterative Doubling to Demonstrate s = U(s)
        // Initial state s is set to 1, and the update function U(s)
        //     doubles it.
        // The loop runs as long as state < threshold.
        threshold := 1000  // Loop continuation condition: s <
        //     threshold
        state := 1          // Initialization: s = 1

        fmt.Println("Example 1: Iterative Doubling (Modeling s =
        //     U(s))")
        // For loop structure: no explicit initialization clause
        //     here since 'state'
        // is already initialized, the condition is state <
        //     threshold, and the
        // update expression applies updateState.
```

```go
for ; state < threshold; state = updateState(state) {
        fmt.Printf("Current state: %d\n", state)
}
fmt.Printf("Loop terminated. Final state: %d\n\n", state)

// Example 2: Accumulating the Sum of the First 10 Natural
↪   Numbers
// This example uses a classic for loop to compute the sum:
//    for i := 1; i <= n; i++ { sum += i }
// Here, the loop invariant is that 'sum' holds the
↪   cumulative total up to i.
sum := 0  // Accumulator initialization
n := 10   // Total numbers to sum

fmt.Println("Example 2: Summing the First 10 Natural
↪   Numbers")
for i := 1; i <= n; i++ {
        sum += i  // Update the accumulator: invariant sum
        ↪   holds the total for i numbers.
        fmt.Printf("After adding %d, cumulative sum: %d\n",
        ↪   i, sum)
}
fmt.Printf("Total sum from 1 to %d is: %d\n", n, sum)
}
```

Chapter 15

Looping Constructs: For Loops with Range

Semantic Overview

The range keyword in the context of a for loop constitutes a fundamental mechanism for iterating over composite data structures. This construct abstracts the notion of sequential traversal by automatically handling the extraction of paired values from the underlying collection. Formally, for any composite data structure C, the range-based iteration yields pairs that may be denoted as (k, v), where k represents an index or key and v corresponds to the associated element of C. This abstraction not only simplifies iteration but also encapsulates the underlying traversal semantics in a unified syntactic form.

Iteration over Arrays and Slices

For arrays and slices, the range construct enforces a deterministic iteration over a contiguous block of memory. Let A denote an array or slice of length n. In each iteration, two values are produced: an index i and the corresponding element $A[i]$, where i ranges over the set $\{0, 1, 2, \ldots, n-1\}$. This correspondence can be formalized through an indexing function $f : \{0, 1, \ldots, n-1\} \to A$, where each $f(i) = A[i]$ is yielded in sequential order. The iteration mechanism guarantees that every element is visited exactly once in a manner that preserves the natural ordering inherent to the underlying structure.

Iteration over Maps

In the case of maps, the range keyword yields a pair of values representing each key and its associated value. Consider a map M defined by the functional relationship $M : D \to V$, where D is the domain of keys and V is the set of corresponding values. The range-based iteration over M produces pairs (k, v) for each $k \in D$, with $v = M(k)$. Importantly, the order of iteration over the map is not specified; it is deliberately nondeterministic, thereby precluding any assumptions regarding the ordering of key-value pairs. This nondeterminism is intrinsic to the map construct and enforces a level of abstraction that prevents dependence on any predictable sequence during iteration.

Iteration over Strings

Strings in Go are sequences of bytes interpreted under the UTF-8 encoding, and range-based iteration over a string is uniquely adapted to accommodate multibyte characters. Given a string s, the range iteration mechanism decodes the UTF-8 sequence starting at a particular byte index to yield a pair (i, r), where i is the starting byte index of a Unicode code point and r denotes the decoded rune. The mapping can be considered as a decoding function d such that each extracted pair satisfies $r = d(s, i)$, with the index i subsequently advancing by the number of bytes that constitute r. This approach ensures that characters encoded using multiple bytes are treated as single, atomic entities during iteration.

Formal Analysis of For Range Semantics

The operational behavior of the for loop employing the range keyword can be analyzed as a higher-order iterative mapping over a given composite data structure. Let C represent an arbitrary collection, which, depending on its type, embodies one of several structures: an array or slice, a map, or a string. For arrays and slices, the iteration process defines a tuple $\phi(C) = (A(0), A(1), \ldots, A(n-1))$, where each element is produced in a sequential and ordered fashion. For a map $M : D \to V$, the range construct yields a permutation of the set $\{(k, v) : k \in D \wedge v = M(k)\}$, with the inherent nondeterminism obviating any assumed ordering. In the context of strings, the extracted collection is given by $\phi(s) = \{(i, r) : r = d(s, i)\}$, where d denotes the UTF-8 decoding function that maps a starting byte index i to its corresponding rune r. This formalization underscores the intrinsic uniformity and elegance of the range-based iteration, encapsulating a variety of data traversal operations within a singular, expressive syntactic framework.

Go Code Snippet

```go
package main

import (
        "fmt"
        "unicode/utf8"
)

// iterateArrayAndSlice demonstrates the formal iteration over
↪    arrays and slices.
// For any array or slice A of length n, the range loop yields pairs
↪    (i, A[i]),
// corresponding to the function f(i) = A[i] where i ranges over {0,
↪    1, ..., n-1}.
func iterateArrayAndSlice() {
        // Define an array of integers.
        arr := [5]int{10, 20, 30, 40, 50}
        // Define a slice of strings.
        slice := []string{"apple", "banana", "cherry"}

        fmt.Println("Iteration over array:")
        for i, v := range arr {
                // Each iteration yields (i, arr[i])
                fmt.Printf("Index %d, Value %d\n", i, v)
        }

        fmt.Println("\nIteration over slice:")
        for i, v := range slice {
                // For slices, similar to arrays, every element is
                ↪    visited in order.
                fmt.Printf("Index %d, Value %s\n", i, v)
        }
}

// iterateMap demonstrates iteration over a map representing a
↪    function M: D -> V.
// The range loop yields key-value pairs (k, M[k]) for each key in
↪    the map.
```

```go
// Note: The order over the map is nondeterministic, aligning with
↪   Go's abstract semantics.
func iterateMap() {
        // Define a map of string keys to integer values.
        m := map[string]int{
                "Alice":   25,
                "Bob":     30,
                "Charlie": 35,
        }

        fmt.Println("\nIteration over map:")
        for key, value := range m {
                // Each pair (key, value) corresponds to (k, M[k])
                fmt.Printf("Key %s, Value %d\n", key, value)
        }
}


// iterateString demonstrates iteration over a UTF-8 encoded string.
// For a string s, each iteration yields (i, r) where i is the
↪   starting byte index
// and r is the decoded rune from the UTF-8 sequence. This is
↪   analogous to applying
// the decoding function d(s, i) = r.
func iterateString() {
        s := "Hello, "
        fmt.Println("\nIteration over string:")
        for i, r := range s {
                // Verify the rune decoding even for multi-byte
                ↪   characters.
                // i: starting byte index, r: decoded rune
                fmt.Printf("Byte index %d, Rune %c (Unicode: %U)\n",
                ↪   i, r, r)
        }
}


// main function orchestrates the demonstration of formal for range
↪   semantics,
// covering arrays/slices, maps, and strings in Go.
func main() {
        fmt.Println("Demonstrating range-based iterations in Go:\n")
        iterateArrayAndSlice()
        iterateMap()
        iterateString()

        // Additional demonstration: Count runes in a string using
        ↪   utf8.RuneCountInString.
        s := "Hello, "
        runeCount := utf8.RuneCountInString(s)
        fmt.Printf("\nTotal number of runes in %q: %d\n", s,
        ↪   runeCount)
}
```

79

Chapter 16

Arrays: Declaration and Usage

Declaration of Fixed-Size Arrays

Fixed-size arrays in Go are defined by an explicit specification of their length and element type. The canonical form of an array declaration is given by the syntax $[N]T$, where N is a nonnegative integer constant representing the number of elements and T is the type of each element. The size N is an intrinsic component of the array's type identity; hence, two arrays with differing bounds, such as $[N]T$ and $[M]T$ for $N \neq M$, are considered distinct types within the type system. This strict type equivalence reinforces strong, static type checking, thereby enabling rigorous compile-time analysis. The semantics of this declaration ensure that memory is allocated in a contiguous block, with the address computation for any element being a deterministic function of its index.

Initialization Strategies for Arrays

The process of initialization in the context of fixed-size arrays permits the assignment of values at the time of declaration. A literal initializer may enumerate values corresponding to each index in the range $0, 1, \ldots, N - 1$. In cases where only a subset of indices is explicitly assigned, the remaining elements are automatically initialized to the zero value of the element type T. This behavior can be formally represented by a partial mapping: for an array A of length N, if a value is specified for indices in a subset $I \subseteq \{0, 1, \ldots, N-1\}$ such that $A(i) = v_i$ for each $i \in I$, then for all $j \notin I$, the assignment $A(j) = 0_T$ holds, where 0_T denotes the zero value corresponding to type T. This scheme of initialization guarantees that every index is associated with a well-defined value immediately following declaration.

Manipulation Techniques for Arrays

Manipulation of fixed-size arrays in Go encompasses operations that modify, access, and compare array elements within their statically determined bounds. Given that an array A is a mapping from the discrete set $\{0, 1, \ldots, N-1\}$ to type T, individual elements are accessed via indexing, denoted by $A(i)$ for $0 \leq i < N$. Assignment operations of the form $A(i) := x$, where $x \in T$, update the value stored at the specified index.

Arrays in Go are value types, meaning that an assignment to a new variable or a parameter passing operation results in a complete copy of the array. This behavior is congruent with the semantic model in which each array is treated as an independent entity, thereby necessitating an element-wise copy even when the arrays share identical structural properties. Furthermore, equality comparisons between arrays are defined in an element-wise manner: two arrays A and B of type $[N]T$ are considered equal if and only if

$$\forall i \in \{0, 1, \ldots, N-1\}, \quad A(i) = B(i).$$

This strict comparison rule applies provided that the element type T supports equality operations.

Manipulative operations also extend to techniques such as swapping elements and iterating through indices to perform collective transformations. The fixed-size nature of arrays precludes resizing operations; thus, any algorithmic adjustments must operate within the confines of the predetermined capacity. The deterministic layout of array elements in memory allows for analysis of computational complexity, particularly in the context of in-place modifications and value comparisons. Such properties underscore the balance between low-level memory management and high-level type safety inherent in Go's design.

Go Code Snippet

```go
package main

import "fmt"

// compareArrays performs an element-wise comparison between two
//   fixed-size arrays.
// It returns true if and only if for all i in {0,1,...,N-1}, a[i]
//   == b[i].
func compareArrays(a, b [5]int) bool {
    for i := 0; i < len(a); i++ {
        if a[i] != b[i] {
            return false
        }
    }
    return true
}


// swapElements swaps the elements at indices i and j in a
//   fixed-size array.
// It returns a new array with the two elements swapped.
func swapElements(arr [5]int, i, j int) [5]int {
    arr[i], arr[j] = arr[j], arr[i]
    return arr
}


// modifyArray doubles each element of the input array. This
//   demonstrates
// in-place manipulation via iteration, while also emphasizing that
//   arrays
// in Go are value types and modifications occur on a copy unless
//   explicitly managed.
func modifyArray(arr [5]int) [5]int {
    for i := 0; i < len(arr); i++ {
        arr[i] = arr[i] * 2
    }
    return arr
}


func main() {
    // Declaration of a fixed-size array of 5 integers.
    var arr1 [5]int
    fmt.Println("Initial arr1:", arr1)

    // Partial initialization: only indices 0, 2, and 4 are set;
    //   others default to zero.
    arr2 := [5]int{0: 10, 2: 20, 4: 30}
    fmt.Println("Initialized arr2:", arr2)

    // Demonstrate assignment by modifying an element (index 1)
    //   explicitly.
```

```go
    arr2[1] = 15
    fmt.Println("After modifying arr2[1]:", arr2)

    // Display each element with its index and corresponding
    ↪    memory address
    // to illustrate the contiguous memory layout.
    for i, v := range arr2 {
        fmt.Printf("Element at index %d: %d, Address: %p\n",
        ↪    i, v, &arr2[i])
    }

    // Swapping elements at index 0 and index 4 in arr2.
    swappedArr := swapElements(arr2, 0, 4)
    fmt.Println("After swapping index 0 and 4 in arr2:",
    ↪    swappedArr)

    // Element-wise comparison of two arrays.
    // According to the formal equality: for all i in
    ↪    {0,1,...,N-1}, arr2[i] == arr3[i].
    arr3 := [5]int{10, 15, 20, 0, 30}
    areEqual := compareArrays(arr2, arr3)
    fmt.Println("Are arr2 and arr3 equal?", areEqual)

    // Demonstrate that arrays are value types (deep copy
    ↪    behavior).
    arr4 := arr2
    arr4[0] = 999 // Modifying arr4 does not affect arr2.
    fmt.Println("arr2 remains unchanged after modifying arr4:",
    ↪    arr2)
    fmt.Println("Modified copy arr4:", arr4)

    // Apply an algorithm (doubling each element) to the array
    ↪    arr3.
    modifiedArr := modifyArray(arr3)
    fmt.Println("After doubling each element in arr3:",
    ↪    modifiedArr)
}
```

Chapter 17

Slices: Introduction and Basic Operations

Fundamental Representation and Semantics

A slice in the Go programming language constitutes a lightweight data structure that provides a dynamic, flexible view into a contiguous sequence of elements residing in an underlying array. Formally, a slice s is represented by a triplet $(ptr(s), len(s), cap(s))$, where $ptr(s)$ is a pointer to the first element of the slice, $len(s)$ denotes the number of elements accessible via the slice, and $cap(s)$ indicates the total number of elements in the underlying array starting from the element addressed by $ptr(s)$. The invariant $len(s) \leq cap(s)$ is strictly maintained, ensuring that operations on the slice remain bounded within the allocated segment of the array. This structural abstraction permits rigorous compile-time reasoning about memory layout while providing the operational flexibility necessitated by dynamic data manipulation.

Creation and Initialization Techniques

The construction of a slice may be performed via a slicing expression on a fixed-size array, thereby enabling the extraction of a contiguous subset from the original data structure. Given an array A of type $[N]T$, a slicing expression of the form $A[i : j]$ yields a slice that encompasses the elements $A[i], A[i+1], \ldots, A[j-1]$, with indices i and j satisfying $0 \leq i \leq j \leq N$. This method of formation results in a slice that preserves a reference to the underlying array, permitting modifications to be reflected across all views that share the same memory region. Alternatively, slices can be established using intrinsic allocation techniques provided by built-in functions that dynamically allocate an underlying array. In either case, the explicit decoupling of the slice's logical length from its capacity permits dynamic adjustment of the accessible portion of the array, thereby facilitating operations that require variable-length data management while retaining the benefits of static memory allocation.

Basic Operations and Underlying Mechanisms

Operations on slices are distinguished by their emphasis on efficiency and controlled memory usage. The indexing operation, denoted by $s[i]$, provides direct access to the ith element of a slice s, with the constraint that $0 \leq i < len(s)$. Slices further support a secondary slicing operation, wherein $s[i : j]$ produces a new slice that represents a subrange of the original slice, thus maintaining a shared reference to the same underlying array. The dynamic properties of slices are governed by their length and capacity; while the length specifies the current number of accessible elements, the capacity indicates the maximum number of elements that can be accommodated within the array segment commencing at $ptr(s)$. Consequently, operations that extend the slice beyond its current length but within its capacity are feasible without necessitating additional memory allocation. However, should an operation attempt to exceed this capacity, the Go runtime enacts a reallocation protocol that involves the creation of a new underlying array with an appropriate capacity, followed by the transfer of existing elements. This approach, combined with the fact that slices are reference types, necessitates prudent management of shared state, as modifications through one slice can propagate to other slices referencing the same memory region. The interplay between these operations underscores the conceptual elegance and practical efficiency embedded in the design of slices as a fundamental building block for dynamic data structures.

Go Code Snippet

```go
package main

import (
    "fmt"
    "unsafe"
)

// printSliceInfo prints the pointer to the first element,
// the length, and the capacity of the given slice.
// This demonstrates the slice representation: (ptr, len, cap)
func printSliceInfo(name string, s []int) {
    // It is safe to assume s is non-empty in these examples.
    fmt.Printf("%s - Ptr: %p, Length: %d, Capacity: %d\n", name,
        unsafe.Pointer(&s[0]), len(s), cap(s))
}

func main() {
    // 1. Create an underlying fixed-size array.
    arr := [10]int{0, 1, 2, 3, 4, 5, 6, 7, 8, 9}

    // 2. Create a slice s1 using a slicing expression on the
    //    array.
    // This slice represents the triplet (ptr, len, cap) where:
    //   ptr: pointer to arr[2]
    //   len: 5 (elements from index 2 to 6)
    //   cap: 8 (from index 2 to the end of the array)
    s1 := arr[2:7]
    fmt.Println("Slice s1 (from arr[2:7])")
    printSliceInfo("s1", s1)
    fmt.Printf("Content of s1: %v\n\n", s1)

    // 3. Create a subslice s2 from s1.
    // s2 references elements from s1[1] to s1[3] (i.e. arr[3]
    //    to arr[5]).
    s2 := s1[1:4]
    fmt.Println("Slice s2 (from s1[1:4])")
    printSliceInfo("s2", s2)
    fmt.Printf("Content of s2: %v\n\n", s2)

    // 4. Demonstrate that slices share the underlying array.
    // Modify an element via s1 and observe the change in s2.
    s1[2] = 100  // This affects arr[4]
    fmt.Println("After modifying s1[2] to 100:")
    fmt.Printf("Updated array: %v\n", arr)
    fmt.Printf("Content of s2 (reflecting change): %v\n\n", s2)

    // 5. Create a slice using the built-in make function.
    // Here, s3 is initialized with length 3 and capacity 5.
    s3 := make([]int, 3, 5)
    fmt.Println("Slice s3 (created with make)")
```

```go
printSliceInfo("s3", s3)
fmt.Printf("Content of s3: %v\n\n", s3)

// 6. Append an element to s3 while staying within its
↪  capacity.
s3 = append(s3, 10)
fmt.Println("After appending 10 to s3 (within capacity):")
printSliceInfo("s3", s3)
fmt.Printf("Content of s3: %v\n\n", s3)

// 7. Append additional elements to s3 to exceed its
↪  capacity.
// This operation triggers reallocation: a new underlying
↪  array is allocated,
// and the contents are copied over.
s3 = append(s3, 20, 30)
fmt.Println("After appending 20 and 30 to s3 (exceeding
↪  capacity):")
printSliceInfo("s3", s3)
fmt.Printf("Content of s3: %v\n\n", s3)

// 8. Demonstrate direct indexing and further slicing.
fmt.Printf("Element at index 0 of s1: %d\n", s1[0])
subSlice := s1[1:3] // Creates a new slice sharing the same
↪  underlying array.
fmt.Printf("Subslice of s1 (s1[1:3]): %v\n\n", subSlice)

// 9. Advanced demonstration: Appending within capacity when
↪  underlying array is shared.
// Create s4 as a full slice copy of s1.
s4 := s1[:]
fmt.Println("Slice s4 (a full copy of s1 referencing the
↪  same array):")
printSliceInfo("s4", s4)
fmt.Printf("Content of s4: %v\n", s4)

// Append an element to s4 without exceeding capacity.
// Since capacity is available, s4 still references the
↪  original array.
s4 = append(s4, 200)
fmt.Println("\nAfter appending 200 to s4 (within
↪  capacity):")
printSliceInfo("s4", s4)
fmt.Printf("Content of s4: %v\n", s4)

// Modify s4 and observe the effect on s1, because they
↪  share the same underlying array.
s4[0] = 999
fmt.Println("\nAfter modifying s4[0] to 999:")
fmt.Printf("s4: %v\n", s4)
fmt.Printf("s1 (affected due to shared underlying array):
↪  %v\n", s1)
```

87

}

Chapter 18

Slices: Manipulation and Growth

Fundamental Mechanics of Slice Mutation

A slice in Go is defined by a triplet $(ptr(s), len(s), cap(s))$, where $ptr(s)$ denotes the pointer to the underlying array, $len(s)$ represents the number of elements currently accessible, and $cap(s)$ specifies the total number of elements available in the underlying storage from the position indicated by $ptr(s)$. The mutable nature of slices arises from their status as reference types, meaning that multiple slice instances can share the same underlying array. Alterations made through one slice—provided these alterations occur within the bounds of $len(s)$—are immediately reflected in any other slice referencing the same memory region. This facet of slice semantics requires that manipulations be conducted with rigorous attention to the invariant $len(s) \leq cap(s)$, thereby ensuring that any extension of the slice remains contained within the allocated segment of memory.

Dynamic Appending of Elements

The process of appending elements to a slice constitutes a fundamental method of dynamic modification, permitting both the expansion of the logical length and, under certain conditions, the reallocation of the underlying array. When an element is appended to a slice, the operation determines whether the new length, denoted as $len(s) + 1$, remains within the current capacity $cap(s)$. Should this condition be satisfied, the appended element occupies the subsequent memory location in the preallocated array, and the slice's length is incremented accordingly. In contrast, if the operation would result in $len(s) + 1 > cap(s)$, the runtime initiates a reallocation protocol. This protocol entails the creation of a new underlying array with increased capacity, typically following a geometric growth strategy, and the subsequent copying of existing elements into the new array. This reallocation step, while usually amortized to constant time over a sequence of operations, introduces a computational overhead that is essential for the flexibility of dynamic data management.

Capacity Management and Memory Reallocation

The management of a slice's capacity is integrally connected to the behavior of its underlying array and has profound implications for both memory utilization and performance. When a slice is first derived—whether by slicing an array or through a built-in allocation—the capacity $cap(s)$ is set either implicitly or according to explicitly provided parameters. As elements are appended, the current capacity is monitored; operations that remain within $cap(s)$ incur no additional allocation cost. However, when an append operation forces $len(s)$ to exceed $cap(s)$, a new array is allocated with a capacity that often exceeds $len(s)$ by a predefined factor, ensuring an efficient amortized cost for subsequent appends. This process mathematically guarantees that even sequences of repeated append operations incur only an infrequent costlier reallocation. The decision-making process implemented by the runtime is both heuristic and adaptive, striking a balance between the minimization of memory overhead and the efficiency of data movement. Consequently, the dynamic adjustment of slice capacity is not merely an incidental detail but a deliberate design feature that underpins the effective manipulation and growth of slices throughout a program's execution.

Go Code Snippet

```go
package main

import (
        "fmt"
        "unsafe"
)

// printSliceInfo prints important details of the slice including
// ↪ its length, capacity,
// pointer to its first element, and the slice's current content.
func printSliceInfo(label string, s []int) {
        if len(s) > 0 {
                fmt.Printf("%s: len=%d, cap=%d, ptr=%p, data=%v\n",
                ↪ label, len(s), cap(s), &s[0], s)
        } else {
                fmt.Printf("%s: len=%d, cap=%d, ptr=nil, data=%v\n",
                ↪ label, len(s), cap(s), s)
        }
}

// customAppend simulates the append operation by incorporating the
// ↪ key algorithm:
// If (len(s) + 1) <= cap(s), it simply extends the slice by one
// ↪ element and assigns the value.
// Otherwise, it reallocates a new underlying array with increased
// ↪ capacity (using geometric growth),
// copies the existing elements, and then appends the new element.
// This reflects the invariants and memory reallocation mechanism
// ↪ described in the chapter.
func customAppend(s []int, elem int) []int {
        // Check the invariant: if len(s)+1 is less than or equal to
        // ↪ cap(s), extend without reallocation.
        if len(s)+1 <= cap(s) {
                s = s[:len(s)+1]
                s[len(s)-1] = elem
                return s
        }
        // Not enough capacity: calculate new capacity (typically
        // ↪ doubling the current capacity).
        newCap := cap(s) * 2
        if newCap == 0 {
                newCap = 1
        }
        newSlice := make([]int, len(s)+1, newCap)
        copy(newSlice, s)
        newSlice[len(s)] = elem
        return newSlice
}

func main() {
```

```go
// Demonstrate dynamic slice manipulation using the built-in
↪ append function.
fmt.Println("=== Built-in Append Demonstration ===")
// Initialize a slice with length 0 and capacity 3.
s := make([]int, 0, 3)
printSliceInfo("Initial s", s)

// Append elements one by one; check for reallocation by
↪ monitoring the pointer of the underlying array.
for i := 1; i <= 10; i++ {
        var prevPtr uintptr
        if len(s) > 0 {
                prevPtr = uintptr(unsafe.Pointer(&s[0]))
        }
        s = append(s, i)
        fmt.Printf("\nAfter appending %d:\n", i)
        printSliceInfo("s", s)
        if len(s) > 1 {
                newPtr := uintptr(unsafe.Pointer(&s[0]))
                if prevPtr != 0 && prevPtr != newPtr {
                        fmt.Println("Note: Underlying array
                        ↪ reallocated!")
                }
        }
}

// Separator for clarity between demonstrations.
fmt.Println("\n=== Custom Append Simulation ===")
// Start with a slice directly initialized with three
↪ elements.
s2 := []int{100, 200, 300}
printSliceInfo("Initial s2", s2)

// Use customAppend repeatedly to simulate manual capacity
↪ management.
for i := 1; i <= 5; i++ {
        fmt.Printf("\nCustom appending %d to s2:\n", i*10)
        var prevPtr uintptr
        if len(s2) > 0 {
                prevPtr = uintptr(unsafe.Pointer(&s2[0]))
        }
        s2 = customAppend(s2, i*10)
        printSliceInfo("s2", s2)
        newPtr := uintptr(unsafe.Pointer(&s2[0]))
        if prevPtr != 0 && prevPtr != newPtr {
                fmt.Println("Note: Underlying array
                ↪ reallocated in customAppend!")
        }
}
}
```

Chapter 19

Maps: Creation and Basic Operations

Declaration and Initialization

1 Type Specification in Map Declarations

Maps are abstract data structures that associate keys with corresponding values and are defined through a type construct of the form $map[K]V$, where K denotes the type of keys and V the type of values. This syntactic construct provides a compile-time guarantee on the nature of the keys and values stored in the map, ensuring that operations on these associations are performed in a type-safe manner. The explicit declaration of a map thereby establishes a contract that the keys are drawn from a specific domain, and that each such key is uniquely associated with a value from a prescribed codomain.

2 Methods of Instantiation

The instantiation of maps involves allocating memory for the internal data structures that underpin the key-to-value associations. Two prevalent methods exist for instantiation. One approach is to declare a map literal that directly specifies initial key-value bindings. An alternative is to adopt a dynamic instantiation method, wherein an allocation function is employed to create an empty map with a predetermined initial capacity. Irrespective of the chosen mechanism, the resultant map is a reference type; consequently, its elements are accessed indirectly via a pointer to the underlying hash table, which is dynamically managed by the runtime environment.

Basic Operations on Maps

1 Insertion and Update Mechanics

The insertion of key-value pairs into a map is foundational to its utility as an associative container. Insertion is executed by making an explicit assignment of a value to a particular key, thereby either establishing a new association or subsequently updating an existing one. This operation, when performed in a well-formed manner, preserves the uniqueness of keys within the map. The inherent property of maps to accommodate updates via key reassignments ensures that the most recent value associated with a particular key is available for future operations, thereby maintaining internal consistency without necessitating explicit removal of the prior binding.

2 Retrieval and Existence Testing

Retrieval of values in the context of maps is achieved by referencing the key of interest. The operation yields the value associated with the key if such an association is present; otherwise, a default value appropriate to the type may be produced. Existence testing is an essential adjunct to retrieval, as it enables the determination of whether a key is present within the map. This duality of operations—retrieval of the value alongside a Boolean indicator of membership—facilitates robust handling of cases where a key may be absent, thereby precluding erroneous accesses or unintentional reliance on default values.

3 Deletion and Structural Modifications

The removal of key-value pairs from a map is implemented by explicitly dissociating a key from its corresponding value. This operation effectively excises the pairing from the internal representation, thereby reducing the overall size of the map. Notably, deletion does not necessarily entail the immediate compaction of the underlying storage; rather, the entry is marked for removal, and the internal hash structure is adjusted accordingly. Such structural modifications preserve the integrity of the data structure while accommodating subsequent insertions and lookups with minimal overhead. The dynamic nature of maps, combined with their efficient memory management strategies, permits a fluid and adaptive manipulation of key-value associations over the course of program execution.

Go Code Snippet

```go
package main

import (
        "fmt"
)

func main() {
        // ---------------------------------------------------------
        // Declaration and Initialization of Maps
        // ---------------------------------------------------------

        // Method 1: Using a map literal
        capitalCities := map[string]string{
                "USA":    "Washington, D.C.",
                "France": "Paris",
                "Japan":  "Tokyo",
        }

        // Method 2: Using make with an initial capacity
        population := make(map[string]int, 3)
        population["USA"] = 331002651
        population["France"] = 65273511
        population["Japan"] = 126476461

        // Display initial maps
        fmt.Println("Initial capitalCities map:")
        for country, city := range capitalCities {
                fmt.Printf("%s: %s\n", country, city)
        }

        fmt.Println("\nInitial population map:")
        for country, pop := range population {
                fmt.Printf("%s: %d\n", country, pop)
        }

        // ---------------------------------------------------------
        // Insertion and Update Mechanics
        // ---------------------------------------------------------

        // Inserting a new key-value pair into capitalCities
```

```go
capitalCities["India"] = "New Delhi"
// Updating an existing key in population
population["USA"] = 332000000 // Updated population for USA

// Display maps after insertion and update
fmt.Println("\nAfter insertion and update:")
fmt.Println("Updated capitalCities map:")
for country, city := range capitalCities {
        fmt.Printf("%s: %s\n", country, city)
}
fmt.Println("\nUpdated population map:")
for country, pop := range population {
        fmt.Printf("%s: %d\n", country, pop)
}

// ---------------------------------------------------------
// Retrieval and Existence Testing
// ---------------------------------------------------------

// Retrieve with existence check: capital of Japan
key := "Japan"
if city, exists := capitalCities[key]; exists {
        fmt.Printf("\nThe capital of %s is %s\n", key, city)
} else {
        fmt.Printf("\n%s was not found in capitalCities
          ↪ map.\n", key)
}

// Attempt retrieval of a non-existent key: capital of
↪ Brazil
key = "Brazil"
if city, exists := capitalCities[key]; exists {
        fmt.Printf("\nThe capital of %s is %s\n", key, city)
} else {
        fmt.Printf("\n%s was not found in capitalCities
          ↪ map.\n", key)
}

// ---------------------------------------------------------
// Deletion and Structural Modifications
// ---------------------------------------------------------

// Show population map before deletion
fmt.Println("\nPopulation map before deletion:")
fmt.Println(population)

// Delete the entry for France from population map
delete(population, "France")
fmt.Println("Population map after deletion of France:")
fmt.Println(population)

// Iterating over the capitalCities map to display each pair
fmt.Println("\nIterating over capitalCities map:")
```

```go
        for country, city := range capitalCities {
                fmt.Printf("Country: %s, Capital: %s\n", country,
                ↪   city)
        }

        // ----------------------------------------------------------
        // Algorithm: Word Frequency Count using Map
        // ----------------------------------------------------------

        // Sample text for word frequency count
        sampleText := "the quick brown fox jumps over the lazy dog,
        ↪   the quick dog did not react"
        // freqMap will hold word frequencies
        freqMap := make(map[string]int)

        // Splitting the sampleText into words (simple tokenization)
        words := splitWords(sampleText)
        for _, word := range words {
                // Insert or update the frequency in the map
                freqMap[word]++
        }

        fmt.Println("\nWord frequency count:")
        for word, count := range freqMap {
                fmt.Printf("%s: %d\n", word, count)
        }
}

// splitWords is a helper function that tokenizes the input text
↪   into words.
// It considers consecutive letters as a word and uses non-letter
↪   characters as delimiters.
func splitWords(text string) []string {
        var words []string
        currentWord := ""
        for _, char := range text {
                // Check if the character is a letter (both
                ↪   uppercase and lowercase)
                if (char >= 'a' && char <= 'z') || (char >= 'A' &&
                ↪   char <= 'Z') {
                        currentWord += string(char)
                } else {
                        if currentWord != "" {
                                words = append(words, currentWord)
                                currentWord = ""
                        }
                }
        }
        // Append the last accumulated word if any
        if currentWord != "" {
                words = append(words, currentWord)
        }
        return words
```

97

}

Chapter 20

Maps: Iteration and Common Patterns

Iteration Mechanisms in Map Data Structures

1 Structural Overview of Map Iteration

Within the theoretical framework of map data structures, iteration is facilitated by an abstraction over the underlying hash table implementation. The fundamental construct of a map is conceived as a collection of key-value bindings, where keys are drawn from a predetermined domain and values are associated in a manner that guarantees constant-time average lookup performance, typically denoted as $O(1)$. The process of iterating over a map entails traversing the internal hash table buckets and yielding each occupied slot in a sequential order. However, by design, the order in which key-value pairs are encountered is non-deterministic. This inherent non-determinism is a deliberate strategy intended to conceal structural details of the hash table, thereby impeding reliance on any fixed ordering. The iterative mechanism systematically accesses each binding without the overhead of maintaining an external index, thereby ensuring that the full traversal of n elements is achieved with a time complexity of $O(n)$.

2　Complexity and Behavioral Properties

From an algorithmic standpoint, the iteration over a map is characterized by both its simplicity and its nuanced performance characteristics. The iteration construct operates over the complete set of entries, and each iteration step is executed in constant time under average conditions. The absence of a guaranteed order is compensated by the efficiency of direct access to each element, which is managed internally by the runtime environment. The traversal algorithm effectively distinguishes between occupied, vacant, and marked-for-deletion slots, thus preserving the integrity of the key-value associations during both read and update operations. This interplay between simplicity and internal complexity reinforces the suitability of maps in domains requiring rapid associative lookups alongside comprehensive traversal capabilities.

Common Patterns for Optimizing Key-Value Data Access

1　Transformation and Aggregation Patterns

A recurring pattern in the utilization of maps is the simultaneous execution of transformation and aggregation operations during iteration. In scenarios where data undergoes a form of computational synthesis—such as summing values, computing averages, or constructing frequency distributions—the iterative process serves a dual purpose. First, it extracts the necessary key-value pairs from the map, and second, it applies a transformation function to accumulate or reconstitute the data. By leveraging a single-pass iteration, the aggregation pattern minimizes redundant memory accesses and circumvents the need for auxiliary loops. The integration of transformation within the iteration loop often results in improved cache utilization and reduced overhead, thereby enhancing overall performance when manipulating large volumes of key-value associations.

2　Filter-Based and Auxiliary Structure Techniques

Iteration over map structures also commonly incorporates filtering mechanisms that selectively identify entries meeting specific predicates. This filtering pattern is instrumental in isolating subsets of data that satisfy domain-specific criteria, allowing subsequent operations to be performed on a refined data set. In instances where a deterministic order is required for further processing—despite the inherent non-determinism of map iteration—the keys extracted during the traversal can be migrated into an auxiliary data structure, such as a slice, which may then be subjected to sorting. This approach not only preserves the efficiency of the initial map traversal but also provides a controlled environment in which ordered operations can be performed. The combined application of filtering and auxiliary structuring exemplifies an optimization strategy that balances the raw efficiency of map iteration with the requisite operational constraints of higher-level data processing tasks.

3 Concurrent and Lazy Evaluation Considerations

In advanced applications, particularly within the realms of distributed systems and high-throughput data processing, iteration over maps is augmented by concurrency and lazy evaluation techniques. When multiple processing units operate concurrently on disparate segments of a map, synchronization strategies ensure that data consistency is maintained while avoiding significant contention. Lazy evaluation further refines this iterative model by deferring computation until the exact data subset is required, thereby optimizing resource utilization. The marriage of concurrent iteration with lazy evaluation facilitates a dynamic access pattern that adapts to runtime conditions, preserving performance even in the presence of large and frequently mutated data sets. These patterns not only optimize the immediate access of key-value pairs but also contribute to the overall scalability of systems reliant on rapid, iterative data access.

Go Code Snippet

```
package main

import (
        "fmt"
        "sort"
        "sync"
        "time"
)
```

```go
// mapEntry represents a key-value pair in the map.
type mapEntry struct {
        key     string
        value int
}


// sumValues aggregates the values of the map by summing them.
// Algorithmic Complexity: O(n) where each lookup is O(1) on
↪   average.
// Equation: total = v, for all v in the map.
func sumValues(m map[string]int) int {
        sum := 0
        for _, v := range m {
                // Aggregation: sum all values.
                sum += v
        }
        return sum
}


// filterMap returns a new map containing only those key-value pairs
// that satisfy the provided predicate function.
func filterMap(m map[string]int, predicate func(string, int) bool)
↪   map[string]int {
        filtered := make(map[string]int)
        for k, v := range m {
                if predicate(k, v) {
                        filtered[k] = v
                }
        }
        return filtered
}


// sortedKeys returns a sorted slice of keys from the map.
// This allows for converting a non-deterministic iteration order
↪   into a
// deterministic one for further processing.
func sortedKeys(m map[string]int) []string {
        keys := make([]string, 0, len(m))
        for k := range m {
                keys = append(keys, k)
        }
        sort.Strings(keys)
        return keys
}


// processMapConcurrently demonstrates a concurrent approach to
↪   processing map entries.
// It uses a worker pool to process each entry sent through a
↪   channel, simulating lazy evaluation.
// The iteration over the map is O(n) with average constant time
↪   O(1) per lookup.
func processMapConcurrently(m map[string]int) {
        // Create a channel for map entries.
```

```go
    ch := make(chan mapEntry)
    var wg sync.WaitGroup
    numWorkers := 3

    // Launch worker goroutines.
    for i := 0; i < numWorkers; i++ {
        wg.Add(1)
        go func(workerID int) {
            defer wg.Done()
            for entry := range ch {
                // Simulate processing each entry.
                fmt.Printf("Worker %d processed: %s
                ↪   => %d\n", workerID, entry.key,
                ↪   entry.value)
                // Introduce a small delay to mimic
                ↪   processing time.
                time.Sleep(50 * time.Millisecond)
            }
        }(i)
    }

    // Lazy iteration: send each map entry into the channel.
    // The iteration itself traverses n elements in O(n) time.
    for k, v := range m {
        ch <- mapEntry{key: k, value: v}
    }
    close(ch)
    wg.Wait()
}

func main() {
    // Sample map representing a collection of items and their
    ↪   associated values.
    data := map[string]int{
        "apple":  3,
        "banana": 5,
        "orange": 2,
        "kiwi":   7,
        "grape":  4,
    }

    // Display the original map.
    fmt.Println("Original Map:")
    for k, v := range data {
        fmt.Printf("%s => %d\n", k, v)
    }

    // Aggregation: Calculate the total sum of values in the
    ↪   map.
    total := sumValues(data)
    fmt.Printf("\nTotal (Aggregation): %d\n", total)
```

```go
    // Filtering: Select key-value pairs where the value exceeds
    ↪  3.
    filtered := filterMap(data, func(key string, value int) bool
    ↪  {
        return value > 3
    })
    fmt.Println("\nFiltered Map (value > 3):")
    for k, v := range filtered {
        fmt.Printf("%s => %d\n", k, v)
    }

    // Sorting: Display map entries in a deterministic order by
    ↪  sorting the keys.
    fmt.Println("\nMap Entries in Sorted Order:")
    keys := sortedKeys(data)
    for _, k := range keys {
        fmt.Printf("%s => %d\n", k, data[k])
    }

    // Concurrent Processing: Process map entries using a worker
    ↪  pool.
    fmt.Println("\nConcurrent Processing of Map Entries:")
    processMapConcurrently(data)
}
```

Chapter 21

Structs: Defining Custom Data Structures

Conceptual Foundations of Structs

Structs represent a foundational mechanism for aggregating multiple, potentially heterogeneous, data elements into a single coherent unit. Within many formal systems, a struct is conceived as a composite type, where each constituent element—commonly referred to as a field—embodies a specific attribute of the overall entity. The purpose of such an aggregation is to encapsulate related data components under a unified interface, thereby reflecting real-world entities or abstract conceptual constructs. This grouping permits the representation of complex entities as a conjunction of simpler parts, facilitating reasoning about the data in a disciplined and structured manner without recourse to ad hoc associations.

The abstraction provided by structs is inherently aligned with the notion of modularity in type theory. By delineating a clear structure for data, structs provide a means to express invariants and semantic relationships between different data components. The well-defined boundaries separating each field contribute both to the clarity of data representation and to the reliability of operations performed upon these custom types. In this regard, a struct is not merely a passive container; it is an active element in the construction of rigorous, self-consistent data models.

Structural Composition and Data Representation

In theoretical terms, the construction of a struct can be formalized by considering it as an ordered collection of fields $(f_1, f_2, \ldots, f_n)$, where each field f_i is associated with a type T_i. Consequently, the struct defines a composite type S that is mathematically equivalent to the Cartesian product

$$S = T_1 \times T_2 \times \cdots \times T_n.$$

In this representation, an instance of S is an n-tuple $(v_1, v_2, \ldots, v_n)$ such that each $v_i \in T_i$. This formalism not only elucidates the organizational structure of a struct but also underscores its role as a precise model for data aggregation. The ordering inherent in the tuple conveys semantic importance to the position of each field even though, in practice, the physical memory layout may be influenced by considerations such as alignment and padding.

The deterministic sequence of fields confers upon the struct a schema that is crucial for static type-checking and for enforcing consistency throughout data manipulation operations. Although the inherent order may be leveraged for direct memory access and optimized field retrieval, it primarily serves to delineate the fixed association between the conceptual model and its concrete instantiation within a computational framework.

Integration within Type Systems

The inclusion of structs within a type system broadens the expressive capacity of programming languages by enabling the definition of custom types that encapsulate multiple attributes in a semantically coherent manner. In advanced type systems, a struct is more than a mere aggregation of data; it forms the basis for constructing domain-specific abstractions that rigorously capture the nuances of real-world entities. The interaction between customized composite types and the overarching type system ensures that invariants remain enforced at compile time, thereby reducing the potential for errors stemming from type inconsistencies.

From the perspective of type safety, the union of distinct data elements within a struct facilitates a clear demarcation between different layers of abstraction. By explicitly defining the relationships among constituent fields, structs allow for the early detection of logical anomalies and provide a robust framework for subsequent operations that act on the custom type. In many formal developments, the struct is studied not only as a data structure but also as a formal construct that enables concise expression of complex properties, thus bridging the gap between theoretical rigor and practical implementation.

Moreover, the construction of structs plays a central role in the design patterns that underlie modular software architectures. By serving as building blocks for larger, more complicated systems, structs contribute to an extensible and maintainable codebase wherein each custom type encapsulates its internal representation. This encapsulation ensures that the implementation details remain hidden, while the externally defined interfaces communicate only the necessary aspects of the compositional structure. Such integration of structural composition into the language's type system embodies a disciplined approach to managing complexity through abstraction and encapsulation.

Go Code Snippet

```go
package main

import (
        "fmt"
)

// DataTuple represents a composite type that aggregates multiple,
↪    heterogeneous data elements.
// It models the formal tuple (v1, v2, v3) as described by the
↪    equation:
//    S = T1 × T2 × T3
// where:
//    Field1   T1 (integer)
//    Field2   T2 (floating-point number)
//    Field3   T3 (string)
// This structured representation mirrors the theoretical construct
↪    for data aggregation.
type DataTuple struct {
        Field1 int      // Corresponds to v1   T1
        Field2 float64 // Corresponds to v2   T2
        Field3 string  // Corresponds to v3   T3
}

// String returns a formatted representation of the DataTuple
↪    instance.
// It encapsulates the data tuple in a human-readable form.
```

```go
func (d DataTuple) String() string {
        return fmt.Sprintf("(%d, %.2f, %s)", d.Field1, d.Field2,
        ↪   d.Field3)
}

// CartesianProduct computes the Cartesian product of two integer
↪   slices.
// Mathematically, for sets A and B, the Cartesian product is
↪   defined as:
//    A × B = { (a, b) | a  A, b  B }
// In this implementation, each resulting pair is represented as a
↪   DataTuple,
// where Field1 holds the element from the first slice and Field2
↪   holds the element from the second slice.
// Field3 is set to a fixed string identifier to denote the pair.
func CartesianProduct(sliceA, sliceB []int) []DataTuple {
        var result []DataTuple
        for _, a := range sliceA {
                for _, b := range sliceB {
                        tuple := DataTuple{
                                Field1: a,
                                Field2: float64(b),
                                Field3: "Pair",
                        }
                        result = append(result, tuple)
                }
        }
        return result
}

// main function demonstrates the core concepts presented in the
↪   chapter:
// 1. Defining and instantiating a struct that encapsulates
↪   heterogeneous data types.
// 2. Utilizing a method associated with the struct for data
↪   presentation.
// 3. Implementing an algorithm (Cartesian product) that leverages
↪   the structured data representation.
func main() {
        // Create a single instance of DataTuple to represent an
        ↪   individual composite entity.
        tuple := DataTuple{Field1: 10, Field2: 3.14, Field3:
        ↪   "Example"}
        fmt.Println("Single instance of DataTuple:", tuple.String())

        // Define two slices of integers to illustrate the Cartesian
        ↪   product algorithm.
        sliceA := []int{1, 2, 3}
        sliceB := []int{4, 5}

        // Compute the Cartesian product using the defined function.
        product := CartesianProduct(sliceA, sliceB)
```

```go
	fmt.Println("Cartesian Product of sliceA and sliceB as
	↪    DataTuples:")

	// Iterate through the resulting slice of DataTuple and
	↪    print each tuple.
	for _, t := range product {
		fmt.Println(t.String())
	}
}
```

Chapter 22

Structs: Initialization and Field Access

Initialization Techniques

The instantiation of a structured composite type is conceptually analogous to the formation of an ordered tuple, where each component is governed by its corresponding type. Given a struct defined by a collection of fields, the process of initialization involves the assignment of a value to each field such that the instance is expressed as

$$s = (v_1, v_2, \ldots, v_n) \quad \text{with} \quad v_i \in T_i, \ 1 \leq i \leq n.$$

Two principal approaches emerge in the initialization regime. In the first approach, an ordered or positional list of values is provided where the sequence reflects the order of declaration of the fields within the struct. This mode of instantiation presupposes that the ordering of values is semantically correlated with the ordering of the corresponding types and emulates the basic tuple formation in set theory.

An alternative strategy employs a designated initialization mechanism in which each field is explicitly associated with an initialization value. In this methodology, the instance is constructed as a mapping

$$s : \{f_1, f_2, \ldots, f_n\} \to \{v_1, v_2, \ldots, v_n\},$$

where the explicit pairing mitigates the ambiguity inherent in positional correspondence. Such a designation not only reinforces type

110

safety by ensuring that each field f_i is bound to a value $v_i \in T_i$, but also enhances the expressive clarity of the initialization process. Additionally, mechanisms for default initialization are integral to robust type systems; fields lacking explicit assignment are initialized to their respective zero or default value, thereby preserving the integrity and predictability of the structured data.

Field Access and Modification

Once an instance of a composite type has been instantiated, the subsequent operations on the data structure are predicated upon accessing and, when required, modifying its constituent fields. The semantics of field access are encapsulated by an accessor operation, wherein the application of a dot operator to an instance yields a particular field value. Formally, if s denotes an instance of a struct type and f represents one of its fields, then the expression $s.f$ is understood as the outcome of the projection function

$$\pi_f(s) = v,$$

with $v \in T_f$. This projection operation is instrumental in isolating specific components of the composite type from the holistic entity.

Modification of struct fields is modeled as an update procedure on the state of the instance. Let s be an existing state and let f_0 be a designated field such that a new value v' (with $v' \in T_{f_0}$) is to be applied. The updated instance s' is then defined by the transformation

$$s' = s\{f_0 \mapsto v'\},$$

which implies that for every field $g \neq f_0$, the equality $s'(g) = s(g)$ holds, while $s'(f_0) = v'$. This operation formalizes the notion of controlled state mutation whereby the integrity of the struct is maintained through the preservation of unmodified fields.

The interplay between field access and modification is underpinned by the invariants imposed by the type system. The accessor function $\pi_f : S \to T_f$ and the corresponding update transformation constitute canonical operations that facilitate both the retrieval and alteration of the structured data. Such rigor in defining these operations ensures that any manipulation of a composite type is performed in a manner that is semantically transparent and consistent with the formal abstraction of the struct as a finite, ordered mapping from field identifiers to type-specific values.

Go Code Snippet

```go
package main

import "fmt"

// Person is a struct that encapsulates a composite type with three
↪   fields.
// It demonstrates both positional and designated initialization,
↪   along with
// field access and update operations.
// Conceptually, an instance of Person can be viewed as:
//    s = (Name, Age, Address)
// where Name  string, Age  int, and Address  string.
type Person struct {
    Name    string // Field f with type T: string
    Age     int    // Field f with type T: int
    Address string // Field f with type T: string
}

// initPositional creates an instance of Person using an ordered
↪   (positional)
// list of values. This mirrors the tuple formation:
//    s = (v, v, v) with v  T, v  T, v  T.
func initPositional() Person {
    // Positional values must follow the declaration order: Name,
    ↪   Age, Address
    return Person{"Alice", 30, "123 Go Street"}
}

// initDesignated creates an instance of Person by explicitly
↪   assigning values
// to each field, analogous to a mapping:
//    s: {Name, Age, Address} → {v, v, v}.
func initDesignated() Person {
    return Person{
        Name:    "Bob",
        Age:     25,
        Address: "456 Gopher Avenue",
    }
}

// accessField demonstrates the projection function: for an instance
↪   s and field f,
// the dot operator s.f retrieves the value v (i.e., _f(s) = v).
func accessField(s Person) {
    fmt.Printf("Name: %s, Age: %d, Address: %s\n", s.Name, s.Age,
    ↪   s.Address)
}

// updateField demonstrates controlled field modification.
```

```go
// Given an instance s and a target field (e.g., Age), updating the
↪  field with a new
// value v yields a new state s such that:
//    s = s{ Age → v }
// where for any field g  Age, s(g) = s(g).
func updateField(s Person, newAge int) Person {
    // Update the Age field; other fields remain unchanged.
    s.Age = newAge
    return s
}

func main() {
    // Demonstrate positional initialization.
    person1 := initPositional()
    fmt.Println("Person1 (Positional Initialization):")
    accessField(person1)

    // Demonstrate designated (explicit) initialization.
    person2 := initDesignated()
    fmt.Println("Person2 (Designated Initialization):")
    accessField(person2)

    // Update the Age of person2 to demonstrate field modification.
    fmt.Println("Updating Person2's Age from 25 to 26 ...")
    updatedPerson2 := updateField(person2, 26)
    accessField(updatedPerson2)
}
```

Chapter 23

Methods: Definitions and Usage on Structs

Associating Functions with Struct Types

Methods serve as a formal mechanism for coupling functions with structured composite types. In this framework, a method is defined as a function that is intrinsically bound to a particular struct type. Let a structured type be denoted by S, characterized by a finite set of fields $\{f_1, f_2, \ldots, f_n\}$. A method m associated with S is conceived as a mapping

$$m : S \to T,$$

where T represents the return type of the operation. In this construction, the method encapsulates behavior that is inherently related to the data represented by S, thereby establishing an intrinsic association between the two. The binding is achieved through the inclusion of a receiver parameter in the method's definition. This receiver acts as an implicit input, endowing the method with contextual awareness of the state encoded by the struct instance. Consequently, the operation defined by m maintains a formal correspondence with the underlying data, ensuring that the method's operational semantics are tailored to the characteristics of S.

Receiver Values and Operational Semantics

The concept of receiver values is central to the association of methods with struct types. The receiver parameter, typically denoted by a variable such as r, is specified in the signature of a method and determines the context in which the method operates. Depending on the intended semantics, the receiver may be passed by value or by reference. When the receiver is passed by value, it represents an immutable copy of the instance, formally expressed as $r \in S$. In this scenario, any modifications effected within the method are confined to the local copy, leaving the original instance unaltered. Conversely, when the receiver is passed by reference, often indicated as $r \in *S$, the method is permitted to incur modifications directly on the original instance. This distinction is mathematically analogous to the difference between a pure function and a stateful transformation within the broader spectrum of computational models.

The operational semantics underlying these two paradigms can be delineated as follows. For a value receiver, the method invocation produces a transformation of the form

$$m : S \to T,$$

where the state of the original instance remains invariant. For a pointer receiver, the transformation can be conceptually modeled as

$$m : *S \to T,$$

with the additional property that the instance may transition from an initial state s to a modified state s' in a manner such that $s' \neq s$ if the method engenders state changes. This formalism underscores the duality inherent in method definitions and accentuates the importance of selecting an appropriate receiver type to accurately reflect the intended behavior of the method.

Semantic Integration in Structured Programming

The integration of methods into the struct paradigm exemplifies a disciplined approach to embedding behavior within composite data types. This amalgamation of data and associated operations is emblematic of advanced abstraction techniques in computer science. The definition of a method as a binding of a function to a structured type not only encapsulates the operational logic but also reinforces the semantic integrity of the type system. More formally, if S is a set representing instances of a structured type, then the collective behavior imparted by methods can be represented as a higher-order mapping

$$M : S \to (S \to T),$$

where each element in S is associated with a function whose domain is likewise S, and T denotes the codomain of possible outcomes.

This formulation imbues the struct type with self-referential capabilities, mirroring the principles of encapsulation and modularity. The explicit incorporation of receiver values ensures that every method is contextually bound to a particular instance, thereby preserving state invariants and facilitating precise control over data mutation. The duality between value and pointer semantics within receiver parameters further refines this integration, allowing for both stateless operations and those that necessitate deliberate alterations of the instance. This rigorous association between functions and their respective structured types epitomizes the systematic approach employed in modern software engineering, combining theoretical robustness with practical expressiveness.

Go Code Snippet

```
package main

import (
        "fmt"
        "math"
)

// Calculator represents a structured type S with a single field
↪   'value'.
// It is used to demonstrate methods and their binding as per the
↪   equations:
//    m : S -> T   (for value receiver methods)
//    m : *S -> T   (for pointer receiver methods)
type Calculator struct {
        value float64
}
```

116

```go
// Square method is defined with a value receiver.
// It represents a pure function mapping from a Calculator instance
↪   (S) to a result (T),
// without modifying the state of the original instance.
// Mathematical notation: m : S -> T
func (c Calculator) Square() float64 {
        // Compute the square of the Calculator's value.
        return c.value * c.value
}


// Add method is defined with a pointer receiver.
// It modifies the state of the Calculator instance by adding delta
↪   to its value.
// Mathematical notation: m : *S -> T, where the state may
↪   transition from s to s'.
func (c *Calculator) Add(delta float64) {
        c.value += delta
}


// SquareRoot method is another example of a pointer receiver
↪   method.
// It computes the square root of the current value, updates the
↪   state,
// and returns the square root. This reflects a stateful
↪   transformation.
func (c *Calculator) SquareRoot() float64 {
        if c.value < 0 {
                fmt.Println("Cannot compute square root of a
                ↪   negative number")
                return math.NaN()
        }
        result := math.Sqrt(c.value)
        // Update the current state with the computed square root.
        c.value = result
        return result
}


// Operation demonstrates a higher-order method.
// It returns a function that accepts a float64 and yields a float64
↪   result.
// This aligns with the concept of a mapping: M: S -> (S -> T),
// where each instance of Calculator returns a function that
↪   operates on float64 values.
func (c Calculator) Operation() func(delta float64) float64 {
        return func(delta float64) float64 {
                return c.value + delta
        }
}


func main() {
        // Create a Calculator instance with an initial value.
        calc := Calculator{value: 16.0}
        fmt.Println("Initial Value:", calc.value)
```

117

```go
    // Using a value receiver method.
    sq := calc.Square()
    fmt.Printf("Square (Value Receiver): %v\n", sq)
    fmt.Println("After calling Square method, Value remains:",
    ↪  calc.value)

    // Using a pointer receiver method to add a value.
    calc.Add(9.0)
    fmt.Printf("After Adding 9, Value is now: %v\n", calc.value)

    // Using another pointer receiver method to compute square
    ↪  root.
    sqrt := calc.SquareRoot()
    fmt.Printf("Square Root (Pointer Receiver): %v\n", sqrt)
    fmt.Println("After calling SquareRoot method, Value is
    ↪  now:", calc.value)

    // Demonstrate higher-order mapping using Operation method.
    operationFunc := calc.Operation()
    result := operationFunc(5.0)
    fmt.Printf("Result of Operation (adding 5): %v\n", result)
}
```

Chapter 24

Pointers: Fundamentals and Usage

Fundamental Concepts of Pointers

In formal computational theory, a pointer is defined as a specialized variable that holds the memory address of another variable. Let V denote the set of variables and M represent the set of memory locations. A pointer may be characterized by a mapping $\phi : P \to M$, where P is the collection of pointer variables. For any variable $x \in V$, an operator $\alpha(x)$ yields the unique memory address at which x is stored, thereby introducing an essential mechanism of indirection in system memory.

This abstraction encapsulates the notion that the identity of a variable is separate from its physical placement in memory. The pointer variable, upon assignment as $p = \alpha(x)$, functions as an indirect reference to the data stored at the particular address $a \in M$. Such a distinction enables sophisticated manipulation and dynamic allocation of memory resources without the prerequisite of copying the variable's actual content.

This theoretical formulation is pivotal in understanding the relationship between a variable x and its associated pointer p, where $p \in P$ satisfies the invariant that $\phi(p) = \alpha(x)$. The existence of this relationship underpins many aspects of modern memory management strategies and serves as a cornerstone in the design of efficient algorithms and data structures.

Referencing and Dereferencing Variables

The operations of referencing and dereferencing are fundamental to the proper manipulation of pointer variables. Referencing refers to the process that obtains the memory address of a variable. Mathematically, if $x \in V$ is a variable, then its reference is defined as $\alpha(x)$, and assigning this address to a pointer is expressed as $p = \alpha(x)$. Such an operation guarantees that the pointer p now holds a valid member of M, ensuring a correct association between p and the original variable x.

Dereferencing, in contrast, is the operation by which the value stored at the memory location pointed to by p is retrieved. Utilizing the dereferencing operator, typically denoted by $*$, the expression $*p$ yields the contents of the memory cell at address $\phi(p)$. Formally, if a pointer $p \in P$ satisfies $\phi(p) = a$ for some $a \in M$, then the operation $*p$ is equivalent to applying an inverse mapping $\phi^{-1}(a)$, which returns the value of x. This bidirectional correspondence between a variable and its address formalizes a crucial aspect of low-level memory manipulation, wherein referencing is the forward mapping from x to a, and dereferencing is the reverse operation.

The interplay of these operations ensures that modifications applied through a pointer are congruent with the intended memory region. Thus, while referencing is inherently non-intrusive and preserves the immutability of the original variable, dereferencing permits both read and write operations on the encapsulated data, a distinction that bears significant implications in contexts where mutable state and side effects are of critical concern.

Pointers in the Context of Memory Management

Within the broader framework of memory management, pointers serve as essential instruments in exerting precise control over resource allocation and deallocation. The ability to store and manipulate memory addresses directly allows for dynamic memory management schemes that optimize the organization and utilization of available hardware resources.

In many memory management models, pointers facilitate the tracking of dynamically allocated memory blocks. The mapping function ϕ, as previously defined, is extended to incorporate time-dependent behaviors, denoted ϕ_t, which model the mutable correspondence between pointer variables and memory addresses during the execution of a program. This dynamic association is instrumental in supporting memory reclamation techniques and in preventing anomalies such as memory fragmentation and leakage.

Furthermore, the use of pointer arithmetic permits structured traversal of contiguous memory regions. By performing arithmetic on pointer values, it becomes possible to iterate through elements of complex data arrangements without incurring the runtime overhead of repeatedly computing memory offsets by higher-level abstractions. Such manipulations are governed by the size of the data types involved and necessitate rigorous adherence to operational semantics in order to maintain consistency and avoid undefined behavior.

The strategic employment of pointers also enables the formulation of sophisticated data structures that efficiently handle variable-sized collections and recursive relationships. The precise management of memory via pointers, when combined with the judicious use of referencing and dereferencing operations, results in systems that exhibit both high performance and robust control over low-level resource interactions. This formal integration of pointer concepts into memory management protocols is central to the design of efficient, scalable, and reliable computational systems.

Go Code Snippet

```
package main

import (
        "fmt"
)

// updateValue demonstrates modifying a variable's value via its
↪    pointer.
// This function accepts a pointer to an integer and adds 10 to the
↪    integer's value.
// In our formal notation, if p is a pointer such that (p) = (x),
↪    then *p (i.e. x)
// is updated by this function.
func updateValue(val *int) {
```

```go
        *val = *val + 10 // Dereference the pointer to modify the
        ↪   value.
}

// Counter is a simple struct to illustrate pointer receivers.
// A method with a pointer receiver can modify the internal state of
↪   the struct.
// This mirrors the idea of dereferencing (i.e., *p) to access and
↪   update data.
type Counter struct {
        count int
}

// Increment increases the count by one.
// Using a pointer receiver ensures the change affects the original
↪   variable.
func (c *Counter) Increment() {
        c.count++
}

func main() {
        // --- Basic Pointer Operations ---
        // Define an integer variable x.
        var x int = 42
        // Create a pointer p that holds the address of x.
        // This is analogous to: p = (x), and formally (p) = address
        ↪   of x.
        p := &x

        // Print initial values: x, address stored in p, and value
        ↪   obtained by dereferencing p.
        fmt.Println("Initial value x:", x)
        fmt.Println("Pointer p holds address:", p)
        fmt.Println("Dereferenced value *p:", *p)

        // Modify the value of x through the pointer p.
        // This operation demonstrates that *p yields the stored
        ↪   value, enabling in-place updates.
        *p = 58
        fmt.Println("Modified value x through pointer:", x)

        // --- Function Call with Pointer Parameter ---
        // Pass the pointer p to the updateValue function.
        // The function dereferences the pointer and updates the
        ↪   underlying variable.
        updateValue(p)
        fmt.Println("Value x after updateValue call:", x)

        // --- Dynamic Memory Allocation using new() ---
        // The new() function allocates memory for an integer and
        ↪   returns its pointer.
        q := new(int) // q now points to a memory location with an
        ↪   initial zero value.
```

```go
    *q = 100       // Set the allocated memory to 100.
    fmt.Println("Value pointed by q:", *q)

    // --- Pointer with Struct and Method Receiver ---
    // Create a Counter instance using a pointer literal.
    counter := &Counter{count: 0}
    fmt.Println("Initial counter:", counter.count)
    // Call the Increment method, which uses a pointer receiver
    ↪   to update counter.count.
    counter.Increment()
    fmt.Println("Counter after Increment:", counter.count)

    // --- Modifying Array Elements Using Pointers ---
    // Define a slice of integers.
    arr := []int{1, 2, 3, 4, 5}
    // Iterate over the slice, using a pointer to each element
    ↪   to modify its value.
    for i := 0; i < len(arr); i++ {
        // Obtain the pointer to the arr[i] element.
        ptr := &arr[i]
        // Double the value of the element via
        ↪   dereferencing.
        *ptr = *ptr * 2
    }
    fmt.Println("Modified array:", arr)
}
```

Chapter 25

Functions: Declaration and Invocation

Formal Declaration of Functions

A function is an abstract computational entity that encapsulates a mapping between an ordered tuple of input values and an output value. In formal terms, a function may be represented as

$$f : \tau_1 \times \tau_2 \times \cdots \times \tau_n \to \tau,$$

where each τ_i denotes the data type associated with the ith parameter and τ specifies the type of the resultant output. The declaration of a function involves the precise specification of its signature, which comprises the function's identifier, the ordered list of formal parameters, and, when applicable, an explicit statement of its return type. The syntactic structure of such a declaration establishes a contract by which the operational semantics of the function are determined, ensuring that every invocation adheres to the prescribed interface.

The signature not only defines the arity of the function but also provides constraints that facilitate static analysis and type checking. This formal specification plays a critical role in both the syntactic parsing and semantic verification during the compilation process. By establishing the correspondence between the formal parameter list and the expected data types, the declaration guarantees that the substitution of actual arguments adheres to the invariant that each argument conforms to the corresponding type

τ_i.

Parameter Specification and Return Types

The definition of a function relies on a meticulous treatment of parameters and return types. Each parameter is declared as a binding between a symbolic name and an associated data type. In many formal systems, parameters are introduced in a manner that permits grouping of multiple variables under a shared type when their semantic role is equivalent. This grouping notion can be expressed as

$$(x_1, x_2, \ldots, x_k) : \tau,$$

indicating that each variable x_i for $1 \leq i \leq k$ belongs to the type τ. The explicit declaration of these parameters is integral to enforcing type safety and for ensuring that the substitution during function invocation is consistent with the function's formal specification.

The return type of a function is similarly pivotal, as it determines the nature of the output produced upon completion of the function's internal evaluation. In many instances, the return type is explicitly stated, thus providing a semantic guarantee that the computed value will be of type τ. In contexts where functions may yield multiple outputs, the return type may be construed as a tuple,

$$\tau = (\tau_1', \tau_2', \ldots, \tau_m'),$$

although the basic treatment here assumes a singular return value for clarity. The formal association between the input parameters and the return type constitutes the essence of the function's behavioral contract and is a fundamental aspect in the analysis of program correctness.

Invocation Semantics and Usage Patterns

The invocation of a function is the process by which a caller provides a set of actual arguments to instantiate the formal parameters and thereby activates the function's computational routine. Formally, given a function f with signature

$$f : \tau_1 \times \tau_2 \times \cdots \times \tau_n \to \tau,$$

an invocation is represented by an expression of the form

$$f(a_1, a_2, \ldots, a_n),$$

125

where each actual argument a_i is required to satisfy the type constraint $a_i \in \tau_i$. The evaluation of such an invocation is carried out by binding the actual arguments to the corresponding formal parameters and subsequently executing the sequence of operations defined in the function's body.

The semantics of a function call involve not only the substitution of the actual values but also the management of the execution context. The local environment within which the function body is executed is distinct from the caller's environment, thereby ensuring that the state encapsulated by the function remains isolated except for explicitly shared data. The discipline of parameter binding and environment setup is crucial, as it governs the flow of data through the program and underpins the correctness of both sequential and nested function invocations.

The established usage pattern for function invocations supports the modular design of software systems. Functions serve as self-contained units of computation that can be composed, reused, and analyzed independently. This paradigm facilitates abstraction and encapsulation by permitting complex operations to be constructed through the systematic combination of simpler function calls. The invocation mechanism, when examined from a rigorous perspective, is an illustrative example of the interplay between syntax and semantics in the construction of reliable and maintainable computational systems.

Go Code Snippet

```go
package main

import (
        "errors"
        "fmt"
        "math"
)

// Add demonstrates a simple function declaration using parameter
↪    grouping.
// It represents the mapping f:  ×  →  where f(x, y) = x + y.
func Add(x, y float64) float64 {
        return x + y
}

// Multiply represents a function that computes the product of two
↪    numbers.
```

126

```go
// It maps × to , exemplifying the grouping of parameters.
func Multiply(x, y float64) float64 {
        return x * y
}


// Power computes the exponentiation of a base raised to a
↪   non-negative integer exponent.
// This function embodies the mapping f:  ×  → . It returns an error
↪   if the exponent is negative.
func Power(base float64, exponent int) (float64, error) {
        if exponent < 0 {
                return 0, errors.New("exponent must be
                ↪   non-negative")
        }
        result := 1.0
        for i := 0; i < exponent; i++ {
                result *= base
        }
        return result, nil
}


// ComputeFormula demonstrates a composite function that uses the
↪   above helper functions.
// Given inputs x and y, it computes the expression:
//     f(x, y) = ((x + y) ~2 + (x * y)) / sqrt(x~2 + y~2)
// This function illustrates formal parameter binding, arithmetic
↪   operations, and error handling.
func ComputeFormula(x, y float64) (float64, error) {
        // Compute the sum and product: f_sum = x + y, f_product = x
        ↪   * y.
        sum := Add(x, y)
        product := Multiply(x, y)

        // Compute (x + y) ~2 using the Power function.
        squareSum, err := Power(sum, 2)
        if err != nil {
                return 0, err
        }

        // Compute the denominator sqrt(x~2 + y~2) using the math
        ↪   package.
        xSquare := math.Pow(x, 2)
        ySquare := math.Pow(y, 2)
        denom := math.Sqrt(xSquare + ySquare)
        if denom == 0 {
                return 0, errors.New("denominator is zero, invalid
                ↪   input values")
        }

        // Calculate the final result by combining the computed
        ↪   values.
        numerator := squareSum + product
        result := numerator / denom
```

127

```go
        return result, nil
}

// makeIncrementer demonstrates the use of an anonymous function and
↪   closure.
// It returns a function that takes a float64 and increments it by
↪   the captured 'increment' value.
// This aligns with the notion f:  →  , where f(x) = x + increment.
func makeIncrementer(increment float64) func(float64) float64 {
        return func(x float64) float64 {
                return x + increment
        }
}

func main() {
        // Demonstrate ComputeFormula with sample inputs.
        x, y := 3.0, 4.0
        computedValue, err := ComputeFormula(x, y)
        if err != nil {
                fmt.Println("Error computing formula:", err)
        } else {
                fmt.Printf("Computed Formula for x=%.2f and y=%.2f
                ↪   is: %.2f\n", x, y, computedValue)
        }

        // Demonstrate the usage of a closure returned by
        ↪   makeIncrementer.
        addFive := makeIncrementer(5.0)
        inputValue := 10.0
        incrementedValue := addFive(inputValue)
        fmt.Printf("Incrementing %.2f by 5 results in: %.2f\n",
        ↪   inputValue, incrementedValue)

        // Additional demonstration: invoking the Power function
        ↪   directly.
        base := 2.0
        exponent := 8
        powerResult, err := Power(base, exponent)
        if err != nil {
                fmt.Println("Error in Power function:", err)
        } else {
                fmt.Printf("%.2f raised to the power of %d is:
                ↪   %.2f\n", base, exponent, powerResult)
        }
}
```

Chapter 26

Functions: Parameters and Return Values

Formal Parameter Specification

In the domain of programming language theory, a function is primarily characterized by its signature, which encapsulates the set of permissible inputs through a formally defined parameter list. Each parameter is rigorously associated with a specific data type, and the collective domain is represented by an ordered Cartesian product of types, namely

$$\tau_1 \times \tau_2 \times \cdots \times \tau_n.$$

This precise association ensures that any substitution of actual values for the formal parameters adheres to well-defined type constraints, thereby enforcing the integrity of data and the consistency of operations. The practice of parameter grouping further allows for compact expression when multiple parameters share an identical type, exemplifying the principle of syntactic abstraction while preserving semantic rigor. This formalism is integral to static type analysis, as it provides the foundation upon which both compiler verification processes and theoretical models of function evaluation are built.

Return Value Articulation

The evaluation of a function culminates in the production of an output, which is governed by the explicit declaration of a return type within the function signature. In scenarios where a single result is intended, the function is characterized by a mapping of the form

$$f : \tau_1 \times \tau_2 \times \cdots \times \tau_n \to \tau.$$

Here, τ denotes the type of the solitary return value, and this specification serves as a critical contract between the function definition and its subsequent usage. Such an unambiguous declaration not only facilitates static verification by ensuring that the computed output conforms to the designated type but also aligns with the theoretical underpinnings of mathematical functions. The explicit articulation of a return type is essential for both semantic clarity and the optimization processes employed during program compilation.

Multiple Return Values

Beyond the conventional single-output paradigm, certain computational models permit functions to yield multiple results in a single invocation. In these cases, the return type is extended to a tuple of types, typically represented as

$$\tau_1' \times \tau_2' \times \cdots \times \tau_m'.$$

This extended form enables the simultaneous transmission of several values directly from the function, each constituent of the tuple conveying distinct computational outcomes. The semantics of such functions are intrinsically linked to the notion of tuple construction, wherein each output value is positioned within an ordered sequence that corresponds to a component of the overall return type. This mechanism is particularly efficacious when the function is intended to deliver both primary results and ancillary data—such as indicators of error or status—and it contributes to the expressive power of the type system by facilitating a clear and concise representation of multivariate outputs. The inclusion of multiple return values thereby enriches the denotational framework of functions, supporting a more nuanced interpretation of computational processes.

Go Code Snippet

```go
package main

import (
        "fmt"
)

// Multiply demonstrates a function with a single return value.
// Its formal signature can be viewed as:
//     f: int × int → int
// where the input domain (int, int) results in an output of type
↪   int.
// This uses parameter grouping since both parameters share the same
↪   type.
func Multiply(a, b int) int {
        return a * b
}

// DivMod demonstrates a function returning multiple values.
// Its signature is analogous to:
//     f: int × int → (int, int)
// where the first return value represents the quotient and the
↪   second the remainder.
func DivMod(a, b int) (quotient int, remainder int) {
        quotient = a / b
        remainder = a % b
        return
}

// ComputeSumAndDifference shows another example of a function with
↪   multiple return values,
// following the mapping:
//     f: int × int → (int, int)
// It computes both the sum and the difference of the two input
↪   integers.
func ComputeSumAndDifference(a, b int) (sum int, diff int) {
        sum = a + b
        diff = a - b
        return
}

func main() {
        // Demonstrate the Multiply function (single return value)
        product := Multiply(3, 4)
        fmt.Println("Multiply(3, 4) =", product)

        // Demonstrate the DivMod function (multiple return values)
        quotient, remainder := DivMod(17, 5)
        fmt.Printf("DivMod(17, 5) returns: quotient = %d, remainder
↪    = %d\n", quotient, remainder)
```

```go
    // Demonstrate the ComputeSumAndDifference function
    // (multiple return values)
    sum, diff := ComputeSumAndDifference(10, 4)
    fmt.Printf("ComputeSumAndDifference(10, 4) returns: sum =
        %d, difference = %d\n", sum, diff)
}
```

Chapter 27

Functions: Working with Multiple Return Values

Formal Characterization of Multi-Valued Functions

Within the theoretical framework of programming language semantics, a function that yields multiple outputs is rigorously modeled as a mapping

$$f : \tau_1 \times \tau_2 \times \cdots \times \tau_n \to (\tau_1', \tau_2', \ldots, \tau_m').$$

In this formulation, the domain is constructed as an ordered Cartesian product of types, while the codomain is expressed as an ordered tuple of types. Each element τ_i' in the output tuple is associated with a precise type, ensuring that every instantiation of the function adheres to strict type constraints. This formalism not only encapsulates the deterministic transformation of input tuples into output tuples but also facilitates a robust abstraction in which composite computational outcomes are naturally decomposed into their constituent types.

Type System and Evaluation Semantics

In the context of a statically typed computational environment, the specification of functions with multiple return values reinforces a rigorous approach to static type verification. Every component of the output tuple is explicitly declared as part of the function signature, which guarantees that the evaluation process yields a collection of values that conform to the predetermined types. The explicit type declaration supports compile-time checking mechanisms, thereby preventing type mismatches and ensuring operational consistency. Evaluation semantics dictate that when a function is invoked, the constructed tuple of return values is assembled in a manner analogous to an implicit tuple construction, reflecting the underlying principles of a Cartesian product. The meticulous alignment between the input domain and the structured output not only underpins the soundness of the type system but also enriches the denotational semantics that characterize function evaluation.

Practical Applications in Computational Design

The capability to return multiple values from a function engenders a diverse array of applications in sophisticated computational design. This feature permits the simultaneous conveyance of a primary result along with supplementary metadata, such as status indicators, error codes, or diagnostic information. Such a mechanism minimizes the necessity for auxiliary data structures whose sole purpose is the aggregation of disparate outputs. Furthermore, the facility to return a tuple of values aligns with advanced error handling paradigms, in which a function is expected to communicate both the computed outcome and an explicit error signal. The conceptual clarity offered by this multi-valued approach enhances modularity and promotes finer granularity in the articulation of computational processes. The resultant architectural simplicity not only contributes to more succinct function interfaces but also bolsters maintainability and verifiability within complex software systems.

Go Code Snippet

```go
package main

import (
        "errors"
        "fmt"
)

// computeResults simulates a multi-valued function as described by
// ↪  the mapping:
// f :  × → (', ', ', ')
// Here, given two integer inputs, it returns their sum, difference,
// ↪  product,
// and quotient. In case of division by zero, an error is returned.
func computeResults(a, b int) (sum int, diff int, prod int, quot
// ↪  float64, err error) {
        // Calculate sum
        sum = a + b

        // Calculate difference
        diff = a - b

        // Calculate product
        prod = a * b

        // Calculate quotient with error handling for division by
        // ↪  zero
        if b == 0 {
                err = errors.New("division by zero is undefined")
                return
        }
        quot = float64(a) / float64(b)
        return
}

// evaluateExpression demonstrates using computeResults to mimic the
// ↪  evaluation
// semantics of multi-valued functions. It collects the returned
// ↪  tuple and prints
// the values in a structured format.
func evaluateExpression(a, b int) {
        // Multi-valued function call captures a tuple of outputs.
        sum, diff, prod, quot, err := computeResults(a, b)

        // Handle error if encountered during evaluation.
        if err != nil {
                fmt.Printf("Error while computing results for inputs
                // ↪  (%d, %d): %s\n", a, b, err)
                return
        }
```

```go
        // Print the results in a tuple-like format.
        fmt.Printf("Inputs: (%d, %d) => (Sum: %d, Difference: %d,
        ↪ Product: %d, Quotient: %.2f)\n", a, b, sum, diff, prod,
        ↪ quot)
}

// advancedCalculation demonstrates an extended use case where
↪ multiple return values
// help convey both the computational outcome and additional
↪ metadata. In this example,
// we pack the result along with a status code into a tuple.
func advancedCalculation(x, y int) (result string, statusCode int,
↪ err error) {
        // Simulate a complex calculation using computeResults
        sum, diff, prod, quot, calcErr := computeResults(x, y)
        if calcErr != nil {
                err = calcErr
                statusCode = 1  // Error status code
                return
        }
        // Build a result message encapsulating the calculation
        ↪ details.
        result = fmt.Sprintf("Calculated Values -> Sum: %d,
        ↪ Difference: %d, Product: %d, Quotient: %.2f", sum, diff,
        ↪ prod, quot)
        statusCode = 0 // Success status code
        return
}

func main() {
        // Demonstration of evaluateExpression with valid inputs.
        fmt.Println("=== Simple Evaluation ===")
        evaluateExpression(10, 2)

        // Demonstration of evaluateExpression with an error
        ↪ scenario.
        fmt.Println("=== Error Handling Demonstration ===")
        evaluateExpression(10, 0)

        // Demonstration of advancedCalculation which returns a
        ↪ tuple with additional metadata.
        fmt.Println("=== Advanced Calculation ===")
        res, status, err := advancedCalculation(20, 4)
        if err != nil {
                fmt.Printf("Advanced calculation failed with error:
                ↪ %s\n", err)
        } else {
                fmt.Printf("Status: %d, Result: %s\n", status, res)
        }
}
```

Chapter 28

Functions: Variadic Functions Explained

Formal Definition of Variadic Parameterization

A variadic function is defined within a formal type system by extending the conventional signature to include a parameter capable of accepting an arbitrary finite sequence of arguments. In a rigorous notation, such a function is represented as

$$f : \tau_1 \times \tau_2 \times \cdots \times \tau_n \times \tau^* \to \sigma,$$

where each of the types $\tau_1, \tau_2, \ldots, \tau_n$ corresponds to the fixed non-variadic arguments and τ^* denotes the collection of zero or more arguments all of type τ. This notation embodies the core idea that the variadic parameter is not a singular entity but an aggregation modeled akin to the Kleene closure on the set of elements of type τ. The collected arguments are formally treated as an ordered sequence or list, whose structure remains invariant under the constraints imposed by the system's static type rules. This formulation guarantees that each instantiation of the function adheres to a deterministic mapping from the composite domain to the codomain σ, thereby preserving the integrity of the function's operational semantics.

Type Semantics and Evaluation Dynamics

The inclusion of a variadic parameter introduces an augmented layer to the standard evaluation semantics and type inference mechanisms inherent in statically typed languages. When a function is invoked with a variable number of arguments, the language runtime or compiler implicitly constructs an ordered data structure encapsulating these extra arguments. In formal terms, if the set of variadic arguments is regarded as an element of τ^*, then type verification ensures that each argument satisfies the requisite type τ, upholding the contractual obligations of the function signature. This process is analogous to the injection of a finite sequence into a larger Cartesian product, and it necessitates a meticulous check during compile time. The evaluation strategy thereby entails an implicit transformation: the scattered variadic arguments are coalesced into a unified entity which is then processed by the function in a manner that is both predictable and consistent with the principles of denotational semantics.

Exemplification in High-Level Computational Patterns

Variadic functions offer a powerful abstraction in the realm of computational design by enabling the encapsulation of operations that inherently require flexibility in the number of inputs. They are particularly instrumental in scenarios where data must be aggregated dynamically without prior knowledge of the count. The breadth of applications includes but is not limited to aggregation operations, logging routines, and those algorithms that necessitate pattern matching over an indeterminate set of parameters. Conceptually, the separation between fixed and variadic inputs enhances modularity by allowing specific components of the function to address invariant parameters, while the variadic portion accommodates extensible data. This paradigm favors a reduction in auxiliary data structures, as the mechanism of variadic argument aggregation naturally provides an ordered collection of inputs. The resulting design exhibits both elegance and efficiency, yielding function interfaces that are intrinsically more adaptable to a wide array of high-level programming tasks while conforming to a strict and robust type system.

Go Code Snippet

```go
package main

import (
        "fmt"
        "strings"
)

// Sum computes the sum of a variable number of integer arguments.
// This function demonstrates the formal variadic parameterization
↪   where the
// signature is conceptually viewed as:
//     Sum : int* -> int,
// meaning that it accepts a finite sequence of integers (*) and
↪   returns an int.
func Sum(values ...int) int {
        total := 0
        for _, value := range values {
                total += value
        }
        return total
}

// Compute multiplies a fixed integer by the sum of additional
↪   variadic integers.
// Its type signature can be seen as:
//     Compute : int x int* -> int,
// corresponding to a fixed parameter followed by an arbitrary
↪   collection of integers.
func Compute(fixed int, values ...int) int {
        // The variadic arguments (values) are implicitly gathered
        ↪   into a slice,
        // preserving their order and ensuring type safety.
        return fixed * Sum(values...)
}

// VariadicConcat concatenates a fixed prefix with a variadic list
↪   of strings.
// This function exemplifies the injection of multiple elements into
↪   a single,
// ordered slice provided by the variadic parameter.
func VariadicConcat(prefix string, items ...string) string {
        // The built-in strings.Join function operates on the slice
        ↪   'items'
        // which represents the variadic arguments.
        return prefix + " " + strings.Join(items, " ")
}
```

```go
func main() {
    // Demonstration of using the Sum function.
    fmt.Println("Sum of numbers:", Sum(5, 10, 15, 20))

    // Demonstration of the Compute function where the first
    ↪  argument is fixed
    // and the following ones are aggregated as variadic
    ↪  arguments.
    result := Compute(2, 3, 4, 5)
    fmt.Println("Result of Compute (fixed multiplier * sum):",
    ↪  result)

    // Demonstration of using VariadicConcat to merge a fixed
    ↪  string with variadic strings.
    greeting := VariadicConcat("Hello",
        "world!",
        "This",
        "is",
        "a",
        "variadic",
        "function.")
    fmt.Println("Concatenated string:", greeting)

    // Passing a slice to a variadic function by using the ...
    ↪  operator.
    numbers := []int{7, 14, 21, 28}
    fmt.Println("Sum from slice:", Sum(numbers...))
}
```

Chapter 29

Functions: Anonymous Functions and Closures

Formalism of Inline Function Definitions

Anonymous functions, often expressed in the form of lambda abstractions, constitute function definitions that are articulated directly at the point of use rather than being separately declared with a distinct identifier. In a formal type-theoretic framework, such a construct is denoted as $\lambda x_1, x_2, \ldots, x_n. E$, where $x_1, x_2, \ldots, x_n$ represent the formal parameters and E denotes the function body. This notation illustrates that the function, although devoid of a bound name, embodies the complete mapping from the domain (formed by the types of the parameters) to the codomain. The shorthand nature of this definition permits the expression of function objects inline, thereby facilitating functional abstraction and the capacity to pass behavior as a parameter. The syntactic and semantic integration of these functions into the host language reinforces the notion that functions are first-class citizens, with their types inferable according to the rules of the underlying type system.

Closures and Lexical Environment Capture

The intrinsic property of anonymous functions to capture the surrounding lexical environment is epitomized by the concept of clo-

141

sures. A closure is formally defined as a pairing of an anonymous function with its referencing environment, the latter being a mapping from free variable identifiers to their corresponding values or memory locations at the time of the function's definition. If E is the expression representing the body of an anonymous function and ρ represents the environment in force during the function's creation, then the closure may be symbolically denoted as $\langle \lambda x_1, x_2, \ldots, x_n.\, E,\, \rho \rangle$. This entity guarantees that any free variables in E—those not bound by the formal parameters $x_1, x_2, \ldots, x_n$—are resolved according to the encapsulated environment ρ. The preservation of environmental bindings ensures that the behavior of the function remains contextually consistent, even when it is subsequently passed to or invoked by different scopes. As such, closures provide a robust mechanism for maintaining state and contextual integrity across disparate temporal and spatial domains of a program.

Evaluation Dynamics and Static Semantics

The evaluation of anonymous functions and closures is rooted in the operational semantics intrinsic to statically typed languages. When an anonymous function is declared inline, a closure is instantiated that captures the pertinent parts of the surrounding environment. The evaluation of this closure, when later applied to a set of arguments, is executed within the composite context comprising both the supplied arguments and the preserved environment. Formally, if a closure is represented as $\langle \lambda x.\, E,\, \rho \rangle$ and is applied to an argument a, then the resulting computation is evaluated under an extended environment $\rho[x \mapsto a]$. This model of evaluation adheres to the principles of substitution and environment extension, ensuring that static type checking remains viable and that the integrity of function composition is maintained. The type system guarantees that the closure's captured variables and the parameters of the anonymous function are fully compatible with the function's declared type, thereby enforcing rigorous adherence to the language's contracts even as the function operates devoid of an explicit identifier.

Go Code Snippet

```go
package main

import (
        "fmt"
)

// makeIncrementer returns a closure that increments an internal
//    counter.
// This demonstrates how an anonymous function captures the
//    surrounding lexical environment.
func makeIncrementer(start int) func() int {
        count := start
        // Anonymous function acting as a closure that updates and
        //    returns count
        return func() int {
                count++
                return count
        }
}

// performCalculations shows inline anonymous function definitions
//    for simple arithmetic operations.
// Each function is defined in place and then immediately utilized.
func performCalculations(a, b int) (sum int, diff int, prod int) {
        // Inline function for addition
        add := func(x, y int) int {
                return x + y
        }
        // Inline function for subtraction
        subtract := func(x, y int) int {
                return x - y
        }
        // Inline function for multiplication
        multiply := func(x, y int) int {
                return x * y
        }
        return add(a, b), subtract(a, b), multiply(a, b)
}

func main() {
        // Demonstrate the closure by creating an incrementer
        //    starting from 10.
        inc := makeIncrementer(10)
        fmt.Println("Closure - Incrementer:")
        fmt.Println("First call:", inc())  // Expected output: 11
        fmt.Println("Second call:", inc()) // Expected output: 12

        // Use inline anonymous functions in performCalculations for
        //    basic arithmetic.
        a, b := 20, 5
```

```go
sum, diff, product := performCalculations(a, b)
fmt.Println("\nInline Anonymous Functions:")
fmt.Printf("Operands: a = %d, b = %d, Sum = %d, Difference =
↪   %d, Product = %d\n",
        a, b, sum, diff, product)

// Demonstrate closures capturing variables within a loop.
// The closure properly captures the current iteration value
↪   to compute its square.
fmt.Println("\nClosures in Loop:")
var funcs []func() int
for i := 0; i < 3; i++ {
        // Create a new variable to capture the current
        ↪   value of i to avoid common pitfalls.
        j := i
        funcs = append(funcs, func() int {
                return j * j
        })
}
for index, f := range funcs {
        fmt.Printf("Square of %d is %d\n", index, f())
}

// Demonstrate dynamic closure evaluation by returning a
↪   function that calculates exponentiation.
// The captured exponent (exp) defines the number of
↪   multiplications performed.
makePowerFunc := func(exp int) func(int) int {
        return func(base int) int {
                result := 1
                for i := 0; i < exp; i++ {
                        result *= base
                }
                return result
        }
}
square := makePowerFunc(2)
cube := makePowerFunc(3)
fmt.Println("\nExponentiation using Closures:")
fmt.Printf("Square (4^2): %d\n", square(4)) // Expected
↪   output: 16
fmt.Printf("Cube (3^3): %d\n", cube(3))        // Expected
↪   output: 27
}
```

Chapter 30

Function Types: First-Class Functions in Go

Functions as Values: A Formal Overview

The concept of first-class functions is predicated on the recognition that functions are not merely syntactic constructs but are entities that can be manipulated like any other value within the language's semantic framework. In Go, a function value is accompanied by a type signature that can be denoted by the mapping $T_1 \to T_2$, where T_1 represents the domain of accepted parameters and T_2 the codomain of produced results. This formal characterization ensures that functions, upon assignment or transmission as parameters, maintain an integrity analogous to algebraic mappings. The intrinsic property of being first-class endows function values with the capacity to be stored in variables, included within data structures, and transmitted between disparate parts of a program without any diminution of their operational semantics.

Assignment and Identity of Function Types

When a function is assigned to a variable, the language semantics guarantee that the variable inherits not only the executable body of the function but also its associated type signature and any captured contextual bindings. The act of assigning a function to a variable, expressed as an operation of the form $g := f$, establishes a correspondence where the variable g becomes a referential alias for the function f. This aliasing preserves the identity and behavior of f, ensuring that successive invocations of g are semantically equivalent to those of f. The statically typed nature of Go requires that the type of the variable, which is expected to be a function from T_1 to T_2, be congruent with the signature of f, thereby enforcing a rigorous discipline in function assignment. Such constraints prevent type mismatches and facilitate optimizations during compile time by assuring that every function assignment adheres to the prescribed type invariants.

Passing Functions as Arguments in Higher-Order Constructs

The treatment of functions as first-class entities is further exemplified by their role as parameters within higher-order constructs. When a function is passed as an argument, its type signature becomes an integral part of the receiving function's interface. Consider a higher-order function h that accepts a parameter f, where f is defined as a function mapping elements from T_1 to T_2. In such a scenario, the formalism of the language dictates that the invocation of h with the function argument f must satisfy the condition of signature compatibility, ensuring that f is an admissible mapping from T_1 to T_2. This mechanism provides the foundation for composing elaborate computational strategies in which functions can encapsulate behavior and be dynamically interchanged. The evaluation of these higher-order constructs is governed by the same substitution and type-checking principles that regulate the application of primitive function values, thus integrating function passing seamlessly into the broader, statically enforced type system.

Static Typing and Function Signature Consistency

A cornerstone of Go's design philosophy is the preservation of function signature consistency through strict static typing. Each function value is intrinsically bound to a unique signature that delineates the number, order, and types of its parameters along with the resultant type. This binding is immutable and serves as a contract that dictates how functions may be composed, assigned, or transmitted. Within this model, any operation that involves function values—whether it be an assignment to a variable or the passage as a parameter—must obey the rules of type congruence. In formal terms, if a function f with type $T_1 \rightarrow T_2$ is to be associated with a variable or parameter declared for that signature, then the type system enforces an isomorphism between the expected and the actual mapping structures. Such rigorous adherence to type consistency not only preserves the internal consistency of the program but also enables compile-time verification of function interactions, thereby contributing to the overall robustness and reliability of programmatic abstractions.

Go Code Snippet

```go
package main

import (
        "fmt"
)

// IntMapper defines a function type that maps an int to an int.
// This reflects the formal notation T1 -> T2.
type IntMapper func(int) int

// square returns the square of its input.
// It demonstrates a basic mapping: x -> x*x.
func square(x int) int {
        return x * x
}

// cube returns the cube of its input.
// It provides another mapping: x -> x*x*x.
func cube(x int) int {
        return x * x * x
}

// higherOrder demonstrates passing a function as an argument.
// It accepts a function f of type IntMapper and an integer x, then
↪   returns f(x).
func higherOrder(f IntMapper, x int) int {
        return f(x)
}

// compose takes two functions f and g (each of type IntMapper) and
↪   returns a new function h.
```

147

```go
// The composed function h applies g first and then f, i.e., h(x) =
↪  f(g(x)).
// This reflects the chaining of mappings: T1 -> T2 composed with T1
↪  -> T2 produces a new mapping.
func compose(f, g IntMapper) IntMapper {
        return func(x int) int {
                return f(g(x))
        }
}


// applyAlias demonstrates function assignment (aliasing).
// It assigns the input function to another variable and applies it
↪  to each element in the slice.
func applyAlias(f IntMapper, values []int) []int {
        results := make([]int, len(values))
        aliasF := f // f is assigned to aliasF; both point to the
        ↪  same function.
        for i, v := range values {
                results[i] = aliasF(v)
        }
        return results
}

func main() {
        // Assignment and Identity of Function Types
        // Here, f is assigned the function square. Both f and
        ↪  square share the same type signature.
        var f IntMapper = square
        fmt.Println("Square of 5:", f(5))

        // Passing Functions as Arguments in Higher-Order Constructs
        // The function cube is passed to higherOrder, which invokes
        ↪  it with the argument 3.
        cubedValue := higherOrder(cube, 3)
        fmt.Println("Cube of 3:", cubedValue)

        // Composing Functions: Creating a composite function that
        ↪  computes square(cube(x)).
        // Since cube(x) returns x^3, and square(x) returns x^2, the
        ↪  composite function computes x^6.
        composedFunc := compose(square, cube)
        fmt.Println("Square of Cube of 2 (2^6):", composedFunc(2))

        // Using function aliasing in a practical example.
        // Each number in the slice is processed using a function
        ↪  alias for square.
        numbers := []int{1, 2, 3, 4, 5}
        squaredNumbers := applyAlias(square, numbers)
        fmt.Println("Squared numbers:", squaredNumbers)

        // Demonstrating anonymous functions and closures.
        // multiplier returns a function that multiplies its input
        ↪  by a predetermined factor.
```

148

```go
	multiplier := func(factor int) IntMapper {
		return func(x int) int {
			return x * factor
		}
	}
	// Create a function that doubles its input.
	double := multiplier(2)
	fmt.Println("Double of 4:", double(4))
}
```

Chapter 31

Method Receivers: Value versus Pointer

Formal Characterization of Receiver Types

Within the design of method definitions, the receiver may be specified in one of two distinct forms: as a value of type T or as a pointer of type $*T$. In a value receiver, the method is invoked on a copy of the original object, whereas a pointer receiver permits the method to operate directly on the memory address of the object. This dichotomy establishes a formal framework in which the type system enforces strict rules regarding parameter passing and state mutation. The formal signature of a method employing a value receiver can be viewed as a mapping from an instance of T to a result, with the operation encompassing a complete duplication of the object's state prior to invocation. In contrast, a method with a pointer receiver is denoted by an implicit reference to an instance of the object, thereby enabling direct manipulation of its memory-resident representation.

Semantics of Value Receivers

A method defined with a value receiver exhibits the property that the receiver is passed by value. Consequently, the method's operational semantics dictate that a complete copy of the receiver is constructed at the time of invocation. This copy, which is of type T, encapsulates the entire state of the object at that moment, and any modifications effected within the method remain confined to the copy. The isolation introduced by copying ensures that the original object, stored in a separate memory location, remains unaltered regardless of transformations applied within the method's execution. This mechanism guarantees referential transparency within the context of the method call, albeit at the potential expense of increased computational overhead when dealing with large or complex data structures. Additionally, the immutable behavior inherent in value receivers can prevent unintended side effects in environments where concurrent operations occur, as each method call operates on an independent snapshot of the object's state.

Semantics of Pointer Receivers

In contrast, a method declared with a pointer receiver utilizes a direct reference to the object's memory address, denoted by a type $*T$. The invocation of such a method does not induce a copying of the object; rather, it provides the method with a pointer that essentially serves as an alias for the original instance. The operational semantics associated with pointer receivers allow for in-place modifications to the object's state, as any changes implemented via the pointer affect the source data in situ. This direct manipulation facilitates efficient state transformations, particularly when the size of the object or the complexity of its structure renders copying prohibitively expensive in terms of performance. However, the mutable nature imparted by pointer receivers introduces a spectrum of considerations related to aliasing and side effects, especially within contexts that demand strict state isolation. The responsibility to manage these side effects falls to the domain of the programmer, who must ensure that such methods are employed with careful attention to the integrity of the overall system state.

Behavioral and Performance Implications

The choice between value and pointer receivers engenders significant behavioral and performance ramifications. From the perspective of behavior, value receivers intrinsically protect the original object from accidental modification due to their copy-by-value semantics. This attribute proves particularly advantageous in scenarios where deterministic behavior and the prevention of unintended mutations are paramount. In contrast, pointer receivers empower methods with the capacity to alter the state of an object, thus enabling more direct and efficient adaptations to the object's properties. The performance implications are equally nuanced: the use of value receivers may incur a non-negligible cost when large data structures are involved, as the overhead associated with copying can degrade performance metrics. Conversely, pointer receivers circumvent this overhead by merely passing the address of the object, thereby reducing memory consumption and enhancing execution speed. Furthermore, the static type system rigorously ensures that the operational semantics of receiver types are preserved throughout method calls, thereby facilitating compile-time validations that contribute to overall system robustness. The interplay between value and pointer receivers ultimately reflects a fundamental trade-off between the safety of isolated state manipulation and the efficiency afforded by direct memory access.

Go Code Snippet

```go
package main

import (
    "fmt"
    "math"
)

// Counter demonstrates the differences between methods with value
//     and pointer receivers.
type Counter struct {
    value int
}

// IncrementByValue uses a value receiver. Its modifications occur
//     on a copy of the original Counter.
func (c Counter) IncrementByValue(n int) {
    c.value += n
    fmt.Printf("Inside IncrementByValue (Value Receiver): %d\n",
        c.value)
}

// IncrementByPointer uses a pointer receiver. Its modifications
//     update the original Counter.
func (c *Counter) IncrementByPointer(n int) {
    c.value += n
```

```go
    fmt.Printf("Inside IncrementByPointer (Pointer Receiver): %d\n",
      ↪  c.value)
}

// QuadraticEquation encapsulates coefficients for a quadratic
↪  equation along with fields to store computed roots.
type QuadraticEquation struct {
    A, B, C       float64
    Root1, Root2  float64
    Solved        bool
}

// SolveCopy demonstrates the use of a value receiver by computing
↪  the roots of the quadratic equation.
// The original QuadraticEquation instance remains unchanged because
↪  the method operates on a copy.
func (q QuadraticEquation) SolveCopy() {
    disc := q.B*q.B - 4*q.A*q.C
    if disc < 0 {
        fmt.Println("No real roots in SolveCopy")
        return
    }
    sqrtDisc := math.Sqrt(disc)
    root1 := (-q.B + sqrtDisc) / (2 * q.A)
    root2 := (-q.B - sqrtDisc) / (2 * q.A)
    fmt.Printf("Computed roots in SolveCopy (value receiver): %f,
      ↪  %f\n", root1, root2)
}

// SolveInPlace demonstrates the use of a pointer receiver by
↪  computing the roots using the quadratic formula and storing
// the results directly in the original QuadraticEquation instance.
func (q *QuadraticEquation) SolveInPlace() {
    disc := q.B*q.B - 4*q.A*q.C
    if disc < 0 {
        fmt.Println("No real roots in SolveInPlace")
        return
    }
    sqrtDisc := math.Sqrt(disc)
    q.Root1 = (-q.B + sqrtDisc) / (2 * q.A)
    q.Root2 = (-q.B - sqrtDisc) / (2 * q.A)
    q.Solved = true
    fmt.Printf("Computed roots in SolveInPlace (pointer receiver):
      ↪  %f, %f\n", q.Root1, q.Root2)
}

func main() {
    // Demonstrate how the method receivers affect state mutation.
    fmt.Println("Demonstrating Counter methods:")
    counter := Counter{value: 10}
    fmt.Printf("Initial Counter value: %d\n", counter.value)
    counter.IncrementByValue(5)
```

153

```
    fmt.Printf("Counter value after IncrementByValue: %d (unchanged
    ↪ because of copy semantics)\n", counter.value)
    counter.IncrementByPointer(5)
    fmt.Printf("Counter value after IncrementByPointer: %d (updated
    ↪ in place)\n", counter.value)

    // Demonstrate solving a quadratic equation using both receiver
    ↪ types.
    fmt.Println("\nDemonstrating Quadratic Equation solving:")
    // Equation: x^2 - 3x + 2 = 0 should have roots 1 and 2.
    eq := QuadraticEquation{A: 1, B: -3, C: 2}
    eq.SolveCopy() // Does not update eq's internal state.
    fmt.Printf("Equation state after SolveCopy: %+v\n", eq)
    eq.SolveInPlace() // Updates eq with the computed roots.
    fmt.Printf("Equation state after SolveInPlace: %+v\n", eq)
}
```

Chapter 32

Type Embedding: Achieving Composition

Theoretical Foundations of Type Embedding

Type embedding constitutes a paradigm that diverges from conventional inheritance by emphasizing composition over hierarchical extension. In this formalism, one type incorporates another by including it as an anonymous field, thereby granting the composite type direct access to the embedded type's members and methods. This structural inclusion is not a mechanism for subclassing but rather a means to reuse functionality while maintaining a clear separation of concerns. The embedded type, denoted by a type E, is assimilated into the composite type C so that the interface of E becomes partially visible in C. Thus, the design decision to employ type embedding is predicated on the belief that code reuse and component modularity can be achieved without the rigid constraints imposed by traditional inheritance systems.

Mechanisms of Composition via Embedding

The process of composition through type embedding is rooted in the structural decomposition of data types. A composite type C is defined such that it contains an embedded type E, where the latter

155

contributes both data attributes and method implementations to C. Formally, given a composite type C and an embedded type E, the effective member set of C can be expressed as

$$M_C = M'_C \cup M_E,$$

where M'_C represents the members explicitly declared in C, and M_E corresponds to the members inherited via embedding E. This relation ensures that any operation defined over E is also available in the context of C, subject to the language's scoping rules and name resolution procedures. The embedding mechanism thereby permits a fluid transfer of functionality without necessitating explicit delegation, and it encourages design decisions that favor modular composition over tightly coupled inheritance hierarchies.

Formal Semantics and Inference of Embedded Types

Within a statically typed setting, the formal semantics of type embedding can be rigorously articulated through the lens of type inference and member resolution. When a type C embeds another type E, the type system extends the environment associated with C by incorporating the mappings defined in the domain of E. Let Γ denote the global type environment; the introduction of an embedded type induces a transformation

$$\Gamma \implies \Gamma \cup \{\mathrm{members}(E)\},$$

where $\mathrm{members}(E)$ is the set of methods and fields that are inherent to E. This process enforces that any member access in a value of type C is first resolved within C itself and subsequently within the scope of E if not found directly. Such a layered approach ensures that type safety is preserved, while the extended member set adheres to the properties of structural type compatibility. Moreover, static analysis tools and compilers are designed to leverage this formal structure so as to guarantee that ambiguities in member resolution are resolvable at compile time, thereby contributing to predictable and robust software design.

Comparative Evaluation with Traditional Inheritance Models

Unlike traditional inheritance, which enforces an is-a relationship through a strict parent-child hierarchy, type embedding facilitates a has-a composition that is inherently flexible and minimally intrusive. Inheritance intrinsically binds a subclass to a supertype, often leading to overgeneralization and inadvertent exposure of internal state. Type embedding, by contrast, enables a composite type to selectively acquire and expose only the necessary aspects of an embedded type. This selective exposure permits a refined control over the interface, ensuring that only relevant functionalities become part of the composite abstraction. The design philosophy underlying embedding can be mathematically characterized by the absence of an implicit subtype relation; instead, the composition is achieved through the union of member sets as previously denoted by

$$M_C = M_C' \cup M_E.$$

This approach not only mitigates the risks associated with deep inheritance hierarchies but also promotes a more maintainable architecture where code reuse is attained without compromising encapsulation or inducing undesired coupling between components.

Go Code Snippet

```go
package main

import (
        "fmt"
)

// Base represents the embedded type E.
// It provides basic fields and methods that will be composed into
↪    Composite.
type Base struct {
        Name   string
        Value int
}

// Show displays the current state of Base.
// This method is defined with a value receiver.
func (b Base) Show() {
        fmt.Printf("Base -> Name: %s, Value: %d\n", b.Name, b.Value)
}
```

157

```go
// Update modifies the Value field of Base.
// This method uses a pointer receiver to allow state change.
func (b *Base) Update(newValue int) {
        b.Value = newValue
}


// In our formal discussion, we denote the effective member set of a
↪    composite type C as:
// M_C = M'_C ∪ M_E,
// where M'_C are the members explicitly declared in C and M_E are
↪    the members inherited from Base.

// Composite type C embeds Base anonymously to achieve type
↪    composition.
// This provides direct access to all methods and fields from Base.
type Composite struct {
        Base                    // Anonymous embedding: acts as the set
        ↪    M_E.
        Additional string // Explicitly declared members: represents
        ↪    M'_C.
}


// Display is a method specific to Composite.
// It demonstrates that Composite has access not only to its own
↪    fields but also to Base's methods.
func (c Composite) Display() {
        fmt.Printf("Composite -> Additional: %s\n", c.Additional)
        // Demonstrate member resolution by calling Base's Show
        ↪    method directly.
        c.Show()
}


// demonstrateEmbedding creates a Composite instance and
// showcases updating embedded fields and method resolution.
func demonstrateEmbedding() {
        // Create a new Composite value with initialized Base
        ↪    fields.
        comp := Composite{
                Base:        Base{Name: "Embedded Base", Value: 100},
                Additional: "Extra Data",
        }

        fmt.Println("=== Before Update ===")
        comp.Display() // Calls Composite.Display, which in turn
        ↪    calls Base.Show.

        // Update the embedded Base's Value using its Update method.
        comp.Update(200)
        fmt.Println("=== After Update ===")
        comp.Display()
}
```

```go
// unionOfMethods demonstrates that the Composite type's effective
↪    method set
// contains both its own methods and those of the embedded Base.
// This is the operational counterpart of the equation: M_C = M'_C
↪    M_E.
func unionOfMethods() {
        comp := Composite{
                Base:        Base{Name: "Union Example", Value: 300},
                Additional: "Union Field",
        }

        fmt.Println("\n=== Union of Methods Demonstration ===")
        // Call Composite's own method.
        comp.Display()

        // Explicitly call the embedded Base's Show method.
        comp.Base.Show()

        // Notice: Through embedding, methods Update, Show, etc. are
        ↪    available directly on comp.
}

// main is the entry point of the program.
// It executes demonstrations of type embedding, member resolution,
↪    and algorithmic composition.
func main() {
        // Demonstrate how type embedding allows for composition.
        demonstrateEmbedding()

        // Further illustrate the union of member sets from the
        ↪    composite and embedded types.
        unionOfMethods()

        // Final note printed to the console to link back to our
        ↪    formal equation.
        fmt.Println("\nNote: In Go, type embedding provides a
        ↪    structural composition mechanism equivalent to")
        fmt.Println("the mathematical union of explicit and embedded
        ↪    member sets (M_C = M'_C  M_E),")
        fmt.Println("thereby promoting code reuse and modular design
        ↪    without the pitfalls of classical inheritance.")
}
```

159

Chapter 33

Interfaces: Defining and Implementing

Conceptual Foundations of Interfaces

Interfaces serve as an abstract mechanism to delineate behavior contracts without prescribing specific implementations. An interface is formally defined as a collection of method signatures that a concrete type may satisfy regardless of its internal structure. In this paradigm, behavior is abstracted from implementation, and the specification of an interface consists solely of the syntactic and semantic descriptions of the operations it mandates. This separation of concerns permits the decoupling of the contract from any particular realization, thereby facilitating modular design and permitting cross-cutting abstractions that transcend concrete type details. The essence of an interface lies in its ability to guarantee that any type conforming to it will exhibit a prescribed set of behaviors, thereby promoting interchangeability and enhancing the overall cohesiveness within a system's architecture.

Formal Specification of Behavior Contracts

Consider an interface I defined as a finite set of method signatures,

$$I = \{\tau_1, \tau_2, \ldots, \tau_n\},$$

where each τ_i encodes the full signature of a method, including its parameter types and return type. A concrete type T is said to implement the interface I if and only if, for every signature $\tau \in I$, there exists a corresponding method in T whose signature is compatible with τ. This compatibility is characterized by a relation that ensures the method in T can be used in every context where the interface's contract is expected. The validity of such an implementation is determined entirely at compile time by the type system, which verifies that the union of method signatures offered by T, denoted as M_T, satisfies the inclusion

$$I \subseteq M_T.$$

This formalism encapsulates the notion of a behavioral contract, wherein the interface I specifies a set of obligations that any conforming type must fulfill.

Mechanisms of Implicit Implementation in Concrete Types

Concrete types adhere to interface contracts through an implicit mechanism that does not mandate an explicit declaration of intent. When a type T provides method implementations whose signatures collectively match those specified in an interface I, it is immediately recognized by the type system as satisfying the contract. This implicit implementation paradigm eliminates the overhead of maintaining explicit interface-type associations and allows for evolutionary software design. By relying solely on the presence of compatible methods, the type system enforces a form of structural typing that underpins polymorphism. The implicit nature of interface satisfaction encourages a design in which types evolve organically to meet emerging interface requirements, ensuring that the abstraction encapsulated by I is maintained through the natural growth of M_T. In this framework, the adherence to an interface is not a declaration but a consequence of method availability and signature conformity.

Static Type Inference and Interface Satisfaction

The process of static type inference plays a pivotal role in verifying the satisfaction of interface contracts by concrete types. Let T be a concrete type and $I = \{\tau_1, \tau_2, \ldots, \tau_n\}$ be an interface. The type inference mechanism scrutinizes T to ascertain that every τ_i has a corresponding method implementation within T. Formally, if M_T is interpreted as the set of all method signatures provided by T, then interface satisfaction is established when

$$I \subseteq M_T.$$

This validation is achieved through a rigorous type-checking process that considers the covariant and contravariant aspects of method signatures. The verification of interface membership relies on an inductively defined set of rules that ensure the semantic integrity of the interaction between abstract contracts and concrete implementations. By embedding these rules into the type system, the language guarantees that all type substitutions and method invocations adhere strictly to the prescribed behavioral contracts. The resultant assurance provides a robust framework within which static analysis yields definitive and predictable outcomes, further solidifying the reliability of interface-based abstraction in complex software systems.

Go Code Snippet

```go
package main

import (
        "fmt"
)

// IBehavior represents an abstract behavior contract.
// Formally, we can view it as:
// I = { GetData(), Compute(value int) int }
// Any concrete type that provides these methods implicitly
↪    satisfies this interface.
type IBehavior interface {
        GetData() string
        Compute(value int) int
}

// ConcreteType is a concrete struct that provides method
↪    implementations
// corresponding to the IBehavior interface. In other words, its
↪    method set M_T
// includes GetData and Compute, thereby fulfilling the contract I
↪    M_T.
type ConcreteType struct {
```

```go
        name string
}

// GetData returns the name associated with the ConcreteType.
// This method satisfies the GetData() signature in IBehavior.
func (ct ConcreteType) GetData() string {
        return ct.name
}

// Compute performs a sample arithmetic operation.
// For demonstration, it calculates: result = value * 2 + len(name)
// This method satisfies the Compute(value int) int signature in
↪   IBehavior.
func (ct ConcreteType) Compute(value int) int {
        return value*2 + len(ct.name)
}

// UseInterface accepts any type that implements the IBehavior
↪   interface.
// This function demonstrates static type inference where the
↪   assignment of ct
// to a variable of type IBehavior is verified at compile time.
func UseInterface(ib IBehavior) {
        fmt.Println("Data:", ib.GetData())
        fmt.Println("Computed Result:", ib.Compute(10))
}

// Compile-time check: This ensures that ConcreteType implements
↪   IBehavior.
// If ConcreteType does not implement all methods in IBehavior,
↪   compilation will fail.
var _ IBehavior = (*ConcreteType)(nil)

func main() {
        // Create an instance of ConcreteType.
        ct := ConcreteType{name: "GoInterface"}

        // Implicit interface satisfaction:
        // The concrete type ConcreteType provides all methods
        ↪   required by IBehavior,
        // hence the assignment is valid.
        var ib IBehavior = ct

        // Use the interface in a function call,
        // demonstrating the interaction between abstract contracts
        ↪   and concrete implementations.
        UseInterface(ib)

        // Additional demonstration: static type inference in
        ↪   action.
        // The compiler verifies that both GetData and Compute
        ↪   methods exist in ct.
        data := ct.GetData()
```

163

```
    result := ct.Compute(5)
    fmt.Println("Direct call - Data:", data, "| Result:",
    ↪   result)
}
```

Chapter 34

Interfaces: Practical Applications

Polymorphism and Interface-Based Substitution

Interfaces serve as an elegant mechanism to achieve polymorphic behavior within statically typed systems. In a rigorous formalization, an interface can be regarded as a set of behavioral contracts, denoted by

$$I = \{\tau_1, \tau_2, \ldots, \tau_n\},$$

where each element τ_i represents a unique method signature. A concrete type T that fulfills the condition

$$I \subseteq M_T,$$

where M_T denotes the complete set of method signatures provided by T, is regarded as substitutable in any context where the interface I is expected. This implicit correspondence between the abstract behavior prescribed by the interface and the actual method set of the concrete type fosters an environment where distinct types may be interchanged seamlessly, thereby facilitating polymorphism. Such substitution does not rely on inheritance hierarchies but rather on a structural matching of method signatures, thus ensuring that disparate types adhering to the same interface exhibit a uniform set of behaviors.

Decoupling Implementation Details Through Abstraction

The intrinsic decoupling of implementation from specification is a primary advantage derived from the utilization of interfaces. By abstracting away the underlying concrete implementations, interfaces enable the delineation of design contracts that remain impervious to changes in the actual codebase. This decoupling is manifested through a separation wherein the interface defines the operational semantics while the concrete types afford varied realizations of those semantics. Consequently, modifications or enhancements within one concrete type do not necessitate alterations in the client code that depends solely on the interface, provided that the contractual obligations defined by the interface remain unaltered. Such a design paradigm facilitates modularity, as the interaction between components is governed by well-defined contracts rather than by tightly integrated coupling of implementations.

Interface-Driven Architectural Patterns in Modern Systems

The abstraction provided by interfaces has significantly influenced the development of architectural patterns in contemporary software systems. Patterns such as dependency injection, strategy, and factory methods exploit interfaces to create loosely coupled and highly configurable systems. In these architectures, the concrete instantiation of behavior is deferred until runtime, and the determination of specific behavior is managed through interface-based references. This results in systems where the decomposition of functionality into interchangeable components not only enhances the maintainability of the system but also promotes a high degree of extensibility. The use of interfaces as a foundation for these patterns ensures that the addition or substitution of components can be achieved with minimal disruption to the overall architecture, as the abstraction serves as an invariant contract amid the variability of concrete implementations.

Go Code Snippet

```go
package main

import (
        "fmt"
)

// Shape interface represents a set of behaviors (method signatures)
// Analogous to the formal definition:
// I = { , }, where  and  correspond to the methods Area and
↪   Perimeter.
// A concrete type T is substitutable (i.e., I M_T) if it provides
↪   implementations for all methods in I.
type Shape interface {
        Area() float64      // : Method to compute the area
        Perimeter() float64 // : Method to compute the perimeter
}

// Circle is a concrete type representing a circle.
// It implements the Shape interface by providing definitions for
↪   Area and Perimeter.
type Circle struct {
        Radius float64
}

// Area computes the area of a circle using the formula:
// A =  * r , where  is approximated as 3.14159.
func (c Circle) Area() float64 {
        return 3.14159 * c.Radius * c.Radius
}

// Perimeter computes the circumference of a circle using the
↪   formula:
// P = 2 *  * r.
func (c Circle) Perimeter() float64 {
        return 2 * 3.14159 * c.Radius
}

// Rectangle is a concrete type representing a rectangle.
// It implements the Shape interface by providing its own versions
↪   of Area and Perimeter.
type Rectangle struct {
        Width, Height float64
}

// Area computes the area of a rectangle using the formula:
// A = width * height.
func (r Rectangle) Area() float64 {
        return r.Width * r.Height
}
```

167

```go
// Perimeter computes the perimeter of a rectangle using the
↪ formula:
// P = 2 * (width + height).
func (r Rectangle) Perimeter() float64 {
        return 2 * (r.Width + r.Height)
}

// PrintShapeDetails demonstrates polymorphism and interface-based
↪ substitution.
// It accepts any type that fulfills the Shape interface, decoupling
↪ the caller from the concrete implementation.
func PrintShapeDetails(s Shape) {
        fmt.Printf("Area:      %.2f\n", s.Area())
        fmt.Printf("Perimeter: %.2f\n", s.Perimeter())
}

// main demonstrates key concepts:
// - Polymorphism via the Shape interface.
// - Decoupling through abstraction where client code depends only
↪ on the interface.
// - Dependency injection by selecting the concrete implementation
↪ at runtime.
func main() {
        // Instantiate concrete types.
        circle := Circle{Radius: 5}
        rectangle := Rectangle{Width: 4, Height: 6}

        // Demonstrate interface-based substitution.
        fmt.Println("Circle details:")
        PrintShapeDetails(circle)

        fmt.Println("\nRectangle details:")
        PrintShapeDetails(rectangle)

        // Dependency injection: Decide which concrete type to use
        ↪ based on configuration.
        var s Shape
        config := "circle" // Change this value to "rectangle" to
        ↪ test the alternative implementation.

        if config == "circle" {
                s = Circle{Radius: 7}
        } else {
                s = Rectangle{Width: 7, Height: 3}
        }

        fmt.Println("\nInjected Shape details:")
        PrintShapeDetails(s)
}
```

Chapter 35

Type Conversion: Converting Between Types

Fundamental Concepts of Type Conversion

In formal terms, type conversion is the process of transforming a value from one type, say A, to another type, say B, via a well-defined mapping. This mapping is typically denoted as $f : A \to B$, where for every element $x \in A$, the conversion produces a corresponding element $f(x) \in B$. Such an operation requires a rigorous mathematical framework in which the domain A is related to the codomain B by a function that, when possible, preserves inherent properties of x. Not all values in A necessarily have a counterpart in B, and in such cases the conversion is defined only on a subset $A_r \subseteq A$ where f is total. This selective mapping underscores the fact that type conversion, while often conceptually simple, must be underpinned by precise domain restrictions and conditions that ensure consistency between the semantics of the two types involved.

Mechanics of Conversion Operations

The mechanics of converting a value across types involve a sequence of defined steps governed by the target type's representational and operational constraints. Given a value x in type A, the conversion is formally expressed as $B(x)$, which represents the reconstitution of x within the confines of type B's domain. This operation can be regarded as a function g such that

$$B(x) = g(x), \quad \text{where } g : A \rightarrow B.$$

The function g must account for the structural differences between A and B, particularly in cases where the two types have distinct ranges, degrees of precision, or underlying memory representations. Moreover, when A and B embody different numerical precisions or data encodings, the conversion mechanism must determine whether the transformation is lossless or if there exist scenarios where values might be rounded, truncated, or otherwise modified in a manner that does not yield a one-to-one correspondence. In many systems, the conversion function is designed to be explicit; that is, it is invoked by a deliberate operator or function call to avoid unintended conversions that could lead to semantic ambiguities.

Implications for Data Integrity

From an integrity standpoint, the process of converting values between types bears significant implications for the preservation of data fidelity. When a conversion is executed under conditions where the value x lies within the subset A_r for which there exists a bijective mapping, the equality

$$B(x) = x$$

holds in the sense of semantic identity, thereby ensuring data integrity. However, if x falls outside this representable subset, the conversion may introduce distortions such as overflow, underflow, or rounding errors, which in turn compromise the integrity of the data. The loss of precision, especially when converting from a type of higher resolution to one of lower resolution, is a critical concern. In such circumstances, the mapping can become non-invertible, implying that the original value cannot be unambiguously recovered from its converted form. These issues necessitate a cautious approach in the design and implementation of type conversion operations, particularly within domains that mandate high precision and fault-tolerant computations.

Furthermore, the careful orchestration of type conversion functions is essential in mitigating accidental data corruption. The maintenance of invariants—properties that remain unchanged under the conversion process—is of paramount importance. Any discrepancy between the properties of $x \in A$ and those of $B(x) \in B$ can lead to subtle bugs or systemic failures in critical applications. By rigorously delineating the boundaries of acceptable conversions and by enforcing explicit and well-documented conversion protocols, it becomes possible to manage potential inconsistencies and preserve the overall consistency of the system's data representations.

Go Code Snippet

```go
package main

import (
        "fmt"
        "math"
)

// floatToInt converts a float64 value to an int.
// It returns the converted value along with a boolean indicating
↪    whether the conversion
// was lossless. A lossless conversion requires that the fractional
↪    part of the number is zero.
// This function demonstrates the theoretical formulation B(x) =
↪    g(x) when x is within a lossless subset.
func floatToInt(x float64) (int, bool) {
        // Check for a zero fractional part using floor comparison.
        if math.Floor(x) != x {
                // The value x is not exactly representable as an
                ↪    int without losing precision.
                return int(x), false
        }
        return int(x), true
}

// intToFloat converts an int value back to a float64.
// This helper function supports the round-trip test of the type
↪    conversion, indicating data integrity.
func intToFloat(y int) float64 {
        return float64(y)
}

// demonstrateConversion illustrates the conversion process and
↪    checks for data integrity.
// For a given input x in type A (float64), it calculates B(x) =
↪    g(x) via floatToInt and verifies if
// converting back (i.e. intToFloat) preserves the original value.
```

171

```go
func demonstrateConversion(values []float64) {
        fmt.Println("Demonstrating Type Conversion and Data
        ↪  Integrity:")
        fmt.Println("---------------------------------------------------")

        for _, x := range values {
                convertedInt, isLossless := floatToInt(x)
                convertedBack := intToFloat(convertedInt)
                if isLossless {
                        // If the conversion is lossless, then data
                        ↪  integrity holds: B(x) == x.
                        fmt.Printf("Original: %v, Converted (int):
                        ↪  %d, Back-Converted: %v [Lossless:
                        ↪  %t]\n",
                                x, convertedInt, convertedBack,
                                ↪  convertedBack == x)
                } else {
                        // When the value includes a fractional
                        ↪  component, conversion truncates it and
                        ↪  data may be lost.
                        fmt.Printf("Original: %v, Converted (int):
                        ↪  %d [Lossy conversion: fractional part
                        ↪  truncated]\n", x, convertedInt)
                }
        }
}

func main() {
        // Test values demonstrating both lossless and lossy type
        ↪  conversions.
        // Values with an exact integer representation should remain
        ↪  invariant under conversion.
        values := []float64{42.0, 42.5, -17.0, 0.0, 1234567890.0,
        ↪  3.9999}
        demonstrateConversion(values)
}
```

Chapter 36

Type Inference and Short Variable Declarations

Type Inference Mechanism

In statically typed languages, type inference plays a vital role in reducing verbosity without compromising the rigor of type safety. In the Go programming language, the compiler employs a systematic procedure whereby the type of a variable is deduced from the accompanying expression. This mechanism may be formalized by introducing an inference function, denoted as $\mathcal{I}$, such that for a given expression E, the associated type T is determined by

$$T = \mathcal{I}(E).$$

This functional mapping is evaluated during the compile-time static analysis phase, ensuring that every variable receives an unambiguous and well-defined type. The determinism inherent in $\mathcal{I}$ is essential to maintain consistency across the program, a fact that reinforces the overall integrity of the type system. Furthermore, the rigidity of such inference ensures that even when numerical literals or composite expressions are presented, their resultant types adhere strictly to the semantic constraints imposed by the language's design.

Short Variable Declarations: Syntactic Simplicity and Semantic Precision

The introduction of the short variable declaration operator, denoted by the symbol :=, provides a syntactically concise alternative for variable initialization. This operator enables the simultaneous declaration and assignment of a variable, obviating the need for redundant type annotations when the type can be unambiguously inferred from the right-hand side expression. Formally, an expression such as

$$x := E$$

instantiates a variable x with a type T determined by the evaluation of E, where $T = \mathcal{I}(E)$. The economy afforded by this syntactic construct not only improves clarity but also minimizes potential sources of error that may arise from manual type specification. The implicit derivation of types through := consolidates the declaration and initialization processes, thereby fostering a programming environment in which code remains succinct yet semantically robust.

Implications for Static Analysis and Code Maintainability

The interplay between type inference and short variable declarations bears significant consequences for both static analysis and long-term maintainability of code. When a variable is instantiated using the shorthand declaration, the association $x : T$ is established as an invariant across the program. This invariant is verifiable by automated analysis tools that rely on type information to perform optimizations, enforce security constraints, and detect inconsistencies. In mathematical terms, if a variable x is initialized with an expression E, the maintained relation

$$x : \mathcal{I}(E)$$

ensures that the semantic properties of x are preserved throughout its scope.

The syntactic brevity offered by the := operator reduces the cognitive overhead required to comprehend variable declarations and promotes cleaner codebases. By eliminating redundant type annotations, developers are able to focus on algorithmic complexity and logical correctness rather than low-level type details. This design paradigm contributes to more maintainable code, where the invariants provided by the type inference mechanism serve as the foundation for rigorous compiler checks and subsequent refactorings. The resultant harmony between syntactic simplicity and semantic precision exemplifies a deliberate architectural decision that enhances both the expressiveness and reliability of the language.

Go Code Snippet

```go
package main

import (
    "fmt"
    "reflect"
)

// typeInference simulates the inference function (E) by returning
//   the runtime type
// of the provided expression. This mimics the formal relation T =
//   (E).
func typeInference(val interface{}) string {
    return reflect.TypeOf(val).String()
}

// addInts demonstrates a simple algorithm: adding two integers.
// It uses explicit types while the caller leverages short variable
//   declarations
// to let the compiler infer the types of the input variables.
func addInts(x, y int) int {
    return x + y
}

func main() {
    // Demonstrating type inference with short variable
    //   declarations.
    intVal := 42            // int is inferred
    floatVal := 3.14        // float64 is inferred
    strVal := "GoLang"      // string is inferred

    // Using typeInference to display the inferred types, aligning
    //   with the equation T = (E).
    fmt.Printf("The inferred type of %v is %s\n", intVal,
        typeInference(intVal))
    fmt.Printf("The inferred type of %v is %s\n", floatVal,
        typeInference(floatVal))
    fmt.Printf("The inferred type of %v is %s\n", strVal,
        typeInference(strVal))
```

```go
// Applying the short variable declaration: x := E, where E is
↪   evaluated and its type is inferred.
result := addInts(intVal, 8)  // result is inferred as int
fmt.Printf("Result of adding %v and 8 is %d; inferred type is
↪   %s\n", intVal, result, typeInference(result))

// Demonstrating an invariant: once a variable is declared using
↪   short assignment,
// its type remains consistent, as in x : (E).
x := 100
fmt.Printf("Variable x is %d and its type is confirmed as %s\n",
↪   x, typeInference(x))

// A composite expression example to illustrate type inference:
a := 10
b := 20
sum := a + b  // sum is inferred as int
fmt.Printf("Sum of a and b is %d, with type %s\n", sum,
↪   typeInference(sum))

// Further demonstrating type inference with a complex
↪   expression:
// Converting result to float64 to combine with floatVal and
↪   perform arithmetic.
complexExpr := floatVal * float64(result) / 2.0  // inferred as
↪   float64
fmt.Printf("Complex expression result is %.2f, with type %s\n",
↪   complexExpr, typeInference(complexExpr))
}
```

Chapter 37

Reexamining Constants: Typed versus Untyped Constants

Typed Constants and Their Formal Characterization

In the Go programming language, constants may be defined with an explicit type annotation. When a constant is declared with a specified type, an invariant of the form

$$c : T$$

is established, where c denotes the constant and T its declared type. This invariant guarantees that every occurrence of c in the program is bound to the precise semantic and syntactic rules ascribed to T. Typed constants provide a level of strictness that enforces, at both compile time and run time, the type consistency inherent in static type systems. The precise declaration of types for constants reduces ambiguity during expression evaluation and ensures that operations involving such constants respect the predetermined arithmetic, logical, or string semantics associated with the type T.

The formal treatment of typed constants adheres to the principles of strong static typing. The declaration is accompanied by a deliberate assignment of a type which, in a conventional setting, may be expressed as

$$\text{const } c : T = E,$$

where E represents the constant expression whose value is computed at compile time. The explicit typing constrains c to behave as an element of T in every evaluative context. As a consequence, the invariants maintained by the type system prevent inadvertent operations that could otherwise result in imprecise or erroneous computations.

Untyped Constants: Ideal Numbers and Contextual Typing

Contrasting with the rigidity of typed constants, untyped constants in Go are defined without an explicit type annotation. Such constants are considered to have an idealized nature; they are not initially bound to a specific type, but rather possess a form of universal applicability. In formal notation, an untyped constant may be introduced as

$$\text{const } c = E,$$

where the absence of an explicit type allows constant c to be treated as an ideal number or ideal value. These ideal values are endowed with the capability to adopt a concrete type according to the context in which they are subsequently employed. In many respects, an untyped constant is endowed with the semantic property that in any valid context, it undergoes an implicit transformation consistent with the underlying rules of type selection as defined by the language specification.

The process of contextual type assignment for untyped constants can be expressed by the equation

$$T = \mathcal{I}(c, E),$$

where $\mathcal{I}$ represents the context-driven type inference mechanism operating at compile time. In scenarios involving operations between untyped constants or between an untyped constant and a typed variable, the untyped constant is coerced into the appropriate default type. These default types are typically derived from a hierarchy of ideal types, such as ideal integers, ideal floats, or ideal complex numbers, each of which is defined with infinite precision within the confines of the language's design. Consequently, untyped constants offer a flexibility that facilitates the construction of expressions without the overhead of redundant type annotations.

Interplay and Contextual Differentiation Between Typed and Untyped Constants

The dichotomy between typed and untyped constants in Go is of both theoretical and practical significance. While typed constants enforce a strict contract between declaration and usage, untyped constants embrace the versatility of context-sensitive type determination. The transition from an untyped ideal value to a concrete typed value occurs during the compilation process as a consequence of contextually inferred type expectations. This contextual transition is governed by a set of formal rules that ensure that untyped constants, when embedded in operations or assigned to variables, inherit the appropriate type without loss of precision or semantic integrity.

In situations where explicit precision and overflow control are critical, the use of typed constants is advantageous. A typed constant's invariant, namely

$$c : T,$$

provides not only clarity but also a robust framework for static analysis, wherein all interactions involving c are subject to stringent type-checking. On the other hand, the utilization of untyped constants proves beneficial in contexts requiring numeral abstraction and mathematical exactness. The mechanism by which an untyped constant is assigned a default type further illustrates the expressive power of Go's type system. The determination of this default type relies on the evaluation of the expression E in a manner that respects the underlying mathematical structure, ensuring that the constant is seamlessly incorporated into arithmetic, logical, or string expressions.

Furthermore, the careful delineation between the two styles also aids in reducing potential ambiguities during complex expression evaluations. The invariants maintained for typed constants, when juxtaposed with the fluidity of untyped constants, create a balanced system where type safety and operational flexibility coexist. The formal properties of each kind of constant underpin a system in which the merits of both strict type enforcement and adaptable expression manipulation can be harnessed effectively within a single language paradigm.

Go Code Snippet

```go
package main

import "fmt"

// This Go code snippet demonstrates the concepts introduced in the
//   chapter concerning
// typed and untyped constants. It shows the invariant c : T for
//   typed constants and the
// contextual inference mechanism for untyped constants,
//   corresponding to the idea that
// for an untyped constant c defined by an expression E, a concrete
//   type T is chosen as per
// the context (i.e., T = (c, E)).

// computeValues takes an integer value x and an integer y (where y
//   may originate from an untyped constant)
// and returns their computed sum along with the average computed in
//   floating-point arithmetic.
func computeValues(x int, y int) (int, float64) {
    // Typed constant: Explicitly declared as int, ensuring the
    //   invariant c : int.
    const typedFactor int = 3

    // Untyped constant: Declared without an explicit type; it acts
    //   as an ideal number.
    // When used in calculations requiring a float, it will be
    //   implicitly converted.
    const divisor = 2.0 // untyped constant acting as an ideal float

    // Perform arithmetic using the typed constant and parameters.
    sum := x + y + typedFactor

    // The untyped divisor is converted to float64 in the context of
    //   division.
    average := float64(sum) / divisor

    return sum, average
}

func main() {
    // Typed constant: its type is explicitly set to int.
    const typedConst int = 100
```

```go
// Untyped constant: without an explicit type annotation, it is
↪ an ideal number.
const untypedConst = 200

// Demonstrating the invariant "c : T" for the typed constant.
fmt.Println("Typed constant (c : int):", typedConst)

// When assigning an untyped constant to a variable with an
↪ explicit type,
// the constant is contextually converted to that type.
var number int = untypedConst // untypedConst is now treated as
↪ an int.
fmt.Println("Untyped constant assigned to int:", number)

// Arithmetic combining typed and untyped values.
// The literal 50 here is untyped and will be treated as an int
↪ in this context.
result1 := typedConst + 50
fmt.Println("Result of typed arithmetic (100 + 50):", result1)

// Demonstrating the usage of an untyped constant in
↪ floating-point arithmetic.
const untypedFloat = 1.5 // untyped, ideal float constant
var pi float64 = 3.14159
floatResult := untypedFloat * pi // untypedFloat is implicitly
↪ converted to float64
fmt.Println("Floating arithmetic (1.5 * pi):", floatResult)

// Using a function where untyped constants are passed in and
↪ combined with typed values.
sum, avg := computeValues(50, untypedConst)
fmt.Printf("Computed values: Sum = %d, Average = %.2f\n", sum,
↪ avg)

/*
    Summary of Demonstrated Principles:
    1. Typed constants (e.g., const c int = 100) strictly adhere
    ↪ to the invariant c : T.
    2. Untyped constants (e.g., const c = 200) are ideal values
    ↪ and adopt a type based on their usage.
    3. When an untyped constant is used in an expression with an
    ↪ expected type,
        the contextual type assignment mechanism (T = (c, E))
        ↪ applies.
*/
}
```

Chapter 38

Control Flow: Loops with Break and Continue

Break Statement: Formal Termination of Iterative Execution

Within the realm of iterative constructs, the break statement represents a control operator that enforces an immediate cessation of further iterative evaluation. When a break operation is encountered, the current loop undergoes an abrupt transition, effectively bypassing any residual computations or evaluations that would otherwise execute in subsequent iterations. Formally, if a loop is represented by a control structure L, the execution of a break statement can be modeled as a transformation function β such that

$$\beta : L \to L',$$

where L' symbolizes the loop state after termination. This function embodies the notion that once the invariant condition for termination is satisfied, the residual block of the loop is disregarded in favor of progressing to the statement immediately following the loop construct.

The semantics of the break statement preserve a clear invariant: in an unlabelled context, the break operation is confined to the innermost active loop. This localized operational effect ensures that in a system of nested loops, the sudden transition induced by break does not propagate beyond the immediate loop boundary. The formal characterization of this behavior requires that the abstract machine semantics accommodate a rule wherein, upon the detection of a break, control is transferred in such a manner that no further iterations are executed for the affected loop. This is concisely expressed in the form of a rewrite rule within the operational semantics framework.

Continue Statement: Controlled Iterative Skipping

The continue statement introduces a nuanced form of control flow alteration by permitting the selective omission of the remaining statements in a current iteration. Rather than terminating the loop entirely, continue instructs the execution engine to suspend the residual operations associated with the iteration and to reinitialize the loop's control evaluation. Formally, given an iterative construct L, the execution of a continue statement may be represented by an operator γ that induces the state transition

$$\gamma : L \to L^*,$$

where L^* denotes the state of the loop after the bypassing of the current iteration's remaining operations and just prior to the re-evaluation of the loop condition.

This mechanism preserves the overall iterative structure while dynamically altering the execution order within each cycle. By effecting the immediate transition to the loop's condition evaluation, the continue statement distinguishes itself from the break operation, which terminates the loop entirely. The operational semantics must, therefore, encapsulate the conditional nature of this transition such that the state after γ reflects the proper reinitiation parameters dictated by the loop's control conditions. The formal apparatus governing this behavior ensures that the continue statement does not disrupt the structural integrity of the loop but rather imposes a controlled modification of its execution sequence.

Interplay in Nested Loop Structures

In scenarios involving nested loop constructs, the semantics of break and continue statements acquire an additional layer of complexity due to their context-sensitive interactions. The absence of explicit labels mandates that both break and continue apply, by default, to the innermost loop in which they are encountered. Within such nested configurations, the formal treatment of control flow relies on a hierarchical decomposition of the loop constructs. Let L_1 denote an outer loop and L_2 an inner loop; then, invoking break in L_2 results in a state transition that exclusively affects L_2, leaving L_1 to proceed with its subsequent iterations based on its own control conditions.

Mathematically, if the operational semantics of the inner loop are denoted by a function such as β_2 for a break operation and γ_2 for a continue operation, the composite behavior in the nested structure is given by the sequential application of these local operators. The overall control transition can be expressed as

$$L_1 \circ \beta_2(L_2) \quad \text{or} \quad L_1 \circ \gamma_2(L_2),$$

which encapsulates the principle that the control effects are restricted to the loop in which they are triggered. This layered approach to control flow ensures that the invariants preserved within each loop are maintained independently, even in the presence of nested structures.

The interplay between break and continue in these contexts requires that the abstract semantic model of loop control permits a clear mapping from local iteration modifications to the broader execution state. The delineation between terminating an iteration and prematurely concluding the entirety of a loop becomes critical in optimizing loop behavior. The formal semantics, therefore, incorporate rules that distinguish the scope of each control operator, ensuring that any deviation from the standard iterative progression is both predictable and unambiguous within the multi-layered loop hierarchy.

Go Code Snippet

```
package main

import "fmt"
```

```go
// simulateLoop demonstrates the operational semantics of break and
↳ continue.
// It relates to the formal transformations discussed in the
↳ chapter:
//   - The break operation () terminates the loop: : L → L'.
//   - The continue operation () skips the remainder of the current
↳ iteration: : L → L*.
func simulateLoop() {
    fmt.Println("Begin simulation of break and continue semantics.")

    // Example 1: Break Statement Demonstration
    // ----------------------------------------
    // This loop iterates over integers 0 to 9.
    // When i equals 5, it simulates the transformation  (break),
    ↳ effectively exiting the loop.
    fmt.Println("\nExample 1: Break Statement")
    for i := 0; i < 10; i++ {
        if i == 5 {
            // Simulate break: the transformation  stops further
            ↳ loop evaluation.
            fmt.Printf("Break condition met at i=%d. Exiting
            ↳ loop.\n", i)
            break
        }
        fmt.Printf("Iteration %d in break loop.\n", i)
    }

    // Example 2: Continue Statement Demonstration
    // -------------------------------------------
    // This loop iterates over integers 0 to 9.
    // When j equals 3, it simulates the transformation  (continue),
    // causing the loop to skip the rest of the current iteration.
    fmt.Println("\nExample 2: Continue Statement")
    for j := 0; j < 10; j++ {
        if j == 3 {
            // Simulate continue: the transformation  skips the
            ↳ remaining code in the loop body.
            fmt.Printf("Continue condition met at j=%d. Skipping
            ↳ iteration.\n", j)
            continue
        }
        fmt.Printf("Iteration %d in continue loop.\n", j)
    }

    // Example 3: Nested Loop Demonstration
    // ------------------------------------
    // This example shows the interplay of break and continue in
    ↳ nested loops.
    // The default behavior applies to the innermost loop unless
    ↳ labels are used.
    fmt.Println("\nExample 3: Nested Loop with Break and Continue")
```

```go
outerLoop:
for a := 0; a < 3; a++ {
    fmt.Printf("Outer loop iteration a=%d\n", a)
    for b := 0; b < 5; b++ {
        // When b equals 2, apply continue in the inner loop (
        ↪   transformation).
        if b == 2 {
            fmt.Printf("  Continue in inner loop at b=%d (
            ↪   applied).\n", b)
            continue
        }
        // When a equals 1 and b equals 3, apply break to exit
        ↪   the inner loop ( transformation).
        if a == 1 && b == 3 {
            fmt.Printf("  Break in inner loop at a=%d, b=%d (
            ↪   applied).\n", a, b)
            break
        }
        fmt.Printf("  Inner loop iteration b=%d\n", b)
    }
    // Demonstrating the use of a labeled break:
    if a == 2 {
        fmt.Printf("Breaking outer loop at a=%d using label.\n",
        ↪   a)
        break outerLoop
    }
}

fmt.Println("\nSimulation complete.")
}

func main() {
    simulateLoop()
}
```

Chapter 39

Defer: Postponed Function Execution

Deferred Execution Mechanism

The defer statement in Go offers a systematic means of scheduling function calls in such a manner that their execution is postponed until the surrounding function concludes its evaluation. In this construct, the deferred call is not executed at the point of its registration but is instead enqueued for later execution. Formally, if an execution context is denoted by C, the application of the defer operator, here represented as δ, transforms the context according to

$$\delta : C \to C',$$

where C' reflects the modified context with the deferred call included in an execution stack. When multiple defer statements are encountered, the language semantics dictate that the functions are executed in a last-in, first-out order, ensuring a deterministic reversal of the registration sequence.

Formal Semantics of Deferred Calls

The operational semantics of the defer statement can be framed within a transition system that models both registration and execution phases. Consider a function f executing within a state σ, and let D denote the set of deferred calls accumulated during its execution. The registration of a new deferred call, corresponding to an expression e, is modeled by the state transition

$$\langle f, D, \sigma \rangle \xrightarrow{\text{defer}} \langle f, D \cup \{e\}, \sigma \rangle.$$

Subsequent to the normal execution of f, a deferred execution rule is applied. At termination, the deferred calls are executed sequentially in reverse order, formalized as

$$\langle \text{end of } f, D, \sigma \rangle \rightarrow \langle \text{post-defer execution}, \sigma' \rangle,$$

where σ' denotes the state after completion of all deferred computations. This formal treatment guarantees that the transformations induced by the defer mechanism maintain the integrity of the program's execution state.

Implications for Resource Management

The employment of the defer statement has notable implications for resource management. By deferring cleanup functions or other resource deallocation procedures until the surrounding function returns, the mechanism ensures that resources such as file handles, network connections, and allocated memory are released in a predictable and consistent manner. In a formal context, the scheduling of a resource deallocation function r can be expressed as an operator acting on the resource state $\mathcal{R}$:

$$\delta_r : \mathcal{R} \rightarrow \mathcal{R}',$$

with $\mathcal{R}'$ capturing the state after execution of the deferred cleanup. This deferred execution model is particularly effective in environments where resource management must obey strict ordering constraints to prevent leaks and maintain system stability.

Interaction with Control Flow Constructs

The defer statement interacts with other control flow elements in a manner that preserves the expected semantics of the enclosing function. When a return statement is encountered within a function, all deferred calls, accumulated during its execution, are guaranteed to execute before the actual return is processed. This behavior may be abstracted by a composite state transition in which the deferred execution is interleaved with the return transition:

$$\langle \text{return } v, D, \sigma \rangle \rightarrow \langle \text{execute deferred calls}, v, \sigma' \rangle,$$

where v is the return value and σ' represents the state after deferred execution. Moreover, in exceptional control flow scenarios such as panic propagation and subsequent recovery, the deferred calls serve as a safeguard for resource deallocation and state restoration. The precise ordering and guaranteed execution of deferred calls ensure that these interactions conform to well-defined operational semantics, thereby underpinning robust error handling and cleanup strategies within the language.

Go Code Snippet

```
// Comprehensive Go code demonstrating defer semantics, resource
↪   management, and panic recovery.
// This code correlates with the following formal equations and
↪   operational semantics:
//
// 1. Registration of deferred calls:
//    ( f, D, ) defer ( f, D {e}, )
//    (Deferred calls are enqueued rather than executed
↪   immediately.)
//
// 2. Deferred execution at function termination:
//    ( end-of-f, D, ) execute deferred calls (LIFO) ( post-defer
↪   execution, ' )
//
// 3. Resource management via deferred cleanup:
//    r: → '
//    (A cleanup function deferred to ensure that resources are
↪   released properly.)
//
// 4. Interaction with control flow (including panic recovery):
//    Even when a panic occurs, deferred calls are executed before
↪   the function finally exits.

package main

import (
        "fmt"
        "os"
)

// Resource simulates a resource (like a file handle or network
↪   connection)
```

189

```go
// that needs explicit cleanup after use.
type Resource struct {
        name string
}

// Cleanup releases the resource. This function is intended to be
// ↪ deferred,
// ensuring it executes after the main processing of the resource.
func (r *Resource) Cleanup() {
        fmt.Printf("Cleaning up resource: %s\n", r.name)
}

// simulateDeferredCalls demonstrates the registration and LIFO
// ↪ execution of defer.
// It mimics the semantic transition: : C → C', where deferred calls
// ↪ are added to C'.
func simulateDeferredCalls() {
        fmt.Println("Entering simulateDeferredCalls")

        // Register deferred calls.
        // According to Go semantics, these will execute in reverse
        // ↪ order when the function returns.
        defer fmt.Println("Deferred Call 1: Executed in LIFO order")
        defer fmt.Println("Deferred Call 2: Registered later, will
        ↪ execute first")

        fmt.Println("Executing main body of simulateDeferredCalls")
        // Defer execution: once the function completes, the
        // ↪ deferred calls will be triggered.
}

// processResource demonstrates resource allocation and clean-up
// ↪ using defer.
// It models the transformation of the resource state: r: → ' after
// ↪ deferred cleanup.
func processResource() {
        // Simulate allocation of a resource.
        res := &Resource{name: "TempFile.txt"}
        fmt.Printf("Allocating resource: %s\n", res.name)

        // Defer the cleanup of the resource.
        defer res.Cleanup()

        // Simulate processing on the resource.
        fmt.Println("Processing resource...")

        // Simulate a file operation: create a file, write to it,
        // ↪ and close it.
        f, err := os.Create("example.txt")
        if err != nil {
                fmt.Println("Error creating file:", err)
                return
        }
```

190

```go
        // Ensure the file is closed via a deferred function.
        defer func() {
                fmt.Println("Closing file example.txt")
                f.Close()
        }()

        // Write a string to the file.
        _, err = f.WriteString("Hello, Go defer mechanism!")
        if err != nil {
                fmt.Println("Error writing to file:", err)
                return
        }
        fmt.Println("File written successfully")
}

// functionWithPanic demonstrates how deferred calls interact with
↪   control flow,
// particularly during panic propagation and recovery.
// It illustrates that deferred cleanup and recovery routines run
↪   before exiting the function.
func functionWithPanic() {
        // Deferred function to recover from panic.
        defer func() {
                if r := recover(); r != nil {
                        fmt.Println("Recovered from panic:", r)
                }
        }()

        fmt.Println("Function with panic: About to panic")
        // Trigger a panic to simulate an exceptional control flow
        ↪   scenario.
        panic("simulated panic")
        // This line is unreachable; deferred recovery will handle
        ↪   the panic.
        fmt.Println("This line will never execute")
}

func main() {
        fmt.Println("Demonstrating defer semantics in Go")

        // Demonstrate multiple deferred calls and their LIFO
        ↪   execution order.
        simulateDeferredCalls()
        fmt.Println("--------")

        // Demonstrate resource management with deferred cleanup.
        processResource()
        fmt.Println("--------")

        // Demonstrate that deferred functions execute even in the
        ↪   presence of a panic.
        functionWithPanic()
```

191

```
    fmt.Println("End of main")
}
```

Chapter 40

Memory Allocation: new and make Functions

Memory Allocation in Go

Memory allocation in Go is characterized by a clear demarcation between low-level memory reservation and the initialization of composite data structures. The language provides two built-in primitives, namely, *new* and *make*. The function *new* is employed to allocate memory for any given type and returns a pointer to a zero-valued instance of that type. In contrast, *make* is expressly designed for constructing and initializing composite data types—specifically slices, maps, and channels—by not only allocating memory but also establishing the internal structure required for their correct operation. This bifurcation introduces a versatile approach to memory management, ensuring that the data structures are instantiated in a state that adheres to the invariants defined by their underlying types.

The new Function: Pointer Allocation and Zero-Initialization

The *new* function provides a low-level mechanism for memory allocation. For an arbitrary type T, the expression $new(T)$ allocates memory sufficient to hold a value of type T and returns a pointer of type $*T$. Importantly, the allocated memory is zeroed, meaning that every bit is set to 0, thereby unequivocally establishing a baseline state for the allocated object. This operation can be formally represented by the transformation function

$$f_{new} : T \to *T,$$

where $f_{new}(T)$ yields a pointer to an instance of T whose memory is completely zero-initialized. The operation performed by *new* is minimalistic in nature; it does not incorporate any further initialization or configuration beyond this zeroing process. Consequently, *new* is ideally suited for allocating memory environments where further explicit initialization is either unnecessary or deferred to subsequent processing stages.

The make Function: Construction and Initialization of Composite Types

In stark contrast to *new*, the *make* function is purposely crafted for the allocation and initialization of composite types such as slices, maps, and channels. The operational semantics of *make* extend beyond mere memory reservation by performing an initialization that satisfies the internal invariants associated with each composite type. For instance, when constructing a slice, *make* not only allocates an underlying array but also configures the slice header to correctly represent its length and capacity. In the context of maps, *make* allocates memory for a hash table and sets up the internal bucket structures, thereby ensuring efficient key-based lookup. For channels, *make* constructs a communication mechanism with a fully established buffer (if specified), priming it for concurrent message passing. This dual process of allocation and initialization can be conceptualized as a mapping function

$$f_{make} : T \to T,$$

where the subsequent value satisfies the compositional requirements and invariants mandated by the type T. The comprehensive initialization provided by *make* guarantees that the returned object is immediately operable and conforms to the semantic expectations imposed on slices, maps, and channels.

Comparative Analysis of new and make

A rigorous examination of the two functions elucidates a fundamental dichotomy in the design of Go's memory allocation facilities. The function *new* offers a straightforward allocation strategy that returns a pointer of type $*T$, ensuring that the memory is set to a uniform zero state. However, this mechanism does not extend to the initialization of internal fields necessary for the proper functioning of composite types. Conversely, *make* is engineered to serve the specific purpose of initializing composite data structures; it produces values that are fully prepared for immediate use by instantiating internal representations in accordance with predefined invariants. The difference is further accentuated by their respective type signatures: *new* returns a pointer, while *make* returns a directly usable object of the composite type. This inherent division in functionality not only delineates the appropriate contexts for their use but also reinforces the overall integrity and safety of memory operations within the Go runtime.

Go Code Snippet

```go
package main

import (
        "fmt"
)

func main() {
        //
    ↪   -----------------------------------------------------------------
        // Demonstration of the use of new:
        // f_{new}: T -> *T
        // The new function allocates memory for the type and
    ↪      returns a pointer
        // to a zero-valued instance of that type.
        //
    ↪   -----------------------------------------------------------------

        // Allocate an integer using new; the returned pointer
    ↪      points to 0.
        numPtr := new(int)
        fmt.Printf("Value allocated by new (should be 0): %d\n",
    ↪      *numPtr)

        // Update the value pointed by numPtr.
        *numPtr = 2023
```

```go
	fmt.Printf("Updated value pointed by numPtr: %d\n\n",
	↪   *numPtr)

	//
	↪   -----------------------------------------------------------------
	// Demonstration of the use of make:
	// f_{make}: T -> T
	// The make function is used to initialize composite types,
	↪   ensuring that
	// their underlying structures (like slices, maps, or
	↪   channels) are properly
	// set up to satisfy their invariants.
	//
	↪   -----------------------------------------------------------------

	// Using make to create and initialize a slice.
	slice := make([]int, 5, 10) // Create a slice of int with
	↪   length 5 and capacity 10
	fmt.Printf("Initial slice: %v, Length: %d, Capacity: %d\n",
	↪   slice, len(slice), cap(slice))

	// Populate the slice with values.
	for i := 0; i < len(slice); i++ {
		slice[i] = (i + 1) * 10
	}
	fmt.Printf("Populated slice: %v\n\n", slice)

	// Using make to create and initialize a map.
	myMap := make(map[string]int)
	myMap["Go"] = 1
	myMap["Rust"] = 2
	myMap["Python"] = 3
	fmt.Printf("Initialized map: %v\n\n", myMap)

	// Using make to create and initialize a channel.
	// Create a buffered channel of strings with capacity 3.
	ch := make(chan string, 3)
	ch <- "Hello"
	ch <- "Go"
	ch <- "Concurrency"

	fmt.Printf("Channel current length: %d, Capacity: %d\n",
	↪   len(ch), cap(ch))

	// Read all messages from the channel.
	for len(ch) > 0 {
		msg := <-ch
		fmt.Printf("Message received from channel: %s\n",
		↪   msg)
	}
}
```

Chapter 41

Arrays vs. Slices: Distinctions and Use Cases

Structural and Typing Characteristics

Arrays in Go are defined by their fixed size, a property intrinsically embedded within their type signature. An array is expressed as $[n]T$, where n signifies the exact number of elements and T represents the type of each element. The immutability of the size parameter n is enforced at compile time, resulting in a data structure whose memory footprint remains constant throughout its lifetime. This rigidity engenders determinism in memory allocation and facilitates compile-time optimizations. In stark contrast, slices are denoted by the type $[]T$ and serve as a dynamic abstraction layered atop an underlying array. A slice is composed of a pointer to the base element of the array, an integer representing the current length, and another integer specifying its maximum capacity. This tripartite representation enables slices to dynamically adjust the range of elements it encapsulates, thereby permitting operations such as re-slicing and incremental expansion. The fundamental distinction in their type systems not only delineates arrays as statically bounded entities but also sanctions slices as flexible, runtime-adjustable constructs.

Memory Layout and Allocation Semantics

The contrasting memory layouts of arrays and slices arise from their distinct allocation semantics and intended use. Arrays, characterized by their fixed length, are allocated as contiguous blocks in memory. This contiguous allocation facilitates predictable addressing and direct pointer arithmetic, attributes that are advantageous in low-level system operations where performance determinism is critical. Conversely, a slice is not a stand-alone data structure but rather a descriptor that identifies a segment of an underlying array. This descriptor consists of a pointer to the first element in the array segment, alongside indicators for its current length and available capacity. The separation between the slice descriptor and the actual storage—which may reside in a distinct memory region—introduces a level of indirection. This indirection, while incurring a negligible runtime overhead due to bounds checking and the potential for reallocation, confers the slice with its characteristic flexibility. The duality of allocation, where the slice itself is a lightweight header and the underlying array can be dynamically managed, enables efficient data manipulation without compromising on the robustness of memory safety guarantees.

Performance Implications and Semantic Considerations

The performance profiles and semantic behaviors of arrays and slices diverge in ways that directly influence their suitability for varied applications. Arrays, by virtue of their compile-time fixed size and contiguous memory arrangement, offer minimal overhead in scenarios that demand maximal predictability and speed. The absence of runtime allocation adjustments obviates the need for bounds checking during iteration when the compiler is able to infer invariant conditions. However, the value semantics inherent to arrays imply that any assignment or function parameter passing results in a complete copy of the array, a factor which can impose significant memory usage penalties when dealing with large data sets. In contrast, slices exhibit reference semantics; when a slice is passed to a function or assigned to another variable, the underlying array is not duplicated, but rather the slice descriptor is copied. This mechanism ensures that the overhead of duplicating large volumes of data is mitigated. Notwithstanding, the abstraction provided by slices necessitates additional runtime checks, such as dynamic bounds verifications and potential reallocations during append operations. The trade-off between the deterministic performance of arrays and the dynamic flexibility of slices is emblematic of the broader design philosophy in Go's type system, wherein the choice of data structure is dictated by the operational requirements and performance constraints of the specific application domain.

Applicability and Design Rationale in System Architectures

The selection between arrays and slices is contingent upon a confluence of design considerations that encompass both static guarantees and dynamic flexibility. Arrays are optimally suited for contexts in which the size of the data set is known a priori and must remain invariant. Their fixed allocation model permits stringent compile-time validations and can inherently reduce the likelihood of runtime errors associated with boundary violations. Such properties are particularly advantageous in systems-level programming, where deterministic memory layouts and minimal overhead are imperative. In contrast, slices offer a versatile mechanism for handling collections of data whose size may vary during execution. The dynamic resizing capability, coupled with the facility to create new views into the underlying array, positions slices as the preferred construct in higher-level abstractions and applications where data growth is unpredictable. The architectural decision to employ slices is further justified in scenarios that demand efficient memory usage through shared references and where the overhead of dynamic checks is acceptable in exchange for enhanced flexibility. The judicious application of arrays or slices reflects a strategic design decision, aligning the choice of data structure with the specific demands of performance, memory efficiency, and operational adaptability within robust software systems.

Go Code Snippet

```
package main
```

```go
import (
        "fmt"
)

// sumArray calculates the sum of a fixed-size array using value
↪  semantics.
// Equation: sum = a[0] + a[1] + ... + a[n-1]
func sumArray(arr [5]int) int {
        sum := 0
        for i := 0; i < len(arr); i++ {
                sum += arr[i]
        }
        return sum
}

// sumSlice calculates the sum of a slice using reference semantics.
// Equation: sum = s[0] + s[1] + ... + s[n-1]
func sumSlice(slice []int) int {
        sum := 0
        for _, value := range slice {
                sum += value
        }
        return sum
}

// reverseSlice reverses the elements of a slice in-place.
// Algorithm: For i from 0 to n/2, swap s[i] with s[n-1-i]
func reverseSlice(s []int) {
        for i, j := 0, len(s)-1; i < j; i, j = i+1, j-1 {
                s[i], s[j] = s[j], s[i]
        }
}

// modifySlice multiplies every element of the slice by 2.
// Formula applied: s[i] = 2 * s[i]
func modifySlice(s []int) {
        for i := range s {
                s[i] = 2 * s[i]
        }
}

func main() {
        // Define a fixed-size array.
        // Arrays in Go are statically sized with a type signature
        ↪  of [n]T.
        array := [5]int{1, 2, 3, 4, 5}
        fmt.Println("Array:", array)
        fmt.Println("Sum of Array:", sumArray(array))

        // Create a slice from the fixed array.
        // Slices in Go, denoted by []T, hold a pointer to an
        ↪  underlying array, length, and capacity.
        slice := array[:] // slice referencing the entire array.
```

200

```go
    fmt.Println("Initial Slice (from array):", slice)
    fmt.Println("Sum of Slice:", sumSlice(slice))

    // Append additional elements to the slice.
    // This demonstrates the dynamic nature of slices as opposed
    ↪  to fixed arrays.
    slice = append(slice, 6, 7)
    fmt.Println("Slice after appending 6 and 7:", slice)
    fmt.Println("Sum of Extended Slice:", sumSlice(slice))

    // Create a sub-slice. This operation re-slices without
    ↪  copying the underlying array.
    subSlice := slice[2:5]
    fmt.Println("Sub-slice (elements 2 to 4):", subSlice)

    // Reverse the slice using an in-place algorithm.
    // This algorithm swaps elements symmetrically from both
    ↪  ends until the middle is reached.
    reverseSlice(slice)
    fmt.Println("Reversed Slice:", slice)

    // Modify the slice by doubling each element.
    // Demonstrates arithmetic manipulation on slice elements:
    ↪  a_i = 2 * a_i.
    modifySlice(slice)
    fmt.Println("Modified Slice (each element multiplied by
    ↪  2):", slice)
}
```

Chapter 42

String Manipulation: Operations and Functions

Representation of Strings in Go

In Go, a string is formally defined as a sequence of bytes that adhere to the UTF-8 encoding standard. The immutable property of strings is embedded in their definition, ensuring that once a string is instantiated, its binary representation remains constant. This design choice guarantees that any operation which appears to modify a string actually results in the creation of a new string instance. The underlying memory representation is optimized for both performance and safety, facilitating efficient data sharing without the risks associated with mutable state. The static type system mandates that a string, denoted by the type `string`, behaves in a rigorously predictable manner, thereby enabling advanced compiler optimizations and robust error detection during compile time.

Fundamental String Operations

A core set of operations on strings forms the foundation for text manipulation in Go. Among these, concatenation emerges as a primary mechanism whereby two distinct strings, such as s_1 and s_2, are combined to yield a new string whose length is given by

$|s_1| + |s_2|$. This operation, although conceptually simple, underscores the intrinsic property of immutability by necessitating the allocation of new memory for the resultant string. Substring extraction is another critical operation; it enables the selection of a contiguous sequence of bytes from an existing string using a half-open interval notation, typically expressed as $s[i : j]$, where the range spans indices i (inclusive) to j (exclusive). Such operations, defined over the immutable byte sequence, play a pivotal role in enabling safe and predictable manipulations within the constraints of the language's type system.

Core Functions of the Go Strings Package

The Go strings package provides a robust collection of functions designed to streamline common text manipulation tasks. Functions for case conversion, for example, systematically transform each character in a string to its corresponding uppercase or lowercase variant without altering the original value due to the immutable nature of strings. Additionally, the package supplies functions to search for substrings, count occurrences of particular patterns, and assess whether a string commences or concludes with a given sequence. These functions are implemented with a focus on minimizing unnecessary allocations and mitigating performance overhead inherent to repeated string processing. Utility functions for trimming extraneous characters from either end of a string further exemplify the package's emphasis on ensuring consistency in text data. Together, these operations conform to a cohesive design that marries high-level abstraction with finely tuned, efficient algorithms.

Performance Considerations and Algorithmic Implications

The design of string operations in Go reflects a nuanced balance between the theoretical underpinnings of immutability and the practical demands of efficient computation. Given that strings are immutable, operations traditionally associated with in-place modification instead yield new strings, rendering certain operations inherently linear in time complexity, specifically $O(n)$ where n denotes the length of the string. This characteristic necessitates algorithmic strategies that minimize redundant memory allocation, particularly in contexts involving iterative concatenation or repeated substring extractions. The strings package leverages pre-allocation and algorithmic optimizations to address these challenges, ensuring that functions operate within acceptable performance bounds even under high load. Such considerations are of paramount importance in large-scale software systems where the precise trade-off between time complexity and memory efficiency must be managed with exacting care.

Go Code Snippet

```go
package main

import (
        "fmt"
        "strings"
)

func main() {
        // Representation of strings in Go:
        // A Go string is an immutable sequence of bytes in UTF-8.
        // Any operation that appears to modify a string actually
        ↪    creates a new string.
        s1 := "Hello, "
        s2 := "World!"

        // Fundamental string operation: Concatenation
        // Important Equation:
        //    len(s1 + s2) = len(s1) + len(s2)
        concatenated := s1 + s2
        expectedLength := len(s1) + len(s2)
        fmt.Printf("Concatenated string: %s\n", concatenated)
        fmt.Printf("Expected length = %d, Actual length = %d\n\n",
        ↪    expectedLength, len(concatenated))

        // Substring Extraction:
        // Using the half-open interval notation s[i:j] where i is
        ↪    inclusive and j is exclusive
        // For example, extracting "World" from "Hello, World!"
        ↪    (indices 7 to 12, since 12 is excluded)
        substring := concatenated[7:12]
        fmt.Printf("Extracted substring (indices 7 to 11): %s\n\n",
        ↪    substring)

        // Using core functions from Go's strings package for
        ↪    various operations:
```

```go
// Case conversion: converting the entire string to
//     uppercase and lowercase.
upper := strings.ToUpper(concatenated)
lower := strings.ToLower(concatenated)
fmt.Printf("Uppercase: %s\n", upper)
fmt.Printf("Lowercase: %s\n\n", lower)

// Counting occurrences:
// Count number of times the letter 'l' (case-sensitive)
//     appears in the string.
countL := strings.Count(concatenated, "l")
fmt.Printf("Count of 'l' in %q: %d\n\n", concatenated,
    countL)

// Searching for substrings:
hasPrefix := strings.HasPrefix(concatenated, "Hello")
hasSuffix := strings.HasSuffix(concatenated, "World!")
fmt.Printf("Starts with 'Hello': %v\n", hasPrefix)
fmt.Printf("Ends with 'World!': %v\n\n", hasSuffix)

// Trimming characters:
// Remove specified characters from the beginning and end.
//     Here we remove '!' if present.
trimmed := strings.Trim(concatenated, "!")
fmt.Printf("Trimmed string (removing '!'): %s\n\n", trimmed)

// Performance Consideration:
// Repeated concatenation can be expensive due to
//     immutability.
// Using strings.Builder helps to efficiently build strings
//     with minimal memory allocations.
words := []string{"Go", "is", "an", "open-source",
    "programming", "language"}
var builder strings.Builder
for i, word := range words {
        builder.WriteString(word)
        if i < len(words)-1 {
                builder.WriteString(" ") // Inserting a
                    space as a separator.
        }
}
sentence := builder.String()
fmt.Printf("Sentence constructed with strings.Builder:
    %s\n\n", sentence)

// Example Algorithm: Iterating and analyzing characters in
//     a string.
// Check if the concatenated string contains the substring
//     "World".
if strings.Contains(concatenated, "World") {
        fmt.Println("The string contains 'World'")
}
```

```go
    // Iterating over the string using range. This properly
    ↪  handles multi-byte UTF-8 characters.
    fmt.Println("\nIterating over characters in the concatenated
    ↪  string:")
    for index, char := range concatenated {
        // The index corresponds to the byte position in the
        ↪  string.
        fmt.Printf("Index %d: %c\n", index, char)
    }
}
```

Chapter 43

Formatted String Construction: Using Sprintf and Scanf

Mechanisms of Formatted Output Synthesis

The Sprintf function within the fmt package provides a deterministic method for the synthesis of new strings based on a specified format and a set of provided values. This function operates by interpreting a format string—a literal template interlaced with conversion specifiers—and mapping each specifier to a corresponding value. The mapping adheres to a well-defined grammatical structure, where conversion verbs such as %d, %f, and %s dictate the translation of numerical and textual data into a human-readable and predictable representation. The formatting directives allow for precision control and field width specification, often expressed in forms such as %.3f to enforce a restricted number of digits after the decimal point. Internally, Sprintf allocates a new immutable string that encapsulates both the literal segments of the format string and the converted representations of the input values. The transformation process can be analyzed in terms of its computational complexity, which is generally linear in the length of the output, that is, $O(n)$ where n represents the total number of output characters produced by concatenating literal elements with the expanded values.

Structured Input Parsing with Scanf

In a complementary fashion, the Scanf function is designed for the extraction of data from formatted strings, operating as an inverse mechanism to Sprintf. This function accepts a format specification that delineates the expected structure of the input text and facilitates the decomposition of that text into discrete, type-specific components. Each conversion specifier, for instance %d for integer values or %f for floating-point numbers, serves as a directive for the parser to identify and convert corresponding segments of the input. The parsing mechanism operates by sequentially scanning the input string, matching substrings against the directives embedded within the format string, and converting them into their native representations. The process is underscored by a formal grammar that governs the tokenization of the input, with whitespace and literal characters playing critical roles in maintaining the fidelity of the extraction process. Error detection is an intrinsic element of this operation; any discrepancy between the specified format and the encountered input triggers an error condition that is propagated back to the calling context. Such error handling is essential to ensuring that only valid representations are admitted, thereby preserving type safety and consistency.

Implications for Data Representation and Processing Efficiency

From a theoretical standpoint, the dual operations of formatted string construction via Sprintf and structured parsing via Scanf serve as pivotal interfaces between data representation and the processing of textual information. The production of a formatted string by means of Sprintf is intrinsically non-mutative, resulting in a new allocation that embodies a direct and immutable representation of the input values. This immutability guarantees that the original data remains unaltered, thereby aligning with principles of referential transparency commonly advocated in functional paradigms. Conversely, the use of Scanf to decompose a formatted string reinforces the necessity for rigorous syntactic adherence, owing to its reliance on predetermined patterns to accurately map segments of the input to corresponding data types.

The performance characteristics of these operations are closely intertwined with the nature of their implementations. Sprintf performs a sequential traversal of the format string, interleaving literal content with formatted output in accordance with each conversion directive. This process can lead to a predictable allocation pattern with an overall cost proportional to the output length. Meanwhile, Scanf employs a scanning algorithm that must contend with variable token lengths and potential irregularities in the input data. The algorithmic design of both functions is optimized to mitigate unnecessary memory allocation and processing overhead; buffering techniques and lookahead mechanisms are often integrated to achieve an efficient balance between speed and accuracy.

The formal symmetry between the output produced by Sprintf and the input expected by Scanf underscores a broader design philosophy within the fmt package. Each conversion specifier is defined with a set of unambiguous rules that govern both the encoding and decoding processes, ensuring that data can be reliably transformed between its in-memory representation and its textual form. This bidirectional consistency is critical in applications that require high assurance of data integrity, as it obviates discrepancies that might otherwise arise from ambiguous formatting or parsing conventions. The mathematical rigor underlying these format functions reinforces their role as essential tools in the domain of string manipulation and input/output processing.

Go Code Snippet

```
package main

import (
        "bufio"
        "fmt"
        "os"
        "strings"
)

// main demonstrates formatted string construction using Sprintf and
↪    structured input parsing using Scanf/Sscanf.
// It also highlights key computational aspects such as immutability
↪    and linear-time processing (O(n)) for formatted output.
func main() {
        // Example 1: Formatted string construction using Sprintf.
```

```go
// Here we format a floating point number (pi) to three
↪    decimal places.
pi := 3.141592653589793
formattedPi := fmt.Sprintf("Pi formatted to three decimal
↪    places: %.3f", pi)
fmt.Println(formattedPi)

// Example 2: Constructing a composite message with multiple
↪    conversion specifiers.
// Demonstrates the use of %s for strings, %d for integers,
↪    and %.2f for floating point numbers.
name := "Gopher"
age := 5
score := 98.7654321
message := fmt.Sprintf("Hello %s, Age: %d, Score: %.2f",
↪    name, age, score)
fmt.Println(message)

// Example 3: Combining literal and dynamic content into an
↪    immutable formatted string.
// The resulting string is a new allocation that does not
↪    alter the original input values.
items := 3
price := 29.99
description := "books"
completeMessage := fmt.Sprintf("You have purchased %d %s at
↪    $%.2f each.", items, description, price)
fmt.Println(completeMessage)

// Note: The Sprintf function processes the format string
↪    and arguments in linear time O(n) relative to
// the total number of output characters, ensuring
↪    deterministic performance.

// Example 4: Structured input parsing using fmt.Sscanf.
// We simulate parsing a formatted string matching a known
↪    pattern.
inputStr := "Order: 1001, Quantity: 7, Total: 59.93"
var orderID int
var quantity int
var total float64

// The format string must exactly match the input structure
↪    to correctly extract values.
n, err := fmt.Sscanf(inputStr, "Order: %d, Quantity: %d,
↪    Total: %f", &orderID, &quantity, &total)
if err != nil {
        fmt.Fprintf(os.Stderr, "Scanning error: %v\n", err)
} else {
        // n should equal 3 if all values are successfully
        ↪    parsed.
```

```
                fmt.Printf("Parsed Values -> OrderID: %d, Quantity:
                ↪  %d, Total: %.2f (Parsed count: %d)\n", orderID,
                ↪  quantity, total, n)
}

// Example 5: Handling error conditions in formatted
↪  scanning.
// Attempt to parse an input string with unexpected
↪  (non-numeric) values.
faultyInput := "Order: ABC, Quantity: seven, Total: sixty"
var faultyOrderID, faultyQuantity int
var faultyTotal float64
count, err := fmt.Sscanf(faultyInput, "Order: %d, Quantity:
↪  %d, Total: %f", &faultyOrderID, &faultyQuantity,
↪  &faultyTotal)
if err != nil {
                fmt.Fprintf(os.Stderr, "Faulty scanning detected:
                ↪  %v\n", err)
} else {
                fmt.Printf("Faulty Parsed Values -> OrderID: %d,
                ↪  Quantity: %d, Total: %.2f (Parsed count: %d)\n",
                        faultyOrderID, faultyQuantity, faultyTotal,
                        ↪  count)
}

// Example 6: Interactive input parsing using Scanf
↪  (commented out for non-interactive execution).
/*
                fmt.Print("Enter your birth year (e.g., 'Year:
                ↪  1990'): ")
                reader := bufio.NewReader(os.Stdin)
                inputLine, _ := reader.ReadString('\n')
                // Trim any extraneous whitespace/newline
                inputLine = strings.TrimSpace(inputLine)
                var birthYear int
                parsedCount, err := fmt.Sscanf(inputLine, "Year:
                ↪  %d", &birthYear)
                if err != nil || parsedCount != 1 {
                        fmt.Fprintf(os.Stderr, "Failed to parse
                        ↪  birth year: %v\n", err)
                } else {
                        fmt.Printf("Your birth year is: %d\n",
                        ↪  birthYear)
                }
*/

// These examples underscore the bidirectional consistency
↪  between Go's formatted output (Sprintf)
// and input parsing (Scanf/Sscanf). They illustrate how
↪  format directives govern the string synthesis
// and parsing operations, ensuring that data is reliably
↪  transformed between its in-memory representation
```

```
    // and its textual form with a predictable performance
    ↪  profile.
}
```

Chapter 44

Working with Numbers: Parsing and Conversion

Techniques for Interpreting Numeric Representations

The process of parsing numeric strings is a critical operation that transforms textual representations into quantifiable numerical data. This transformation encompasses the identification and segmentation of digit sequences, sign indicators, and potential symbols used for decimal separation or scientific notation. Underlying these techniques is the rigorous application of formal grammars and finite state automata, which govern the stepwise evaluation of each character in a string. In many implementations, the complexity of the parsing operation is linear, denoted as $O(n)$, where n represents the total number of characters processed. Critical to this analysis is the consideration of input normalization, including the treatment of leading zeros, whitespace, and locale-specific conventions. The deterministic nature of these algorithms ensures that each well-formed numeric string is accurately interpreted according to an established rule set derived from both automata theory and numerical analysis.

Conversion Between Numeric Types: Methodologies and Precision Considerations

Conversion between various numeric types involves a meticulous mapping of a number's in-memory representation to an alternative format that may vary in precision and range. Such conversions may occur between integer types of different widths or between integers and floating-point representations. The conversion process must address the intrinsic limitations of fixed-width representations, including overflow and underflow conditions, as well as the challenges posed by the finite precision inherent in floating-point arithmetic. In particular, conversions that truncate or round a number require a careful assessment of the potential loss of significance and the propagation of rounding errors. The underlying arithmetic for floating-point numbers adheres to standards such as IEEE-754, which prescribes both the representation and the rounding modes for binary floating-point arithmetic. As a result, the conversion techniques are underpinned by mathematical rigor that ensures an optimal balance between computational efficiency and numeric fidelity.

Error Detection and Algorithmic Considerations in Parsing and Conversion

Robust error detection is an integral component of both numeric parsing and type conversion. The mechanisms for identifying invalid input—such as non-numeric characters, malformed digit groupings, or values exceeding the representable range—rely on predefined validation rules embedded within the parsing algorithm. These rules are derived from formal language theory and are implemented using deterministic or nondeterministic finite automata that ensure consistency with the expected numeric syntax. Errors encountered during the parsing phase trigger recovery or propagation routines, which are vital for maintaining system stability and preventing the corruption of subsequent computational processes. Similarly, during type conversion, the evaluation of potential precision loss or overflow conditions is accomplished through systematic checks, ensuring that the conversion adheres to the specifications of the target data type. The algorithms employed in these tasks are analyzed not only by their asymptotic performance but also by their ability to manage error conditions effectively, thereby preserving both the integrity and the consistency of numerical computations.

Go Code Snippet

```go
package main

import (
        "errors"
        "fmt"
        "math"
        "strings"
)

// parseNumber manually parses a numeric string into a float64
↪    value.
// It supports an optional sign, an integer part, a fractional part,
↪    and scientific notation (e/E).
// The parsing algorithm operates in O(n) time, where n is the
↪    length of the input string.
func parseNumber(s string) (float64, error) {
        // Trim leading and trailing whitespace.
        s = strings.TrimSpace(s)
        if len(s) == 0 {
                return 0, errors.New("input string is empty")
        }

        var result float64 = 0.0
        var sign float64 = 1.0
        idx := 0

        // Handle optional sign.
        if s[idx] == '-' {
                sign = -1
                idx++
        } else if s[idx] == '+' {
                idx++
        }

        // There must be at least one digit.
        if idx >= len(s) || (s[idx] < '0' || s[idx] > '9') {
                return 0, errors.New("invalid input: no digits
                ↪    found")
        }

        // Parse integer part.
        hasDigits := false
        for idx < len(s) && s[idx] >= '0' && s[idx] <= '9' {
                hasDigits = true
```

215

```go
                        result = result*10 + float64(s[idx]-'0')
                        idx++
        }

        // Parse fractional part if a decimal point is encountered.
        if idx < len(s) && s[idx] == '.' {
                idx++
                if idx >= len(s) || s[idx] < '0' || s[idx] > '9' {
                        return 0, errors.New("invalid format: no
                            ↪  digits after decimal point")
                }
                factor := 0.1
                for idx < len(s) && s[idx] >= '0' && s[idx] <= '9' {
                        hasDigits = true
                        result += float64(s[idx]-'0') * factor
                        factor /= 10
                        idx++
                }
        }

        // Parse exponent part if present.
        if idx < len(s) && (s[idx] == 'e' || s[idx] == 'E') {
                idx++
                expSign := 1
                if idx < len(s) {
                        if s[idx] == '-' {
                                expSign = -1
                                idx++
                        } else if s[idx] == '+' {
                                idx++
                        }
                }
                if idx >= len(s) || s[idx] < '0' || s[idx] > '9' {
                        return 0, errors.New("invalid format in
                            ↪  exponent")
                }
                var exponent int
                for idx < len(s) && s[idx] >= '0' && s[idx] <= '9' {
                        exponent = exponent*10 + int(s[idx]-'0')
                        idx++
                }
                result *= math.Pow(10, float64(expSign*exponent))
        }

        // Ensure there are no invalid trailing characters.
        if !hasDigits || idx != len(s) {
                return 0, errors.New("invalid character encountered
                    ↪  in input")
        }

        return sign * result, nil
}
```

```go
// intToFloat demonstrates a straightforward conversion from an
//    integer to a float64.
func intToFloat(n int) float64 {
        return float64(n)
}

// safeFloatToInt converts a float64 to an int ensuring no
//    fractional loss is present.
// It returns an error if the float has a fractional component or is
//    outside a safe integer range.
func safeFloatToInt(f float64) (int, error) {
        // Check if the float has a fractional part.
        if math.Trunc(f) != f {
                return 0, errors.New("precision loss: float value
                    has a fractional component")
        }
        // For demonstration, we consider a safe range based on
        //    int32 limits.
        const maxInt = int(^uint32(0) >> 1)
        const minInt = -maxInt - 1
        if f > float64(maxInt) || f < float64(minInt) {
                return 0, errors.New("value out of int range")
        }
        return int(f), nil
}

func main() {
        // Demonstrate numeric parsing with various examples.
        examples := []string{
                "123",
                "-45.67",
                "  3.14159  ",
                "2.5e2",
                " -0.00123e-2",
                "invalid",
                "123abc",
        }

        fmt.Println("Numeric Parsing Examples:")
        for _, ex := range examples {
                value, err := parseNumber(ex)
                if err != nil {
                        fmt.Printf("Input: %q -> Error: %v\n", ex,
                            err)
                } else {
                        fmt.Printf("Input: %q -> Parsed Value:
                            %f\n", ex, value)
                }
        }

        // Demonstrate conversion between int and float.
        fmt.Println("\nConversion Examples:")
        intVal := 42
```

```go
        floatVal := intToFloat(intVal)
        fmt.Printf("Converted int %d to float: %f\n", intVal,
        ↪   floatVal)

        // Attempt safe conversion from float to int.
        testFloats := []float64{123.0, 456.789}
        for _, f := range testFloats {
                iv, err := safeFloatToInt(f)
                if err != nil {
                        fmt.Printf("Float: %f -> Conversion Error:
                        ↪   %v\n", f, err)
                } else {
                        fmt.Printf("Float: %f -> Converted int:
                        ↪   %d\n", f, iv)
                }
        }
}
```

Chapter 45

Loop Patterns: Infinite Loops and Early Exit

Theoretical Foundations of Unbounded Iterative Constructs

Infinite loops represent a class of control structures deliberately designed without an intrinsic halting condition, thereby engendering an iterative process that perpetuates until an external or internal intervention dictates cessation. The essential property of an infinite loop is that the conditional expression governing its execution is invariantly true, leading to a nonterminating sequence of iterations. This phenomenon finds its roots in the formal apparatus of automata theory, where state transitions occur in a perpetual cycle unless disrupted by a designated break condition. By modeling the loop as a finite state automaton with a self-referential transition, one may rigorously state that the standard exit criteria are absent, thereby assigning the loop an iterative complexity that, in the absence of intervention, is theoretically unbounded.

Mechanisms for Controlled Termination via Conditional Disruption

Embedded within the framework of infinite loops, the application of early exit strategies, notably through the use of break statements, introduces a mechanism to disrupt the otherwise unending cycle.

The break construct serves as a conditional interrupt, enabling the evaluation of runtime states or auxiliary predicates that determine the moment at which it is computationally judicious to cease further iterations. This construct is formally analogous to a function call within the state transition diagram of an automaton that diverts the process to an absorbing state. Such strategies embody a controlled form of nonlocal transfer of execution, ensuring that even within a loop whose inherent condition is perpetually satisfied, an ordered and deterministic termination is attainable when a predetermined criterion—such as a convergence threshold or error flag—is met.

Design Considerations and Computational Implications

The deliberate design of infinite loops accompanied by early exit conditions necessitates a rigorous scrutiny of both the theoretical and practical implications. On a theoretical level, the incorporation of a break mechanism renders the infinite loop tractable within the bounds of algorithmic analysis. A precise determination of the conditions under which the break is invoked is essential to guarantee that the loop adheres to expected termination constraints, particularly in scenarios where computation is subject to side effects or stateful mutations. In practical computational systems, the integration of such mechanisms demands careful attention to the invariants preserved during iteration; these invariants are critical for ensuring that the premature termination does not precipitate inconsistencies in the program state. Furthermore, the interplay between the potentially unbounded nature of the loop and the deterministic invocation of the break condition must be formally characterized, often through complexity analyses expressed as $O(n)$ in the average or worst-case scenarios, where n denotes the number of iterations executed prior to termination.

Analytical Examination of Safety and Termination Properties

The deployment of infinite loops, when furnished with appropriate break conditions, invites an analytical examination of safety and termination properties from both a numerical and logical perspective. Formal methods, such as loop invariants and inductive reasoning, play a pivotal role in affirming that each iteration of the loop preserves the intended computational semantics and that the break statement is reached under all feasible execution paths. The evaluation of these properties is closely aligned with well-established principles in theoretical computer science, particularly within the realms of algorithm analysis and formal verification. By establishing stringent conditions for the invocation of an exit mechanism, it becomes possible to demonstrate that the otherwise infinite iterative process converges to a defined state under specified constraints. Such analysis proves indispensable, especially in concurrent or time-critical applications where the predictability of loop termination is directly correlated with system robustness and operational safety.

Go Code Snippet

```go
package main

import (
        "fmt"
        "math"
)

// This program demonstrates an iterative algorithm using an
↪    infinite loop
// with early exit conditions. It approximates the square root of a
↪    given
// number using Newton's method. The algorithm embodies key aspects
↪    discussed
// in this chapter:
//    - An infinite loop is created using the "for" construct without
↪    a condition.
//    - A break statement is used to interrupt the loop when
↪    convergence is achieved.
//    - Loop invariants ensure that the estimate remains positive and
↪    converges.
//    - A maximum iteration guard prevents an unintended
↪    non-terminating loop
//      in pathological scenarios.

func main() {
        // The number for which we compute the square root.
        number := 25.0
```

```go
// Tolerance defines the acceptable difference between
↪   successive estimates.
tolerance := 1e-6

// Initial estimate for the square root; starting with half
↪   of the number.
estimate := number / 2.0

// Iteration counter to track the number of iterations.
iterations := 0

// Maximum allowed iterations to safeguard against
↪   non-termination.
maxIterations := 1000

// Infinite loop representing the iterative process.
for {
        // Compute a new estimate using Newton's method:
        //    newEstimate = 0.5 * (estimate + (number /
        ↪   estimate))
        newEstimate := 0.5 * (estimate + number/estimate)

        // Check for convergence:
        // The loop invariant ensures that the estimates are
        ↪   converging,
        // and the break condition is equivalent to reaching
        ↪   an absorbing state
        // in a finite state automaton.
        if math.Abs(newEstimate-estimate) < tolerance {
                fmt.Printf("Converged: sqrt(%.2f)  %.6f
                ↪   after %d iterations.\n",
                        number, newEstimate, iterations)
                break
        }

        // Increment the iteration counter.
        iterations++

        // Safety check: exit if maximum iterations are
        ↪   exceeded.
        if iterations >= maxIterations {
                fmt.Printf("Maximum iterations reached. Last
                ↪   estimate: %.6f\n", newEstimate)
                break
        }

        // Update the estimate for the next iteration,
        ↪   preserving the loop invariant.
        estimate = newEstimate
}
}
```

Chapter 46

Goroutines: Lightweight Concurrency

Conceptual Underpinnings of Goroutines

Goroutines constitute an intrinsic mechanism within the Go programming language for the realization of concurrent computation. They represent an abstraction that enables the execution of independent functions in parallel, without incurring the substantial memory and processing overhead characteristic of traditional operating system threads. In contrast to heavyweight threads, each goroutine is provisioned with a small initial stack—commonly on the order of a few kilobytes—and the stack is permitted to dynamically expand in response to nested function calls. This minimalistic resource allocation permits the creation of a vast number of concurrent execution contexts, each managed efficiently by the Go runtime system. The abstraction inherent in goroutines is grounded in advanced principles of concurrent process theory, wherein the decoupling of execution streams promotes both computational efficiency and the parallelism required in modern high-performance applications.

Mechanisms for Goroutine Invocation and Launch

The instantiation of a new goroutine is achieved through a distinctive syntactic construct that precedes a function invocation with an explicit keyword. This directive instructs the runtime to initiate the function as an independent concurrent process, thereby enabling the asynchronous execution of its logic. The launch mechanism obviates the need for manual thread management, ensuring that the overhead associated with context switching and resource allocation is minimized. As each goroutine commences execution, its initial state is established with a bare minimum of stack memory, and the system subsequently undertakes the management of its execution lifecycle. The process of launching a goroutine encapsulates the core idea of nonblocking execution, where the primary control flow is not impeded by the concurrent activity of spawned routines.

Runtime Scheduling and Execution Model

Goroutines are scheduled for execution by an adaptive runtime scheduler that maps these lightweight processes onto available operating system threads. The scheduler employs refined algorithms, such as work stealing and multiplexing, to distribute computational load evenly across processor cores. This runtime system is responsible for monitoring the state of each goroutine—whether it is runnable, waiting on synchronization primitives, or engaged in input/output operations—and for effecting context switches as necessary. The dynamic nature of the scheduler allows it to rapidly reassign execution priorities and to suspend and resume goroutines with negligible latency, thus ensuring high throughput even under heavy concurrency. The execution model is characterized by the capacity to handle thousands or millions of concurrently executing goroutines, each operating under a uniform and deterministic allocation scheme that abstracts away the complexities of system-level thread management.

Implications for Concurrent System Design

The lightweight concurrency model provided by goroutines engenders significant implications for the design and architecture of concurrent systems. By reducing the cost of context creation and facilitating rapid asynchronous execution, goroutines enable the formulation of highly granular concurrent algorithms. This paradigm supports the construction of modular systems in which individual units of computation may be developed, tested, and verified in isolation, yet composed into a coherent whole through the orchestration of the runtime scheduler. Furthermore, the inherent isolation and low overhead of each goroutine promote robust system design by mitigating common concurrency hazards such as race conditions and deadlocks, provided that inter-goroutine communication and synchronization are managed through well-defined constructs. The theoretical efficiency of this model is often expressed as an amortized cost approximating $O(1)$ for routine creation, a characteristic that underpins its suitability for applications demanding scalable and high-performance concurrent processing.

Go Code Snippet

```go
package main

import (
        "fmt"
        "math/rand"
        "sync"
        "time"
)

// task defines a unit of work used to simulate processing in a
↪    goroutine.
// Each task has an identifier and a payload representing the
↪    computation "input".
type task struct {
        id      int
        payload int // Payload used in our sample equation
        ↪    computation.
}

// worker simulates a concurrent worker processing tasks received
↪    from the jobs channel.
// It computes a simple mathematical function on the payload:
```

```go
//     f(x) = (x + 1)^2   i.e., f(x) = x^2 + 2x + 1
// This represents an example of performing an "important equation"
// ↪   during asynchronous execution.
// Each worker runs as an independent goroutine; as discussed in the
// ↪   chapter,
// the creation of such goroutines incurs an amortized cost of
// ↪   approximately O(1).
func worker(workerID int, jobs <-chan task, results chan<- string,
↪   wg *sync.WaitGroup) {
        defer wg.Done() // Ensure that the worker signals when it is
        ↪   finished.
        for job := range jobs {
                // Simulate a processing time that depends on the
                ↪   task's payload.
                processTime := time.Duration(job.payload) *
                ↪   time.Millisecond
                time.Sleep(processTime)

                // Evaluate the equation f(x) = (x + 1)^2.
                computed := (job.payload + 1) * (job.payload + 1)

                // Prepare a result string with relevant details.
                result := fmt.Sprintf("Worker %d processed Task %d
                ↪   (payload: %d); f(x) = (x+1)^2 = %d",
                        workerID, job.id, job.payload, computed)

                // Send the result back to the collector.
                results <- result
        }
}

func main() {
        // Seed the random number generator for variable payload
        ↪   simulation.
        rand.Seed(time.Now().UnixNano())

        const (
                numTasks   = 20  // Total number of tasks to be
                ↪   processed.
                numWorkers = 5   // Total number of concurrent
                ↪   workers.
        )

        // Create buffered channels for jobs and results.
        jobs := make(chan task, numTasks)
        results := make(chan string, numTasks)

        // WaitGroup to coordinate the completion of worker
        ↪   goroutines.
        var wg sync.WaitGroup

        // Launch a fixed number of worker goroutines.
        for w := 1; w <= numWorkers; w++ {
```

226

```go
        wg.Add(1)
        go worker(w, jobs, results, &wg)
}

// Dispatch tasks with variable payloads to simulate
// ↪ differing work durations.
for t := 1; t <= numTasks; t++ {
        payload := rand.Intn(100) // Random payload between
        // ↪ 0 and 99 (in milliseconds).
        jobs <- task{
                id:      t,
                payload: payload,
        }
}
// Close the jobs channel to indicate no further tasks will
// ↪ be sent.
close(jobs)

// Launch a goroutine to close the results channel once all
// ↪ workers have finished.
go func() {
        wg.Wait()
        close(results)
}()

// Collect and display results as they are produced by the
// ↪ workers.
for res := range results {
        fmt.Println(res)
}

// Final message indicating that all tasks have been
// ↪ processed.
fmt.Println("All tasks have been processed concurrently
// ↪ using lightweight goroutines.")
}
```

Chapter 47

Concurrency Primitives: Channels Overview

Theoretical Underpinnings and Design Rationale

Channels serve as a foundational mechanism for inter-goroutine communication, providing a structured medium through which discrete computational tasks may exchange data. The conceptual framework of channels is predicated on the theory of message passing concurrency, wherein channels act as conduits that facilitate the transfer of values between concurrently executing processes. Within this paradigm, channels are envisioned as typed conduits that enforce a disciplined interaction protocol, thereby ensuring that data exchanges comply with predetermined interfaces and formats. This design choice inherently mitigates risks associated with shared memory concurrency, such as race conditions, by channeling all inter-process communication through well-defined, isolated pathways.

The mathematical abstraction underlying channel operations can be conceptualized as a relation $R \subseteq S \times T$, where S represents the set of send events and T signifies the set of receive events. The correspondence between these events is governed by operational semantics that specify the conditions under which a sending operation, denoted by the symbol $\leftarrow$, synchronizes with a corresponding receiving operation. Such formalization provides a rigorous foundation for reasoning about the correctness and performance of concurrent systems designed using channels as their primary communication primitive.

Operational Semantics of Channel Operations

The operational semantics of channels intricately detail the behavior of send and receive operations. A channel that is instantiated without an explicit buffer exhibits synchronous characteristics, in which the issuance of a send operation results in a blocking state until a receiver is available to accept the data. Conversely, with the allocation of a nonzero capacity n, a channel accommodates asynchronous communication up to n buffered elements. In this buffered mode, the send operation remains nonblocking until the buffer reaches its maximum capacity, at which point subsequent sends are forced to wait for corresponding receives.

These basic operations are defined by their atomic execution guarantees, ensuring that the concurrent interactions mediated through a channel are free of race conditions and state inconsistencies. The semantics further imply that a receive operation on an empty channel will block until a send operation becomes available, thereby establishing a deterministic synchronization pattern between concurrently executing goroutines. The interplay between the channel's intrinsic buffering capacity and the blocking behavior of its operations is central to the design of efficient, concurrent algorithms that rely on message passing rather than shared state.

Channels as Synchronization Primitives

Beyond their fundamental role as data conduits, channels possess the inherent ability to function as synchronization primitives. By orchestrating the timing and order of operations between sender and receiver, channels facilitate the coordination of concurrent processes without resorting to explicit lock-based mechanisms. This property is particularly valuable in the context of orchestrating complex interactions among multiple goroutines, where channels can be used to signal the completion of computational tasks, propagate events, or enforce mutual exclusion in a manner that is both intuitive and scalable.

The synchronization semantics of channels are underscored by the deterministic association between send and receive events. When a sender dispatches a value via the channel, the corresponding receiver is guaranteed to eventually observe the transmitted data, subject to the constraints imposed by the channel's buffering strategy and the scheduling policies of the runtime system. This deterministic behavior underpins the reliability of concurrent systems that employ channels as their primary means of ensuring that the system state evolves in a coordinated and predictable manner.

Channels thus emerge not only as an efficient mechanism for transferring data between independent execution threads but also as a robust theoretical construct that encapsulates the principles of synchronization in concurrent computation. The alignment of channel operations with the broader tenets of formal process theory reinforces their significance in the design of high-performance, concurrent architectures.

Go Code Snippet

```
package main

import (
        "fmt"
        "sync"
        "time"
)

// This program demonstrates key channel operations in Go based on
↪   the theoretical underpinnings
// discussed in this chapter. It simulates the mathematical relation
↪   R  S × T, where S represents
// send events and T represents receive events. In Go, the send
↪   operator (conceptually represented
// by "⊢") is implemented as "ch <- value", ensuring synchronization
↪   between sender and receiver.

// synchronousChannel sends a value on an unbuffered (synchronous)
↪   channel.
// The send operation represents a send event (S) and will block
↪   until a corresponding receive event (T) occurs.
func synchronousChannel(ch chan int, wg *sync.WaitGroup) {
        defer wg.Done()
        // Send event (S): sending the integer 42 through the
        ↪   channel.
```

```go
        ch <- 42
        fmt.Println("Synchronous send completed with value 42")
}

// synchronousReceiver receives a value from the unbuffered channel,
↪    representing a receive event (T).
func synchronousReceiver(ch chan int, wg *sync.WaitGroup) {
        defer wg.Done()
        // Receive event (T): retrieving the sent value.
        val := <-ch
        fmt.Printf("Synchronous receive obtained value %d\n", val)
}

// bufferedChannelDemo demonstrates a buffered channel where
↪    non-blocking sends are possible until the buffer is full.
// Once the buffer capacity is reached, further sends will block
↪    until space is freed by corresponding receive events.
func bufferedChannelDemo(ch chan int, wg *sync.WaitGroup) {
        defer wg.Done()
        // Fill the buffered channel up to its capacity.
        for i := 0; i < cap(ch); i++ {
                ch <- i
                fmt.Printf("Buffered send: %d\n", i)
        }
        // Start an additional goroutine to send an extra value,
        ↪    which will block until a receiver clears some space.
        go func() {
                ch <- 999
                fmt.Println("Buffered send completed for value 999
                ↪    (after blocking)")
        }()
        // Allow some time to ensure the extra send is blocking.
        time.Sleep(100 * time.Millisecond)
        // Drain the channel, receiving all buffered values
        ↪    including the extra one.
        for i := 0; i < cap(ch)+1; i++ {
                val := <-ch
                fmt.Printf("Buffered receive: %d\n", val)
        }
}

// selectChannelDemo demonstrates the use of the select statement
↪    for non-deterministic channel operations.
// It attempts to receive messages from two channels and, if none
↪    are available, executes a default case.
func selectChannelDemo(ch1, ch2 chan string, wg *sync.WaitGroup) {
        defer wg.Done()
        for i := 0; i < 4; i++ {
                select {
                case msg := <-ch1:
                        fmt.Printf("Select received from channel 1:
                        ↪    %s\n", msg)
                case msg := <-ch2:
```

```go
                        fmt.Printf("Select received from channel 2:
                        ↪  %s\n", msg)
                default:
                        fmt.Println("Select default case: no data
                        ↪  available, continuing...")
                        time.Sleep(50 * time.Millisecond)
                }
        }
}

func main() {
        var wg sync.WaitGroup

        // Demonstrate unbuffered (synchronous) channel operations.
        unbufCh := make(chan int)
        wg.Add(2)
        go synchronousChannel(unbufCh, &wg)
        go synchronousReceiver(unbufCh, &wg)
        wg.Wait()

        // Demonstrate buffered channel operations, highlighting
        ↪  non-blocking sends until the buffer is full.
        bufCh := make(chan int, 5)
        wg.Add(1)
        go bufferedChannelDemo(bufCh, &wg)
        wg.Wait()

        // Demonstrate the select statement over channels for
        ↪  concurrent, non-deterministic message handling.
        ch1 := make(chan string, 2)
        ch2 := make(chan string, 2)
        ch1 <- "message 1 from ch1"
        ch2 <- "message 1 from ch2"
        ch1 <- "message 2 from ch1"
        ch2 <- "message 2 from ch2"
        wg.Add(1)
        go selectChannelDemo(ch1, ch2, &wg)
        wg.Wait()
}
```

Chapter 48

Channels: Buffered versus Unbuffered

Conceptual Distinctions Between Buffered and Unbuffered Channels

In the paradigm of concurrent computation, channels embody the mechanism for inter-goroutine communication, each instantiated with distinct operational characteristics. An unbuffered channel, by its very construction, is defined with a capacity of zero. Such a channel enforces an immediate rendezvous protocol; that is, every send operation is intrinsically coupled with a corresponding receive operation. Formally, if the send events are denoted by the set S and the receive events by the set T, then an unbuffered channel ensures that every $s \in S$ is paired atomically with an element $r \in T$, thereby epitomizing a strictly synchronous communication relation.

In contrast, buffered channels are constructed with a positive capacity n, where $n \in \mathbb{N}_{>0}$. This design permits the channel to temporarily store up to n elements, thereby decoupling the temporal dependencies between senders and receivers. The channel state in this context can be represented by a function $B : \{0, 1, \ldots, n\} \to \mathcal{V}$, with $\mathcal{V}$ representing the domain of values transmissible through the channel. The intrinsic semantics of a buffered channel allow send operations to proceed without the immediate presence of a receiving counterpart, so long as the aggregate of buffered elements does not exceed n. Once this boundary is reached, subsequent sends are forced to block until sufficient capacity is relinquished via corresponding receive operations.

Formal Operational Semantics

The operational semantics governing channel operations provide a rigorous framework to distinguish between the synchronous behavior of unbuffered channels and the quasi-asynchronous dynamics of buffered channels. In the case of an unbuffered channel, the execution of a send operation, denoted symbolically as $s : v \mapsto ch$ for some value v, is predicated on the simultaneous execution of a receive operation $r : ch \mapsto v$. This duality assures that the transaction is executed atomically, a property essential for preserving data consistency under concurrent execution.

Conversely, when a channel is buffered, its operational semantics evolve into a state-dependent system. A send operation may enqueue a value v into the channel if the current number of enqueued elements $|B|$ satisfies $|B| < n$, where n represents the channel's capacity. The channel thereby functions as a stateful queue, and its state transitions can be viewed as mappings within the discrete set $\{0, 1, \ldots, n\}$. Once the buffer is saturated, that is, when $|B| = n$, subsequent send operations must block until a receive operation reduces the occupancy of the buffer. This state-transition model underpins the analysis of race conditions and synchronization policies inherent in channel-based communication.

Synchronization and Performance Characteristics

The divergent synchronization properties intrinsic to unbuffered and buffered channels fundamentally impact system performance and correctness guarantees. Unbuffered channels, by necessitating an immediate pairing of send and receive operations, enforce a robust synchronization discipline. The atomic nature of communication in this modality provides strong assurances against race conditions, as no message can be transmitted without explicit acknowledgement through reception. This property is particularly salient in scenarios where coordinated, stepwise execution is paramount.

Buffered channels, on the other hand, relax this stringent synchrony by enabling a finite degree of asynchrony through their

buffering capability. This decoupling permits senders to operate independently of receivers until the buffer reaches capacity,
thereby potentially enhancing throughput in high-concurrency environments. However, this increased flexibility introduces additional complexity. The intermediary storage of messages can ob-
scure the instantaneous state of inter-goroutine communication and
may lead to transient inconsistencies if the buffer management is
not meticulously calibrated. The performance benefits of buffered
channels, therefore, must be judiciously balanced against the overhead associated with managing intermediate states.

Guidelines for Channel Type Selection

The decision to employ unbuffered or buffered channels within a
concurrent system is dictated by a synthesis of performance ob-
jectives, synchronization requirements, and system architecture.
Unbuffered channels are ideally suited for systems where strict sequential interaction is essential. Their inherent design, which necessitates the immediate synchronization of send and receive operations, makes them the optimal choice in contexts where atomicity
and deterministic ordering are non-negotiable.

Buffered channels are preferable in architectures where producer and consumer routines operate at divergent speeds, or where
peak throughput is required. Their capacity to transiently store
messages permits a degree of temporal decoupling, allowing send
operations to proceed independently until the constraint of the
buffer capacity is encountered. However, this deferred synchronization mandates a careful analysis of buffer sizing and system load.
Inadequate provisioning may lead to unintended blocking behavior, while excessive buffering can complicate state management and
diminish the clarity of inter-process communication dynamics.

Go Code Snippet

```go
package main

import (
        "fmt"
        "sync"
        "time"
)
```

```go
// demoUnbufferedChannel demonstrates the synchronous behavior of an
↪  unbuffered channel.
// In an unbuffered channel, send and receive operations are paired
↪  atomically.
// This reflects the formal equation: for every send s  S, there is
↪  a corresponding receive r  T.
func demoUnbufferedChannel() {
        fmt.Println("=== Unbuffered Channel Demo Start ===")
        // Create an unbuffered channel of int (capacity = 0)
        ch := make(chan int)

        var wg sync.WaitGroup
        wg.Add(1)

        // Launch a receiver goroutine that will wait to receive
        ↪   from the channel.
        go func() {
                defer wg.Done()
                // Simulate delay to illustrate that the sender
                ↪   blocks until a receiver is ready.
                time.Sleep(1 * time.Second)
                val := <-ch
                fmt.Printf("Receiver received: %d\n", val)
        }()

        // The sender sends a value on the unbuffered channel.
        // This send operation will block until the receiver is
        ↪   ready to receive.
        fmt.Println("Sender sending value: 42")
        ch <- 42
        fmt.Println("Sender completed sending")

        wg.Wait()
        fmt.Println("=== Unbuffered Channel Demo End ===\n")
}

// demoBufferedChannel shows the behavior of a buffered channel.
// A buffered channel with capacity n can be viewed as a function
// B: {0,1,...,n} -> V, where len(ch) represents |B|, the current
↪  number of buffered elements.
// If len(ch) < cap(ch), sending does not block; if len(ch) ==
↪  cap(ch), the next send blocks.
func demoBufferedChannel() {
        fmt.Println("=== Buffered Channel Demo Start ===")
        capacity := 3
        // Create a buffered channel of int with capacity = 3
        ch := make(chan int, capacity)

        var wg sync.WaitGroup

        // Producer goroutine: sends values into the buffered
        ↪   channel.
        wg.Add(1)
```

236

```go
    go func() {
        defer wg.Done()
        // Send 5 values to illustrate buffering; notice
        ↪  when len(ch) reaches capacity.
        for i := 1; i <= 5; i++ {
            fmt.Printf("Producer attempting to send: %d
            ↪  | Current Buffer Length: %d, Capacity:
            ↪  %d\n", i, len(ch), cap(ch))
            ch <- i // Non-blocking until the buffer is
            ↪  full.
            fmt.Printf("Producer sent: %d | Updated
            ↪  Buffer Length: %d\n", i, len(ch))
            // Sleep simulates work and gives the
            ↪  consumer time to receive values.
            time.Sleep(500 * time.Millisecond)
        }
        // Once done, close the channel.
        close(ch)
    }()

    // Consumer goroutine: receives values from the buffered
    ↪  channel.
    wg.Add(1)
    go func() {
        defer wg.Done()
        for val := range ch {
            fmt.Printf("Consumer received: %d | Current
            ↪  Buffer Length after receive: %d\n", val,
            ↪  len(ch))
            // Delay to simulate processing time and to
            ↪  show potential blocking when the
            ↪  producer overflows.
            time.Sleep(800 * time.Millisecond)
        }
    }()

    wg.Wait()
    fmt.Println("=== Buffered Channel Demo End ===")
}

// selectDemo demonstrates handling multiple channel operations
↪  concurrently
// using a select statement. This function contrasts unbuffered and
↪  buffered channel usage.
func selectDemo() {
    // Create an unbuffered channel.
    unbuffered := make(chan string)
    // Create a buffered channel with capacity 2.
    buffered := make(chan string, 2)

    var wg sync.WaitGroup
    wg.Add(2)
```

237

```go
        // Start a goroutine to populate both channels.
        go func() {
                defer wg.Done()
                // Launch a separate goroutine to send to the
                ↪   unbuffered channel.
                go func() {
                        time.Sleep(500 * time.Millisecond)
                        unbuffered <- "message from unbuffered
                        ↪   channel"
                }()
                // Send messages to the buffered channel; these are
                ↪   non-blocking until the buffer is full.
                buffered <- "first buffered message"
                buffered <- "second buffered message"
        }()

        // Start a receiver goroutine that employs select to receive
        ↪   messages from either channel.
        go func() {
                defer wg.Done()
                // Use a timeout to avoid indefinite blocking.
                timeout := time.After(3 * time.Second)
                // Attempt to receive three messages.
                for i := 0; i < 3; i++ {
                        select {
                        case msg := <-unbuffered:
                                fmt.Println("Select received
                                ↪   (unbuffered):", msg)
                        case msg := <-buffered:
                                fmt.Println("Select received
                                ↪   (buffered):", msg)
                        case <-timeout:
                                fmt.Println("Select timeout reached,
                                ↪   exiting loop")
                                return
                        }
                }
        }()

        wg.Wait()
}

func main() {
        fmt.Println("=== Go Channel Demonstration ===")

        // Demonstrate unbuffered channel behavior.
        // This aligns with the equation where every send is paired
        ↪   atomically with a receive.
        demoUnbufferedChannel()

        // Demonstrate buffered channel behavior.
        // Here, the channel state is managed as a queue where
        ↪   len(ch) reflects the current count of buffered elements.
```

238

```
    demoBufferedChannel()

    // Additional demonstration with select to process messages
    ↪  from both channel types concurrently.
    fmt.Println("\n=== Select Statement Demo Start ===")
    selectDemo()
    fmt.Println("=== Select Statement Demo End ===")
}
```

Chapter 49

Channels: Directional Usage

Conceptual Underpinnings of Channel Directionality

Channels provide a fundamental mechanism for inter-goroutine communication in concurrent systems. By default, channels support bidirectional data transfer, thereby permitting both send and receive operations. However, restricting a channel to a unidirectional mode imposes a clear operational contract that delineates the roles of the communicating entities. In this formal setting, consider a channel ch that conveys messages of type T. When ch is constrained to transmit values only, it embodies a sending channel, denoted abstractly as $ch_s : T$, while a channel exclusively designated for reception is represented as $ch_r : T$. Such directional restrictions serve to eliminate ambiguity in the data flow, enforcing an explicit separation of producer and consumer responsibilities within the system. The type system, through these constraints, guarantees that each channel is used exclusively as either a sender or a receiver, thereby fostering clarity in the overall communication architecture.

Formal Semantics and Type Restrictions

Directional channel types refine the conventional channel abstraction by reducing the admissible set of operations. Let $C(T)$ denote the conventional bidirectional channel type transmitting values of type T. The transformation into a directional channel involves decomposing $C(T)$ into two distinct subsets: $C_s(T)$ and $C_r(T)$. Formally, one may define:

$$C_s(T) = \{\text{operations } ch \mapsto \text{send}(v), \ v \in T\}$$

$$\text{and} \quad C_r(T) = \{\text{operations } ch \mapsto \text{receive}() = v, \ v \in T\}.$$

This bifurcation restricts any channel declared as $C_s(T)$ to only permit send operations, whereas a channel of type $C_r(T)$ allows solely receive operations. The operational semantics associated with these directional types ensure that any attempt to perform a non-designated action is precluded at compile time. Consequently, the type system enforces a mathematical discipline whereby the allowed operations on a channel are the direct consequence of its declared direction, thereby facilitating rigorous static analysis and reasoning about concurrent behavior.

Implications on Communication Patterns in Concurrent Systems

The enforcement of directional constraints on channels has profound implications for the design and analysis of communication patterns. By partitioning a channel into $C_s(T)$ and $C_r(T)$, the system architects impose an explicit contract that clearly defines which part of the system may produce values and which part may consume them. This separation reduces the cognitive load during system verification and simplifies the state-space analysis when proving properties such as absence of race conditions and deadlocks.

Moreover, the directional restriction enhances modularity by ensuring that functions and components interact through clearly defined interfaces. In particular, when a function is specified to accept a channel of type $C_r(T)$, it immediately conveys that the function is intended to act as a consumer, thereby precluding any inadvertent attempt to transmit data through that interface. This rigorous partitioning not only minimizes the risk of inadvertent misuse but also contributes to the overall determinism of concurrent algorithms.

The static guarantees provided by directional channels also allow optimization opportunities at the compiler level. With the assurance that a channel's operations are confined to a single direction, the compiler may perform more aggressive dead-code elimination and inlining optimizations, given the reduced potential for side effects. In aggregate, the use of directional channels establishes a framework wherein communication patterns are both mathematically sound and operationally efficient, thereby underpinning the design of robust concurrent systems.

Go Code Snippet

```go
package main

import (
        "fmt"
        "time"
)

// sendData sends a series of integer values to a send-only channel.
// This function adheres to the formal specification for a sending
↪   channel:
// C_s(int) = { operations ch -> send(v), where v  int }
func sendData(ch chan<- int) {
        for i := 1; i <= 5; i++ {
                fmt.Printf("Sending: %d\n", i)
                ch <- i
                time.Sleep(300 * time.Millisecond) // Simulate
                ↪   processing delay.
        }
        // Close the channel to signal that no more values will be
        ↪   sent.
        close(ch)
}

// squareWorker receives integers from a receive-only channel,
// squares them, and sends the result to a send-only channel.
// This illustrates the combination of directional channels:
// - Input: C_r(int) = { operations ch -> receive() = v, where v
↪   int }
// - Output: C_s(int) = { operations ch -> send(v), where v  int }
func squareWorker(in <-chan int, out chan<- int) {
        for num := range in {
                squared := num * num
                fmt.Printf("Worker: %d squared is %d\n", num,
                ↪   squared)
```

242

```go
                out <- squared
                time.Sleep(200 * time.Millisecond) // Simulate
                ↪   processing delay.
        }
        // Close the output channel once processing is complete.
        close(out)
}


// receiveResults consumes values from a receive-only channel and
↪   prints them.
// This aligns with the formal definition for a receiving channel:
// C_r(int) = { operations ch -> receive() = v, where v  int }
func receiveResults(ch <-chan int) {
        for result := range ch {
                fmt.Printf("Received Result: %d\n", result)
        }
}


func main() {
        // Create bidirectional channels for initial data and
        ↪   processed results.
        dataCh := make(chan int)
        squaredCh := make(chan int)

        // Launch the producer goroutine using a send-only channel.
        go sendData(dataCh)

        // Launch the squareWorker goroutine to process and forward
        ↪   data.
        go squareWorker(dataCh, squaredCh)

        // Collect and print the results from the receive-only
        ↪   channel.
        receiveResults(squaredCh)

        fmt.Println("Pipeline processing complete.")
}
```

243

Chapter 50

Concurrency Control: Select Statement

Structural Foundations and Syntactic Formulation

The select construct in Go forms a pivotal syntactic mechanism that permits concurrent evaluation of multiple channel operations. Formally, consider a finite set of channel operations

$$\mathcal{O} = \{o_1, o_2, \ldots, o_n\},$$

where each o_i represents an atomic channel operation, such as a send $ch< -v$ or a receive $v = ch$. The semantics of the select statement mandate that the evaluation of the entire construct involves the simultaneous monitoring of all operations in $\mathcal{O}$. The structure intrinsically embodies a disjunctive control operator, whereby the progress of the concurrent system is determined by the earliest enabled operation among those presented. In circumstances where no operation is immediately eligible, the select statement imposes suspension of the executing goroutine, thereby ensuring that the concurrent process adheres to precise synchronization constraints.

Operational Semantics and Formal Behavior

Within the operational framework, each operation $o_i \in \mathcal{O}$ is assigned an evaluation predicate, denoted by $\mathcal{E}(o_i)$, which determines the readiness state of the operation with respect to its associated channel. Should a subset $\mathcal{R} \subseteq \mathcal{O}$ satisfy the condition

$$\forall o_i \in \mathcal{R}, \ \mathcal{E}(o_i) = \texttt{true},$$

then the runtime selects one operation $o_j \in \mathcal{R}$ following nondeterministic selection rules. The intrinsic nondeterminism is a deliberate design choice that both simplifies the concurrent model and ensures that the construct remains free from arbitrary priority among competing operations. This behavior can be formally captured by the transition rule

$$\langle \texttt{select} \ \{o_i\}_{i=1}^n \rangle \to \langle o_j \rangle,$$

where o_j is an element of the set of enabled operations, thereby making the select construct an embodiment of commutative and idempotent operation in the context of concurrent computational transitions.

Non-determinism and Fairness Considerations

The nondeterministic selection intrinsic to the select statement introduces a layer of probabilistic fairness which critically influences the concurrent execution environment. When multiple operations are simultaneously ready, the decision function employed by the scheduler does not exhibit deterministic bias. Rather, the selection reflects an abstract fairness property, ensuring that all enabled operations are eventually executed. In formal terms, consider the set $\mathcal{R}$ as earlier, with the scheduler implementing a function

$$f : \mathcal{P}(\mathcal{R}) \to \mathcal{R},$$

where f yields an arbitrarily chosen operation from $\mathcal{R}$. The fairness embedded in this formulation guarantees that over an unbounded sequence of select invocations, the probability measure associated with the selection of each $o_i \in \mathcal{R}$ approximates uniform distribution. This property not only mitigates starvation phenomena but also simplifies the theoretical examination of concurrent state spaces by circumscribing the combinatorial explosion that might otherwise result from complex interleavings of channel operations.

Analytical Implications for Concurrent Systems

The ramifications of employing the select statement extend deeply into the realm of concurrent system design and analysis. By enabling multiple channel operations to be considered simultaneously, the select construct facilitates the formulation of communication patterns that inherently avoid arbitrary sequencing of events. This level of abstraction permits the concise expression of complex synchronization protocols, effectively reducing the likelihood of deadlock and race conditions in formal models. Additionally, the select construct serves as a foundation for advanced concurrency patterns, where the interplay of readiness predicates and nondeterministic choices can be analyzed using formal verification methods. Specifically, the property

$$\exists o_j \in \mathcal{R} : \langle \texttt{select } \{o_i\}\rangle \rightarrow \langle o_j\rangle,$$

assures that the execution state transitions can be precisely characterized, thereby offering fertile ground for static analysis and model checking techniques. The integration of these analytical tools contributes to the development of robust concurrent systems that are both mathematically sound and operationally efficient.

Go Code Snippet

```go
package main

import (
        "fmt"
        "math/rand"
        "time"
)

// simulateChannelOperation simulates an atomic channel operation.
// In our formal model, we consider a set of operations:
```

246

```go
//    O = { o, o, ..., o }
// and each operation o has an evaluation predicate E(o) that turns
↪    true
// when the operation becomes enabled. This function waits a random
↪    delay
// (simulating the predicate E(o)) and then sends a result on its
↪    channel.
func simulateChannelOperation(ch chan int, opName string, result
↪    int) {
        // Simulate the readiness delay of operation o.
        delay := time.Duration(rand.Intn(400)) * time.Millisecond
        time.Sleep(delay)

        // Once the evaluation predicate E(o) holds true, send the
        ↪    result.
        ch <- result
        fmt.Printf("%s completed after %v, sending result: %d\n",
        ↪    opName, delay, result)
}

func main() {
        // Seed the random number generator to ensure
        ↪    nondeterministic delays,
        // reflecting the inherent nondeterminism in the select
        ↪    construct.
        rand.Seed(time.Now().UnixNano())

        // Define channels representing distinct operations in the
        ↪    set O.
        ch1 := make(chan int)
        ch2 := make(chan int)
        ch3 := make(chan int)

        // Launch goroutines simulating the channel operations.
        // These correspond to operations such as:
        //    o: ch1 <- 10, o: ch2 <- 20, o: ch3 <- 30
        go simulateChannelOperation(ch1, "Operation o (send)", 10)
        go simulateChannelOperation(ch2, "Operation o (send)", 20)
        go simulateChannelOperation(ch3, "Operation o (send)", 30)

        // The select statement below embodies the formal
        ↪    transition:
        //    (select { o }) → ⟨o⟩,
        // where o is nondeterministically chosen from the set of
        ↪    enabled operations.
        fmt.Println("Waiting for any operation to complete...")
        select {
        case res := <-ch1:
                fmt.Printf("Selected o with result: %d\n", res)
        case res := <-ch2:
                fmt.Printf("Selected o with result: %d\n", res)
        case res := <-ch3:
                fmt.Printf("Selected o with result: %d\n", res)
```

247

```
        // The following case represents a fallback for when
        ↪ no channel is ready.
case <-time.After(500 * time.Millisecond):
        fmt.Println("Timeout: No channel operation was
        ↪ ready.")
}

// To ensure all goroutines finish execution before the main
↪ function exits,
// we add a final sleep. In production code, synchronization
↪ primitives like
// sync.WaitGroup would be more appropriate.
time.Sleep(1 * time.Second)

// This implementation illustrates key properties:
// - The readiness evaluation of each operation (E(o)).
// - The nondeterministic selection (fairness) of one
↪ enabled operation o.
// - The alignment with formal concurrent models using
↪ select to manage
//   multiple communication events.
}
```

Chapter 51

Concurrency Patterns: Basic Channel Usage

Channel Communication as a Synchronization Mechanism

Channels constitute a fundamental construct in concurrent systems, serving as the primary medium for synchronization and data exchange without resorting to explicit locking mechanisms. The dual modalities of channel communication—synchronous and asynchronous—are distinguished by the presence or absence of buffering. In unbuffered channels, the transmission expression $ch \leftarrow v$ and the corresponding reception $v' = ch$ are intrinsically coupled, enforcing a strict rendezvous condition between the sender and receiver. Buffered channels, by contrast, instantiate an intermediate storage of capacity C, allowing a decoupling of send and receive operations. This intrinsic design affords the construction of robust concurrency patterns that ensure safety in data exchange while minimizing contention among concurrently executing processes.

Formalisms Underpinning Channel-Based Concurrency

An analytical formulation of channel operations is imperative for a rigorous understanding of their role in concurrent programming.

Each channel operation, whether it be sending a value or receiving one, can be modeled as an atomic action within a transition system. For instance, the operation $ch \leftarrow v$ represents an instantaneous state change contingent upon the successful matching with a corresponding receive operation. Similarly, the operation $v' = ch$ may be conceived as a state transition contingent upon the availability of data within the channel buffer or a synchronizing sender. The composite behavior resulting from the interplay of multiple channel operations can be systematically examined through nondeterministic scheduling models, where fairness assumptions and probabilistic selection criteria ensure that all enabled operations are eventually executed. This formalism undergirds the verification of invariants such as data consistency and absence of deadlock within complex systems.

Architectural Patterns and Channel Composition

The composition of channels into higher-order communication structures is pivotal in realizing scalable and efficient concurrent architectures. Patterns such as fan-out and fan-in exhibit how multiple concurrent entities can coordinate through channels to distribute workload and aggregate results. In the fan-out paradigm, several independent senders channel data concurrently to a set of receivers, effectively dispersing computational tasks across multiple processing units. Conversely, the fan-in model consolidates outputs from multiple senders into a singular stream, facilitating centralized processing or further dissemination. The algebraic properties of channel composition—such as associativity and distributivity in the context of data flow—provide a solid foundation for analyzing the throughput and latency characteristics of such systems. These properties enable the derivation of performance bounds and the assurance of safety properties under diverse operational regimes.

Advanced Operational Dynamics and Pattern Integration

The efficacy of channel-based concurrency patterns is further enhanced by mechanisms that introduce dynamic control over channel interactions. Among these are timeouts, selective reception, and conditional operations, which collectively contribute to the adaptability of concurrent systems. The incorporation of timed operations, defined mathematically as transitions that are conditioned on a temporal threshold τ, permits the graceful degradation of system responsiveness in scenarios where channel readiness is uncertain. Moreover, the integration of selective reception—akin to a nondeterministic choice mechanism—facilitates the concurrent evaluation of multiple channel states, thereby ensuring that the overall system remains both safe and efficient even under variable workloads. The synthesis of these advanced operational dynamics yields a rich tapestry of interaction patterns, wherein the deterministic ordering of data flow is balanced against the inherent nondeterminism of concurrent execution.

Go Code Snippet

```
package main

import (
        "fmt"
        "sync"
        "time"
)

func main() {
        //
  ↪     -------------------------------------------------------------
        // Unbuffered Channel: Synchronous Communication
        //
  ↪     -------------------------------------------------------------
        // Here, the send operation "unbufferedChan <- 42" and the
        // receive operation "value := <-unbufferedChan" occur in a
        // coupled manner, emulating the mathematical form:
        //    ch ← v     and     v' = ch
        unbufferedChan := make(chan int)
        go func() {
                fmt.Println("Unbuffered Sender: Sending 42")
                unbufferedChan <- 42 // Synchronous send
          ↪     (rendezvous)
                fmt.Println("Unbuffered Sender: Finished sending")
        }()

        fmt.Println("Unbuffered Receiver: Waiting for a value")
        value := <-unbufferedChan // Synchronous receive
        fmt.Printf("Unbuffered Receiver: Received %d\n", value)

        //
  ↪     -------------------------------------------------------------
```

```go
// Buffered Channel: Asynchronous Communication
//
// ↪  --------------------------------------------------------------
// Buffered channels decouple send and receive operations.
// The expressions remain analogous to:
//   ch ← v   (with buffering) and   v' = ch
bufferedChan := make(chan int, 3)
fmt.Println("\nBuffered Channel: Sending values 100 and
↪  200")
bufferedChan <- 100
bufferedChan <- 200
fmt.Printf("Buffered Channel: Capacity %d, Length %d\n",
↪  cap(bufferedChan), len(bufferedChan))

// Receiving values from the buffered channel
for i := 0; i < 2; i++ {
        val := <-bufferedChan
        fmt.Printf("Buffered Receiver: Received %d\n", val)
}

//
// ↪  --------------------------------------------------------------
// Select with Timeout: Advanced Operational Dynamics
//
// ↪  --------------------------------------------------------------
// Demonstrates how a select statement can incorporate a
↪  timeout,
// representing a timed transition conditioned on a temporal
↪  threshold .
done := make(chan bool)
go func() {
        time.Sleep(2 * time.Second)
        done <- true
}()

fmt.Println("\nSelect Statement: Waiting for done signal
↪  with 1 second timeout")
select {
case <-done:
        fmt.Println("Select: Received done signal")
case <-time.After(1 * time.Second):
        fmt.Println("Select: Timeout reached, no signal
            ↪  received")
}

//
// ↪  --------------------------------------------------------------
// Fan-Out and Fan-In Patterns: Coordinating Multiple
↪  Goroutines
//
// ↪  --------------------------------------------------------------
// Fan-Out: Multiple workers process jobs concurrently.
// Fan-In: Aggregating results back from all workers.
```

252

```go
    jobs := make(chan int, 10)
    results := make(chan int, 10)
    var wg sync.WaitGroup

    // Worker function represents a concurrent process that:
    // - Receives a job via "job := range jobs"
    // - Processes the job (e.g., applies an operation: result =
    ↪  job * 2)
    // - Sends the result using "results <- result"
    worker := func(id int, jobs <-chan int, results chan<- int)
    ↪  {
        defer wg.Done()
        for job := range jobs {
            fmt.Printf("Worker %d: Processing job %d\n",
            ↪  id, job)
            // Simulate work with time delay; operation
            ↪  analogous to:
            //   result = job * 2
            time.Sleep(time.Millisecond *
            ↪  time.Duration(100+id*10))
            result := job * 2
            results <- result
        }
    }

    // Launch a fixed number of workers (fan-out)
    numWorkers := 3
    wg.Add(numWorkers)
    for w := 1; w <= numWorkers; w++ {
        go worker(w, jobs, results)
    }

    // Dispatch jobs to the workers
    for j := 1; j <= 9; j++ {
        jobs <- j
    }
    close(jobs)

    // Close the results channel once all workers have finished
    ↪  (fan-in)
    go func() {
        wg.Wait()
        close(results)
    }()

    fmt.Println("\nFan-In Aggregation: Collecting results from
    ↪  workers")
    for res := range results {
        fmt.Printf("Aggregated Result: %d\n", res)
    }
    fmt.Println("All jobs processed successfully.")
}
```

Chapter 52

Module Management: Using Go Modules

Foundations of the Module System

The Go module system marks a significant evolution in software construction by establishing a formalized framework for dependency management, version control, and project organization. At its core, every module is identified by a distinctive module path, a string that serves as a unique key within the ecosystem. This approach not only replaces legacy mechanisms but also introduces a structured environment in which dependency relationships and module boundaries are explicitly defined. The resultant framework permits the precise specification of inter-module interactions, thereby enabling developers to manage extensive codebases with a high degree of rigor and clarity.

Dependency Resolution and Graph-Theoretic Analysis

The process of dependency resolution within the Go module paradigm can be rigorously modeled using principles from graph theory. Let $G = (V, E)$ be a directed graph where each vertex $v \in V$ represents an individual module and each edge $(v_i, v_j) \in E$ denotes an explicit dependency from the source module v_i to the target module v_j. By incorporating precise version identifiers and constraint specifications, the Go module system enforces determinism in dependency resolution. The underlying algorithms ensure that potential conflicts are addressed by maintaining a consistent and acyclic dependency graph, thus upholding critical invariants that guarantee both data consistency and the integrity of the overall build process.

Semantic Versioning and Dependency Isolation

An integral aspect of the module system is its strict adherence to semantic versioning, a methodology that captures the evolution of modules in an unambiguous format, typically $v_{\mathrm{major}}.v_{\mathrm{minor}}.v_{\mathrm{patch}}$. Changes to the major version number indicate modifications that are not backward-compatible, whereas increments in the minor or patch numbers denote the introduction of new features or fixes, respectively, without breaking existing contracts. Embedding these semantic guidelines within module metadata ensures robust dependency isolation by clearly delineating compatibility boundaries. This mechanism not only facilitates reproducible builds but also minimizes the risk of runtime inconsistencies, thereby promoting long-term maintainability and stability across complex, interdependent projects.

Project Organization and Modular Encapsulation

Beyond the resolution of dependencies, the organizational capabilities of Go modules play a central role in structuring project code. The modular decomposition provided by the system allows for the segmentation of a large codebase into smaller, self-contained units, each with its own set of dependencies and version controls. Such encapsulation of functionality encourages the development of loosely coupled components, which can be evolved independently while maintaining a coherent overall architecture. This design paradigm supports a disciplined approach to abstraction, wherein the explicit declaration of inter-module relationships aids in the preservation of clean interfaces and the containment of side effects. The resultant structure fosters an environment in which parallel development and continuous integration are not only feasible but are also inherently supported by the module system.

Go Code Snippet

```go
package main

import (
        "errors"
        "fmt"
        "strconv"
        "strings"
)

// Module represents a Go module with a name (module path), semantic
// ↪  version,
// and a list of dependencies (other modules by name).
type Module struct {
        Name         string
        Version      string
        Dependencies []string
}

// parseVersion parses a semantic version string in the format
// ↪  "v{major}.{minor}.{patch}".
// It returns the major, minor, and patch components as integers.
func parseVersion(v string) (int, int, int, error) {
        // Remove the leading 'v' if present.
        if len(v) > 0 && v[0] == 'v' {
                v = v[1:]
        }
        parts := strings.Split(v, ".")
        if len(parts) != 3 {
                return 0, 0, 0, errors.New("invalid version format;
                        ↪  expected format v{major}.{minor}.{patch}")
        }
        major, err := strconv.Atoi(parts[0])
        if err != nil {
                return 0, 0, 0, err
        }
        minor, err := strconv.Atoi(parts[1])
        if err != nil {
                return 0, 0, 0, err
        }
        patch, err := strconv.Atoi(parts[2])
        if err != nil {
                return 0, 0, 0, err
        }
        return major, minor, patch, nil
}
```

```go
// compareVersions compares two semantic version strings.
// It returns -1 if v1 is older than v2, 1 if v1 is newer than v2,
↪   and 0 if they are equal.
func compareVersions(v1, v2 string) int {
        maj1, min1, patch1, err1 := parseVersion(v1)
        maj2, min2, patch2, err2 := parseVersion(v2)

        // If either version fails to parse, default to considering
        ↪   them equal.
        if err1 != nil || err2 != nil {
                return 0
        }

        if maj1 != maj2 {
                if maj1 < maj2 {
                        return -1
                }
                return 1
        }
        if min1 != min2 {
                if min1 < min2 {
                        return -1
                }
                return 1
        }
        if patch1 != patch2 {
                if patch1 < patch2 {
                        return -1
                }
                return 1
        }
        return 0
}

// topologicalSort performs dependency resolution using Kahn's
↪   algorithm.
// Modules are represented as vertices in a directed graph where an
↪   edge from module A to module B
// indicates that A depends on B. It returns an ordering of modules
↪   such that each module appears
// only after all its dependencies have been listed.
func topologicalSort(modules map[string]*Module) ([]string, error) {
        inDegree := make(map[string]int)
        // Initialize inDegree for each module to zero.
        for name := range modules {
                inDegree[name] = 0
        }

        // Build a reverse graph to know which modules are dependent
        ↪   on a given module.
        // Also update the inDegree counts.
        reverseGraph := make(map[string][]string)
```

```go
	for name, mod := range modules {
		for _, dep := range mod.Dependencies {
			// Only consider dependencies that exist
			↪ within our defined modules.
			if _, exists := modules[dep]; !exists {
				continue
			}
			inDegree[dep]++
			reverseGraph[dep] =
			↪ append(reverseGraph[dep], name)
		}
	}

	// Queue for modules with in-degree zero (i.e., no
	↪ dependencies).
	var queue []string
	for name, degree := range inDegree {
		if degree == 0 {
			queue = append(queue, name)
		}
	}

	var order []string
	// Process modules in queue using Kahn's algorithm.
	for len(queue) > 0 {
		// Dequeue a module.
		current := queue[0]
		queue = queue[1:]
		order = append(order, current)

		// Reduce in-degree for modules that depend on the
		↪ current module.
		for _, neighbor := range reverseGraph[current] {
			inDegree[neighbor]--
			if inDegree[neighbor] == 0 {
				queue = append(queue, neighbor)
			}
		}
	}

	// If not all modules are processed, a cycle exists.
	if len(order) != len(inDegree) {
		return nil, errors.New("cycle detected in module
		↪ dependencies")
	}
	return order, nil
}

func main() {
	// Define sample modules illustrating dependency
	↪ relationships.
	modules := map[string]*Module{
```

258

```go
        "moduleA": {Name: "moduleA", Version: "v1.0.0",
        ↪    Dependencies: []string{"moduleB", "moduleC"}},
        "moduleB": {Name: "moduleB", Version: "v1.2.3",
        ↪    Dependencies: []string{"moduleD"}},
        "moduleC": {Name: "moduleC", Version: "v1.1.0",
        ↪    Dependencies: []string{"moduleD"}},
        "moduleD": {Name: "moduleD", Version: "v2.0.0",
        ↪    Dependencies: []string{}},
        "moduleE": {Name: "moduleE", Version: "v1.0.1",
        ↪    Dependencies: []string{"moduleA"}},
}

// Resolve dependencies by determining a load order.
order, err := topologicalSort(modules)
if err != nil {
        fmt.Println("Error during dependency resolution:",
        ↪    err)
        return
}
fmt.Println("Modules initialization order:")
for i, name := range order {
        module := modules[name]
        fmt.Printf("%d: %s (version: %s)\n", i+1,
        ↪    module.Name, module.Version)
}

// Demonstrate semantic versioning by comparing moduleB and
↪    moduleC versions.
cmp := compareVersions(modules["moduleB"].Version,
↪    modules["moduleC"].Version)
switch cmp {
case -1:
        fmt.Printf("%s (%s) is older than %s (%s)\n",
        ↪    modules["moduleB"].Name,
        ↪    modules["moduleB"].Version,
        ↪    modules["moduleC"].Name,
        ↪    modules["moduleC"].Version)
case 1:
        fmt.Printf("%s (%s) is newer than %s (%s)\n",
        ↪    modules["moduleB"].Name,
        ↪    modules["moduleB"].Version,
        ↪    modules["moduleC"].Name,
        ↪    modules["moduleC"].Version)
default:
        fmt.Printf("%s and %s have the same version (%s)\n",
        ↪    modules["moduleB"].Name,
        ↪    modules["moduleC"].Name,
        ↪    modules["moduleB"].Version)
}
}
```

259

Chapter 53

Standard Library Tour: Overview of Packages

Core I/O and Data Formatting Packages

The foundational packages of the standard library establish an integrated framework for input/output operations and data formatting. Within this domain, the design of the formatted output routines exemplifies mathematical precision and consistency. The underlying mechanisms are architected to support diverse data types, enabling transformations from internal representations to textual or binary formats. The systematic methodology inherent in these packages reinforces deterministic behavior during the construction of output strings and buffered streams, ensuring that primitive types and composite structures are rendered in a uniform format. This consistency facilitates not only the accurate presentation of information but also the subsequent consumption by other components that expect tightly defined input structures.

A detailed examination reveals that the compositional philosophy in these packages is founded upon a strict separation between formatting logic and data conversion routines. Abstractions are provided that allow for the systematic translation of numerical, boolean, and string data into their corresponding formatted representations. The rigor of the formatting paradigm is underpinned by an adherence to conventional formatting directives and parameterized templates, which collectively assure that output remains both predictable and adaptable to a wide range of application scenarios.

System Interaction and File Management Modules

Modules dedicated to system-level interaction and file management serve as the interface between the application and the operating environment. These packages encapsulate low-level functionalities required for the opening, reading, writing, and manipulation of files and directories, thereby abstracting the idiosyncrasies of underlying hardware and operating system interfaces. The methodologies employed are designed to promote both efficiency and fault tolerance. By providing a uniform set of operations for handling file descriptors, directory traversal, and permission management, these modules resolve the inherent complexities of file system interactions.

The architectural decisions underlying these interfaces emphasize modularity and robustness, ensuring that system calls are shielded from direct exposure to higher-level application logic. This stratification maintains clean boundaries, where core system interactions are mediated through well-defined function calls that manage resource allocation and error recovery. Consequently, the design enforces a rigorous contract between the application and the host environment, facilitating rigorous error checking and predictable resource deallocation.

Concurrency, Synchronization, and Runtime Interfaces

A profound aspect of the standard library is its comprehensive approach to concurrency and the management of parallel execution. The packages in this category provide a multitude of constructs for orchestrating synchronization among concurrently executing entities. Built upon principles of lightweight concurrency and deterministic scheduling, these modules integrate seamlessly with the runtime system to offer both fine-grained locking mechanisms and higher-level abstractions. The synchronization primitives are engineered to minimize contention and ensure thread-safe interactions without compromising performance.

The interplay between these packages and the runtime environment is critical in the orchestration of goroutines and the management of asynchronous events. The approach favors a coopera-

261

tive model, where concurrency is leveraged through well-structured channel-based communications and careful coordination of shared memory. The synchronization strategies employed reflect a deep understanding of concurrent system design, wherein race conditions and deadlocks are meticulously mitigated by enforcing invariant properties that govern process interactions.

Mathematical, Cryptographic, and Data Computation Utilities

The suite of mathematical and computational utilities provided within the standard library exemplifies a commitment to numerical precision and algorithmic efficiency. Packages in this sector extend capabilities for elementary arithmetic, complex number computations, and operations on high-precision integers. The design of these libraries provides exact arithmetic routines and exposes intricate algorithms for tasks that require rigorous error bounds and reproducible computational results. Such modules are indispensable in environments where quantitative analysis and algorithmic correctness are of paramount importance.

The cryptographic components within the standard library similarly enforce strict mathematical formulations. These modules implement cryptographic primitives that are rooted in theoretical foundations, providing secure hashing, encryption, and digital signature functionalities. The rigorous standards applied in the construction of these packages ensure that cryptographic algorithms maintain both their theoretical integrity and practical robustness when integrated into broader system architectures.

Network Communication and External Protocol Handling

Network communication is addressed by an array of packages that encapsulate the multifaceted requirements of modern protocol-based interactions. These modules furnish the necessary abstractions for establishing connections, sending and receiving data over diverse network topologies, and adhering to standardized communication protocols. The design accommodates both the intricacies of low-level socket management and the high-level constructs required for HTTP and related protocols. The coherent integration of these functionalities is achieved through a systematic layering that lends itself to both scalability and modularity.

The intrinsic design of these networking packages is oriented toward a clear demarcation between connection management and data transmission protocols. This architectural separation ensures that the processes of connection establishment, data encoding, and protocol negotiation are handled in discrete, yet interrelated, layers. The result is an interface that is capable of efficiently managing network traffic, thereby facilitating the development of distributed systems with reliable and secure communication channels.

Data Encoding, Serialization, and Parsing Frameworks

Data exchange and structured information processing receive comprehensive support through dedicated packages that specialize in encoding, serialization, and parsing. These modules are responsible for converting complex data structures into transferable formats, as well as reconstructing those formats back into native representations. The design of the serialization frameworks is characterized by a meticulous balance between human-readability and machine efficiency. By conforming to established data interchange formats, the packages ensure that consistency is maintained across heterogeneous systems.

The strategies employed in these encoding and parsing libraries emphasize both flexibility and precision. Robust error handling and the enforcement of strict schema validations are integral to their operation. The implementation of these mechanisms reflects a deep theoretical grounding in formal language theory, where parsers and serializers are constructed as deterministic finite automata capable of recognizing well-formed expressions. Through this approach, data integrity is preserved across various stages of processing, rendering these frameworks essential for applications that operate in distributed and data-intensive environments.

Go Code Snippet

```
package main

import (
```

```go
    "crypto/sha256"
    "encoding/json"
    "fmt"
    "io/ioutil"
    "math"
    "net/http"
    "os"
    "sync"
    "time"
)

// quadraticRoots computes the roots of a quadratic equation: ax^2 +
//     bx + c = 0.
// If the discriminant is negative, the equation has no real roots
//     and valid is false.
func quadraticRoots(a, b, c float64) (float64, float64, bool) {
        discriminant := b*b - 4*a*c
        if discriminant < 0 {
                return 0, 0, false
        }
        sqrtDisc := math.Sqrt(discriminant)
        root1 := (-b + sqrtDisc) / (2 * a)
        root2 := (-b - sqrtDisc) / (2 * a)
        return root1, root2, true
}

// computeSHA256 returns the SHA256 hash of the input string.
func computeSHA256(s string) string {
        hash := sha256.Sum256([]byte(s))
        return fmt.Sprintf("%x", hash)
}

// httpGetExample performs an HTTP GET request, reads the response
//     body,
// and returns the first 100 characters of the content as a preview.
func httpGetExample(url string) (string, error) {
        client := http.Client{
                Timeout: 5 * time.Second,
        }
        resp, err := client.Get(url)
        if err != nil {
                return "", err
        }
        defer resp.Body.Close()
        body, err := ioutil.ReadAll(resp.Body)
        if err != nil {
                return "", err
        }
        content := string(body)
        if len(content) > 100 {
                content = content[:100]
        }
        return content, nil
```

```go
}

// ComputationResult aggregates the outcomes of various computations
↪   and operations.
type ComputationResult struct {
        // Coefficients for the quadratic equation: ax^2 + bx + c =
        ↪   0.
        QuadraticCoefficients []float64
        ↪   `json:"quadratic_coefficients"`
        // The discriminant computed from the quadratic
        ↪   coefficients.
        Discriminant float64 `json:"discriminant"`
        // The real roots of the quadratic equation, if available.
        QuadraticRoots []float64 `json:"quadratic_roots,omitempty"`
        // Base text for which SHA256 is computed.
        SHA256BaseText string `json:"sha256_base_text"`
        // Computed SHA256 hash for the base text.
        SHA256Hash string `json:"sha256_hash"`
        // SHA256 hashes computed concurrently for a list of
        ↪   messages.
        ConcurrentHashes []string `json:"concurrent_hashes"`
        // A preview of content fetched from a network HTTP GET
        ↪   request.
        HTTPContentPreview string
        ↪   `json:"http_content_preview,omitempty"`
}

func main() {
        // --- Quadratic Equation Computation ---
        a, b, c := 1.0, -3.0, 2.0
        discriminant := b*b - 4*a*c
        root1, root2, valid := quadraticRoots(a, b, c)
        var roots []float64
        if valid {
                roots = []float64{root1, root2}
        }

        // --- SHA256 Hashing Example ---
        baseText := "GoLang Standard Library"
        shaHash := computeSHA256(baseText)

        // --- Concurrency Example: Compute SHA256 hashes
        ↪   concurrently ---
        messages := []string{"Concurrency", "Efficiency",
        ↪   "Scalability", "Robustness"}
        concurrentHashes := make([]string, len(messages))
        var wg sync.WaitGroup
        for i, msg := range messages {
                wg.Add(1)
                go func(index int, text string) {
                        defer wg.Done()
                        concurrentHashes[index] =
                        ↪   computeSHA256(text)
```

```go
        }(i, msg)
    }
    wg.Wait()

    // --- HTTP GET Request Example ---
    url := "https://www.example.com"
    httpContent, err := httpGetExample(url)
    if err != nil {
        fmt.Fprintf(os.Stderr, "HTTP GET error: %v\n", err)
        httpContent = "Error retrieving content"
    }

    // --- Aggregate Computation Results ---
    result := ComputationResult{
        QuadraticCoefficients: []float64{a, b, c},
        Discriminant:          discriminant,
        QuadraticRoots:        roots,
        SHA256BaseText:        baseText,
        SHA256Hash:            shaHash,
        ConcurrentHashes:      concurrentHashes,
        HTTPContentPreview:    httpContent,
    }

    // --- Format and Display Results in JSON ---
    resultJSON, err := json.MarshalIndent(result, "", "  ")
    if err != nil {
        fmt.Fprintf(os.Stderr, "JSON Marshaling error:
        ↪  %v\n", err)
        return
    }
    fmt.Println("Computation Result:")
    fmt.Println(string(resultJSON))

    // --- Write Results to a File ---
    err = ioutil.WriteFile("result.json", resultJSON, 0644)
    if err != nil {
        fmt.Fprintf(os.Stderr, "File write error: %v\n",
        ↪  err)
        return
    }
    fmt.Println("Results written to result.json")
}
```

266

Chapter 54

File Operations: Reading and Writing Data

Systemic Abstractions and the os Package for File I/O

The os package in the Go programming environment encapsulates the intricacies of file system interactions through a well-defined abstraction layer that maps system-level primitives to language-level constructs. This abstraction permits the manipulation of file descriptors, wherein each file is represented by an opaque handle. Underlying system calls—such as *open*(2), *read*(2), and *write*(2)—are interwoven with Go's type system and error management paradigms, thereby ensuring that operations on disk are both semantically consistent and rigorously verified. The architectural design emphasizes strong typing and deterministic error propagation, which are essential for the construction of reliable file input/output subsystems.

Mechanisms for Data Retrieval: Reading Techniques

Reading data from disk is conceptualized as a multi-stage process that begins with the allocation of a file handle followed by the execution of read operations. The Go runtime supports both buffered and unbuffered read techniques, which are instrumental in mitigating the inherent latency associated with frequent system calls. Buffered reading aggregates smaller byte sequences into larger chunks, thereby optimizing input throughput and reducing the overhead of repetitive kernel transitions. The strategy involves a delicate interplay between in-memory buffers and the physical storage medium, and it is quantitatively modelled such that the overall read complexity approximates $O(n)$, where n is the number of bytes processed. This framework permits a systematic translation from raw byte streams to higher-order data structures, while maintaining fidelity with respect to the underlying file metadata.

Mechanisms for Data Recording: Writing Techniques

Writing data to disk is an operation that necessitates precise coordination between transient in-memory representations and their persistent archival on storage media. The process is delineated into distinct phases that include data preparation, buffering, and the eventual dispatch of write commands to the operating system. In the domain of buffered writing, temporary caches are employed to consolidate successive write requests into single, atomic transactions. This methodology not only improves performance but also enforces a form of transactional integrity, wherein the collective write operation can be conceptually represented as a sequence $W = (b_1, b_2, \ldots, b_n)$, with each b_i denoting a contiguous block of data. The rigorous orchestration of these steps ensures that once data is committed, subsequent read operations retrieve an unambiguous and consistent state from disk.

Contending with Error Handling and Resource Synchronization

Robust file operations are predicated on a disciplined regime of error handling and resource synchronization. Within the Go environment, error conditions are detected and propagated through explicit return values, thereby facilitating immediate corrective action or safe degradation of functionality. File descriptor management is executed in a controlled lifecycle that mandates the closure of opened resources, thereby preventing leakage and ensuring that system-level limits are respected. In concurrent contexts, the synchronization of file operations is achieved via locking primitives and coordinated access to critical sections. These mechanisms enforce invariants such that even under conditions of simultaneous read-write collisions, the file system maintains a consistent and deterministic state. The theoretical underpinning of such synchronization protocols is often analogous to classical semaphore or mutex models, typically symbolized as σ and μ, which serve to demarcate protected sections of operation.

Buffer Management and Performance Considerations

Optimizing performance in file input/output operations requires a nuanced approach to buffer management. Data buffering serves as a conduit between high-level application logic and the low-level mechanics of disk access. Internally, the os package orchestrates memory segments—allocated as buffers—to aggregate data sufficiently before engaging in intensive system-level interactions. The efficiency of these operations is governed by factors such as the buffer size B and the intrinsic latency L of the storage hardware. Empirical models indicate that throughput, denoted by T, can be approximated by a function $T = f(B, L)$, wherein an increase in B up to an optimal threshold results in a reduction in the relative impact of L. This relationship underscores the importance of selecting appropriate buffer sizes to achieve a balance between minimizing system calls and maximizing data throughput. The dynamic tuning of these parameters is essential in environments characterized by variable I/O loads and diverse storage architectures.

Go Code Snippet

```
package main

import (
        "bufio"
        "fmt"
        "io"
        "os"
        "sync"
```

```go
        "time"
)

// This program demonstrates several key concepts discussed in the
↪  chapter:
// 1. Buffered reading and writing to model the abstraction of file
↪  I/O (with underlying system calls like open, read, write).
// 2. The reading complexity O(n) when processing the input file
↪  with a buffer of size B.
// 3. Buffered writing of data represented as a sequence W = (b1,
↪  b2, ..., bn).
// 4. Throughput calculation T = f(B, L) where T is approximated by
↪  total bytes processed divided by the elapsed time.
// 5. Error handling and resource synchronization through proper
↪  file closing and a simple worker pool using mutex locking.
//
// To run this example, ensure that an "input.txt" file exists in
↪  the working directory.
// The program reads the contents of "input.txt" and writes them to
↪  "output.txt" using buffered I/O,
// then simulates concurrent processing of the file data using a
↪  worker pool.

func main() {
        // Define the buffer size (B) in bytes.
        bufferSize := 4096 // You may adjust this value to test
        ↪  different buffer sizes

        // Open the input file for reading.
        inputFile, err := os.Open("input.txt")
        if err != nil {
                fmt.Printf("Error opening input.txt: %v\n", err)
                return
        }
        defer inputFile.Close()

        // Create or truncate the output file for writing.
        outputFile, err := os.Create("output.txt")
        if err != nil {
                fmt.Printf("Error creating output.txt: %v\n", err)
                return
        }
        defer outputFile.Close()

        // Create buffered reader and writer with the specified
        ↪  buffer size.
        reader := bufio.NewReaderSize(inputFile, bufferSize)
        writer := bufio.NewWriterSize(outputFile, bufferSize)

        // Start performance measurement.
        startTime := time.Now()

        // Read from the input and write to the output in chunks.
```

270

```
totalBytes := 0
for {
        // Allocate buffer for each read. Using make ensures
        ↪   a fresh slice each time.
        buffer := make([]byte, bufferSize)
        n, err := reader.Read(buffer)
        if err != nil {
                if err == io.EOF {
                        // Finished reading the file.
                        break
                }
                fmt.Printf("Error during reading: %v\n",
                ↪   err)
                return
        }
        totalBytes += n

        // Write the read bytes as a block b_i to simulate
        ↪   writing sequence W = (b1, b2, ..., bn).
        written, werr := writer.Write(buffer[:n])
        if werr != nil {
                fmt.Printf("Error during writing: %v\n",
                ↪   werr)
                return
        }
        if written != n {
                fmt.Printf("Warning: Written bytes (%d) do
                ↪   not match read bytes (%d).\n", written,
                ↪   n)
        }
}

// Flush the buffered writer to ensure all data is written.
writer.Flush()

// Calculate elapsed time.
elapsed := time.Since(startTime)
// Throughput (T) is approximated as: T = totalBytes /
↪   elapsedSeconds.
throughput := float64(totalBytes) / elapsed.Seconds()

fmt.Printf("File I/O Completed.\n")
fmt.Printf("Total Bytes Processed: %d bytes\n", totalBytes)
fmt.Printf("Elapsed Time: %v\n", elapsed)
fmt.Printf("Throughput T = f(B, L)   %.2f bytes/sec\n",
↪   throughput)

// Simulate concurrent processing to demonstrate
↪   synchronization (using mutex)
// to handle file descriptor reading in a worker pool.
simulateConcurrentProcessing(inputFile, bufferSize)
}
```

271

```
// simulateConcurrentProcessing demonstrates error handling and
↪  resource synchronization.
// It uses a simple worker pool where each worker reads a block of
↪  data safely by synchronizing
// access to the shared file using a mutex. This models the
↪  synchronization protocols (like semaphore or mutex)
// mentioned in the chapter.
func simulateConcurrentProcessing(file *os.File, bufferSize int) {
        // Reset file offset to beginning for concurrent processing.
        _, err := file.Seek(0, 0)
        if err != nil {
                fmt.Printf("Error resetting file offset: %v\n", err)
                return
        }

        var wg sync.WaitGroup
        var mu sync.Mutex

        // Worker function: each worker reads a chunk, simulating a
        ↪  processing step.
        worker := func(workerID int) {
                defer wg.Done()
                mu.Lock()
                buffer := make([]byte, bufferSize)
                n, err := file.Read(buffer)
                mu.Unlock()
                if err != nil {
                        if err != io.EOF {
                                fmt.Printf("Worker %d encountered
                                ↪  error: %v\n", workerID, err)
                        }
                        return
                }
                if n > 0 {
                        // Simulate data processing.
                        fmt.Printf("Worker %d processed %d
                        ↪  bytes.\n", workerID, n)
                }
        }

        // Define number of workers for concurrent processing.
        numWorkers := 4

        // Continue launching workers until we reach the end of
        ↪  file.
        for {
                mu.Lock()
                currentPos, err := file.Seek(0, io.SeekCurrent)
                mu.Unlock()
                if err != nil {
                        fmt.Printf("Error retrieving file position:
                        ↪  %v\n", err)
                        break
```

272

```go
	}
	// Check if the entire file has been processed.
	info, statErr := file.Stat()
	if statErr != nil {
		fmt.Printf("Error stating file: %v\n",
		↪	statErr)
		break
	}
	if currentPos >= info.Size() {
		break
	}

	// Launch a group of workers.
	for i := 0; i < numWorkers; i++ {
		wg.Add(1)
		go worker(i + 1)
	}
	// Wait for this batch of workers to finish before
	↪	launching the next.
	wg.Wait()
	}
}
```

Chapter 55

JSON Handling: Encoding and Decoding

Foundational Characteristics of JSON as a Data Interchange Format

JSON is a lightweight, text-based format that encodes structured data using a minimal set of universal constructs. At its foundation, JSON employs name–value pairs and ordered lists, which allow for the representation of hierarchical and heterogeneous data. The syntax is deliberately concise, yet semantically expressive, making it suitable for a wide range of applications in distributed systems and networked environments. The inherent simplicity of JSON facilitates both human readability and machine parsing, thereby providing an effective medium for data interchange.

Architectural Overview of the encoding/json Package in Go

The encoding/json package in Go presents a principled approach to bridging the gap between native Go data structures and the JSON format. Internally, it leverages the reflective capabilities of the language to inspect types and their associated metadata. By

274

mapping exported struct fields to corresponding JSON keys, the package enforces a clear separation between internal representations and external serialization formats. The implementation emphasizes type safety and deterministic error propagation, ensuring that every serialized or deserialized value adheres to the semantic constraints imposed by both the Go type system and the JSON specification.

Marshaling: Serializing Go Data Structures into JSON

Marshaling refers to the process of converting native Go data structures into a JSON-encoded representation. This procedure involves traversing composite types such as structs, maps, and slices, while applying rules that dictate how each data element is to be formatted in JSON. The algorithm relies on introspection to determine the visibility and layout of the data, with special consideration given to struct field tags that can override default mappings. Beyond straightforward field-to-key conversion, the marshaling process also addresses issues of cyclic dependencies and type compatibility, ensuring that the resulting JSON is both syntactically valid and semantically faithful. The computational complexity of marshaling is typically linear, denoted as $O(n)$, where n quantifies the aggregate size of the input data.

Unmarshaling: Reconstituting Go Data Structures from JSON

Unmarshaling is the converse operation, entailing the parsing of a JSON document into its corresponding Go representation. The encoding/json package implements a dynamic type inference mechanism to map JSON arrays, objects, and primitive literals back to the appropriate Go types. During this process, the parser reconciles the hierarchical structure of the JSON input with the static definitions provided in the target Go data structures. In the event of discrepancies—such as type mismatches or missing keys—the unmarshaling mechanism generates explicit error signals that propagate through the call stack. This stringent adherence to error signaling ensures that any deviation from the expected format is identified and reported, thereby preserving the integrity of the reconstructed data.

Error Propagation, Resource Constraints, and Performance Considerations

The serialization and deserialization stages embody critical performance and reliability trade-offs. Error propagation within the encoding/json package is systematically handled through explicit return values, such that any anomalies encountered during marshaling or unmarshaling are comprehensively recorded. This model enforces a disciplined approach to resource management, particularly in the context of dynamic memory allocation and garbage collection. Furthermore, the efficiency of JSON handling is influenced by the interplay between buffer management and I/O latency. In scenarios involving large-scale data transfers, the optimization of throughput is achieved by minimizing redundant operations and streamlining the conversion pipeline, ensuring that the overall processing time remains proportional to $O(n)$, where n represents the size of the data payload.

Go Code Snippet

```go
package main

import (
        "encoding/json"
        "fmt"
        "log"
        "time"
)

// Person represents a basic data structure with JSON tags.
// It includes fundamental types demonstrating how data is
↪   serialized.
type Person struct {
        Name      string    `json:"name"`
        Age       int       `json:"age"`
        Email     string    `json:"email"`
        CreatedAt time.Time `json:"created_at"`
}

// Employee embeds a Person and adds additional fields.
```

```go
// This struct illustrates how nested data structures are marshaled
↪   and unmarshaled.
type Employee struct {
        Person
        Company  string `json:"company"`
        Position string `json:"position"`
}

func main() {
        // Create an instance of Employee with a nested Person
        ↪   struct.
        employee := Employee{
                Person: Person{
                        Name:      "Alice Johnson",
                        Age:       30,
                        Email:     "alice@example.com",
                        CreatedAt: time.Now(),
                },
                Company:  "GoTech",
                Position: "Software Engineer",
        }

        // MARSHALING: Convert the Employee struct to a JSON-encoded
        ↪   representation.
        // The marshaling process traverses the composite types and
        ↪   applies the rules based on JSON struct tags.
        // The computational complexity is typically O(n), where n
        ↪   is the size of the input data.
        startTime := time.Now()
        jsonData, err := json.MarshalIndent(employee, "", "    ")
        if err != nil {
                log.Fatalf("Error during marshaling: %v", err)
        }
        elapsedMarshal := time.Since(startTime)
        fmt.Println("Marshaled JSON data:")
        fmt.Println(string(jsonData))
        fmt.Printf("\nMarshaling took: %v\n\n", elapsedMarshal)

        // UNMARSHALING: Reconstitute the Go data structure from the
        ↪   JSON document.
        // The unmarshaling mechanism maps the JSON keys back to the
        ↪   corresponding struct fields.
        var employeeCopy Employee
        startTime = time.Now()
        if err := json.Unmarshal(jsonData, &employeeCopy); err !=
        ↪   nil {
                log.Fatalf("Error during unmarshaling: %v", err)
        }
        elapsedUnmarshal := time.Since(startTime)
        fmt.Println("Unmarshaled Employee struct:")
        fmt.Printf("%+v\n", employeeCopy)
        fmt.Printf("\nUnmarshaling took: %v\n\n", elapsedUnmarshal)
```

```go
// DYNAMIC TYPE INFERENCE:
// Unmarshal JSON into an empty interface{} to perform
↪  dynamic type inspection.
var dynamicData interface{}
if err := json.Unmarshal(jsonData, &dynamicData); err != nil
↪  {
        log.Fatalf("Error during dynamic unmarshaling: %v",
        ↪  err)
}
fmt.Println("Dynamically unmarshaled data:")
fmt.Printf("%+v\n\n", dynamicData)

// ERROR PROPAGATION EXAMPLE:
// Attempt to unmarshal malformed JSON to demonstrate error
↪  handling.
malformedJSON := []byte(`{"name": "Bob, "age": 27}`)
if err := json.Unmarshal(malformedJSON, &employeeCopy); err
↪  != nil {
        fmt.Printf("Expected error during unmarshaling
        ↪  malformed JSON: %v\n", err)
}

// CYCLIC DEPENDENCY REMINDER:
// Note: The encoding/json package does not support cyclic
↪  data structures.
// Developers must ensure that the data structures used for
↪  JSON conversion do not contain cycles.
// This note reinforces design practices to avoid pitfalls
↪  in serialization.

// SUMMARY:
// The code above encapsulates the following important
↪  aspects:
// 1. Marshaling: Converting Go structs into JSON format
↪  with O(n) complexity.
// 2. Unmarshaling: Parsing JSON back into Go structs and
↪  managing type safety.
// 3. Dynamic Type Inference: Leveraging interface{} to
↪  handle various JSON structures.
// 4. Error Handling: Proper propagation and logging of
↪  errors during conversion processes.
}
```

Chapter 56

XML Handling: Parsing and Generation

Fundamentals of XML Structure and Semantics

XML is a markup language designed to describe data in a hierarchical and self-descriptive manner. At its core, an XML document is comprised of a prolog followed by a nested structure of elements, each defined by a start tag, content, and an end tag. This construct enables the representation of complex structured data while maintaining both syntactic simplicity and extensibility. The formal underpinning of XML can be understood via the lens of context-free grammars, where an XML document conforms to a grammar represented as $G = (V, \Sigma, R, S)$ with S denoting the start symbol, and the production rules R governing the construction of nested elements and attributes. The intrinsic flexibility of XML enables the explicit declaration of attributes, mixed content, and namespace associations, which collectively contribute to a robust medium for data interchange.

Parsing XML Documents with the Go Standard Library

The process of parsing XML documents in Go is facilitated by the language's standard library, which implements a token-based parser that systematically traverses the input stream. This strategy involves reading the document sequentially and decomposing it into discrete tokens such as start elements, character data, and end elements. A significant design decision is the employment of a linear scanning algorithm, which ensures that the computational complexity is $O(n)$, where n corresponds to the size of the input data. Reflection is employed internally to accommodate the mapping between XML tags and corresponding Go data structures. The parser's architecture is optimized to enforce well-formedness, ensuring that every document adheres to the syntactic constraints defined by XML standards. Such a meticulous approach guarantees that any deviation encountered during parsing—whether arising from incorrect nesting or malformed tags—is detected through a rigorous error-propagation mechanism.

Generating XML Content Using Go's Standard Libraries

The generation of XML content from native Go data structures is achieved through a systematic encoding process. This process involves reflecting on the structure's metadata, where field tags provide explicit instructions for the conversion between Go types and XML elements. During the encoding phase, the hierarchy of the Go data structure is methodically translated into a corresponding XML document such that each struct field is converted into an element or attribute as specified by the metadata annotations. The generation mechanism ensures compliance with W3C XML standards by enforcing strict rules regarding tag pairing and attribute quoting. Moreover, the engine responsible for XML generation is designed to operate in a streaming fashion, which minimizes memory overhead and maintains a linear processing time of $O(n)$ relative to the size of the data structure being serialized.

Mapping XML Constructs to Go's Type System

An essential aspect of XML processing in Go is the seamless integration between XML constructs and Go's type system. The encoding and decoding routines utilize reflection to inspect the structure of Go types, thereby enabling an automatic mapping between XML elements and struct fields. This mapping is influenced by the declarative field tags which specify XML element names, attribute roles, and nested relationships. The translator systematically converts character data, element attributes, and nested elements into their equivalent representations in Go. The ability to map these constructs is crucial, especially for dealing with mixed content and optional elements where the absence or presence of a tag must be managed dynamically. This reflective process ensures both type safety and fidelity in preserving the semantic nuances of the original XML document.

Error Propagation and Conformance Verification in XML Processing

In the realm of XML handling, stringent error propagation mechanisms are paramount to maintain data integrity and to enforce compliance with established schema constraints. The Go standard library encases the parsing and generation routines with comprehensive error-checking procedures. During the parsing phase, any structural anomaly—such as mismatched tags or violations of the well-formedness criteria—is immediately conveyed through explicit error returns. In parallel, the generation routines perform verification steps to ensure that the produced XML adheres to the strict syntactic and semantic requirements stipulated by the XML standard. This robust error propagation is complemented by validation techniques that cross-reference document constructs against optional schema or DTD specifications. The systematic handling of errors, along with the retention of detailed error information, enables precise conformance verification and bolsters the reliability of XML transformations in computational environments.

Go Code Snippet

```
// This Go program demonstrates XML parsing and generation following
↪    the concepts
// discussed in the chapter. It implements a token-based parsing
↪    algorithm with
// O(n) complexity for processing XML input, in line with the idea
↪    of scanning
// a document that conforms to the context-free grammar:
//
//    G = (V, , R, S)
//
// where S is the start symbol and R is the set of production rules
↪    defining the
// nested structure of XML elements. The program also shows how to
↪    map XML constructs
// to Go types using struct tags and how to handle errors during
↪    parsing and generation.

package main

import (
        "encoding/xml"
        "fmt"
        "io"
        "os"
        "strings"
)

// Person defines a Go struct that maps to an XML "person" element.
// The XML field tags indicate how each struct field corresponds to
↪    an XML element or nested element.
type Person struct {
        XMLName    xml.Name `xml:"person"`
        Name       string   `xml:"name"`
        Age        int      `xml:"age"`
        Interests  []string `xml:"interests>interest"`
}

// parseXML demonstrates XML parsing using a token-based approach.
// The decoder processes the XML input with a linear scan, ensuring
↪    O(n) complexity.
func parseXML(xmlData string) {
        decoder := xml.NewDecoder(strings.NewReader(xmlData))
        for {
                // Retrieve the next token from the XML input.
                token, err := decoder.Token()
                if err == io.EOF {
                        break // End of document.
                }
                if err != nil {
```

```go
                    fmt.Fprintf(os.Stderr, "Error during token
                    ↪    parsing: %v\n", err)
                    return
            }

            // Process tokens according to their type.
            switch t := token.(type) {
            case xml.StartElement:
                    fmt.Printf("Start Element: <%s>\n",
                    ↪    t.Name.Local)
            case xml.EndElement:
                    fmt.Printf("End Element: </%s>\n",
                    ↪    t.Name.Local)
            case xml.CharData:
                    content := strings.TrimSpace(string(t))
                    if len(content) > 0 {
                            fmt.Printf("Character Data: %s\n",
                            ↪    content)
                    }
            }
        }
}

// generateXML converts a Go data structure into its XML
↪    representation.
// The encoding/xml package uses reflection to map struct fields to
↪    XML elements.
func generateXML(data Person) {
        // MarshalIndent produces a well-formatted XML output.
        output, err := xml.MarshalIndent(data, "", "  ")
        if err != nil {
                fmt.Fprintf(os.Stderr, "Error during XML generation:
                ↪    %v\n", err)
                return
        }
        // Prepend the XML header to guarantee well-formedness.
        xmlOutput := xml.Header + string(output)
        fmt.Println(xmlOutput)
}

func main() {
        // Sample XML document for parsing.
        sampleXML := ` + "`" + `<?xml version="1.0"
        ↪    encoding="UTF-8"?>
<person>
  <name>John Doe</name>
  <age>30</age>
  <interests>
    <interest>Coding</interest>
    <interest>Reading</interest>
  </interests>
</person>` + "`" + `
```

283

```go
	fmt.Println("Parsing Sample XML Document:")
	parseXML(sampleXML)

	fmt.Println("\nGenerating XML from Go Data Structure:")
	// Create an instance of Person to serialize into XML.
	personData := Person{
		Name:      "Jane Smith",
		Age:       28,
		Interests: []string{"Hiking", "Photography",
		↪  "Traveling"},
	}
	generateXML(personData)
}
```

Chapter 57

Regular Expressions: Pattern Matching

Overview of Regular Expressions

Regular expressions constitute a formal mechanism for specifying patterns within textual data, derived from the theoretical framework of regular languages. In formal language theory, a regular expression is a concise representation denoting a set of strings over an alphabet Σ, and it is closely related to the concept of finite state automata. The mathematical underpinnings are encapsulated by the equivalence between regular expressions and deterministic or nondeterministic finite automata, wherein any regular expression corresponds to an automaton that recognizes exactly the language defined by that expression. This intrinsic relationship lays the groundwork for the systematic analysis and synthesis of patterns within strings.

The Architecture of the Regexp Package

The Go programming language provides a dedicated package for regular expression processing that embodies a robust implementation of pattern matching. The architecture of this package is founded on methods that translate a textual regular expression into an operational finite automaton. This translation involves a two-phase process: parsing of the input pattern and subsequent compilation into an internal representation optimized for execution. During the parsing phase, the pattern is decomposed into a series of tokens reflecting its constituent elements such as literals, metacharacters, and quantifiers. In the compilation phase, these tokens are used to construct a finite state machine where transitions are defined based on the input characters. This internal model is then utilized to systematically evaluate input strings against the defined pattern, ensuring that matching operations are both precise and efficient.

Syntax and Semantics in the Go Context

Within the Go ecosystem, the syntax of regular expressions adheres to conventions that blend historical precedence with practical considerations for performance and expressiveness. The language supports a variety of constructs which include, but are not limited to, character classes, quantifiers, anchors, grouping, and alternation. Each construct is designed to capture specific semantic notions; for instance, quantifiers express the degree of repetition and range by which a preceding element is expected to occur, while grouping operations enable the formation of sub-patterns that can be subsequently referenced or manipulated. Special characters have predefined roles that are essential for denoting boundaries of matches, and modifiers may be applied to alter the default behavior. The careful design underlying these elements ensures that the semantic interpretation of a regular expression remains unambiguous and consistent with the formal definitions established in automata theory.

Mechanics of the Matching Process

The operational mechanics that govern pattern matching are embedded in the finite automata produced during the compilation process. When an input string is presented, the matching engine traverses the string in a sequential fashion, evaluating each character against the transition functions of the automaton. This process involves computing the set of active states at each step, with transitions occurring in accordance with the structure of the regular expression. Notably, the matching engine often employs a strategy that minimizes backtracking through the use of precomputed transition tables, thereby enforcing an efficient matching process whose complexity typically adheres to linear time with respect to the length of the input string, denoted by $O(n)$. The inherent design is capable of handling both the simplest and more elaborate patterns, as it dynamically adjusts the internal state based on the precise structure of the regular expression.

Error Handling and Validation of Patterns

A critical component in the design of the regexp package is the rigorous validation of input patterns in order to enforce syntactic correctness before execution. The parser scrutinizes the regular expression for conformity with the prescribed grammatical rules, ensuring that all metacharacters, quantifiers, and grouping symbols are appropriately balanced and contextually valid. In cases where the pattern deviates from the expected syntax, an error is generated, thereby precluding any further processing of ill-formed patterns. This precautionary measure serves to maintain the integrity of the matching process and prevents runtime anomalies that may arise due to ambiguous or contradictory pattern definitions. The systematic propagation of these errors is central to the robustness of the regular expression engine, ensuring that only well-defined patterns are sanctioned for subsequent matching operations.

Go Code Snippet

```
package main

import (
        "fmt"
        "log"
        "regexp"
)

// This program demonstrates key aspects of regular expression
↪    processing as described in the chapter.
// It covers pattern validation, compiling a regex into a finite
↪    automaton, matching input strings,
// extracting submatches (reflecting the notion of state transitions
↪    in a finite automaton), and performing
// replacements. The underlying process of the regexp package mimics
↪    the formal theory where a regular
// expression is parsed into tokens and compiled into an internal
↪    transition-based model ensuring an
```

```go
// efficient, typically O(n), matching process.

func main() {
        // Define a regular expression pattern.
        // The pattern is designed to match a simplified version of
        ↪ an email address, reflecting:
        // - A username: composed of alphanumeric characters along
        ↪ with characters like ._%+-.
        // - The '@' symbol as a literal separator.
        // - A domain: allowing letters, dots, and hyphens, ending
        ↪ with a top-level domain of at least 2 characters.
        pattern := `^([\w.%+\-]+)@([\w.\-]+\.[A-Za-z]{2,})$`

        // Compile the pattern to produce a regex object.
        // At this stage, the pattern is parsed and translated into
        ↪ an internal state machine.
        re, err := regexp.Compile(pattern)
        if err != nil {
                // Handle error: This ensures that only
                ↪ syntactically valid regular expressions enter
                ↪ the matching process.
                log.Fatalf("Error compiling regex: %v", err)
        }

        // Define a set of input strings to demonstrate the matching
        ↪ algorithm.
        inputs := []string{
                "alice@example.com",
                "bob.example@sub-domain.co.uk",
                "invalid-email@.com",     // This should fail as it
                ↪ violates expected syntax.
                "another.invalid@site",   // This should fail due to
                ↪ missing valid TLD.
                "user+mailbox@domain.com", // Valid email with a '+'
                ↪ symbol in the username.
        }

        // Process each input string using the compiled regular
        ↪ expression.
        for _, input := range inputs {
                fmt.Printf("Testing input: %s\n", input)

                // The MatchString method checks if the entire input
                ↪ conforms to the pattern,
                // analogous to initiating a state traversal in a
                ↪ finite automata.
                if re.MatchString(input) {
                        // Extract submatches: the full match and
                        ↪ the captured groups (username and
                        ↪ domain).
                        submatches := re.FindStringSubmatch(input)
                        fmt.Printf("Match found: %v\n", submatches)
```

288

```go
                        // Example: Demonstrate extraction of
                        ↪   captured groups.
                        // Here, submatches[1] contains the username
                        ↪   and submatches[2] holds the domain.
                        if len(submatches) == 3 {
                                fmt.Printf("  Username: %s, Domain:
                                ↪   %s\n", submatches[1],
                                ↪   submatches[2])
                        }
                } else {
                        // When there is no match, it indicates that
                        ↪   the input failed the syntactic or
                        ↪   semantic checks
                        // enforced by the finite automata
                        ↪   underlying the regexp engine.
                        fmt.Println("No match found.")
                }
                fmt.Println()
        }

        // Demonstrate text substitution using ReplaceAllString.
        // In this example, matched email addresses within a block
        ↪   of text are redacted.
        text := "Contact us at support@example.com or
        ↪   sales+promo@shop-domain.com for further assistance."
        fmt.Println("Original Text:")
        fmt.Println(text)

        // Replace all substrings that match the regular expression
        ↪   with the placeholder "[REDACTED]".
        redactedText := re.ReplaceAllString(text, "[REDACTED]")
        fmt.Println("\nText after redaction:")
        fmt.Println(redactedText)

        // Demonstrate retrieval of match indices using
        ↪   FindAllStringIndex.
        // This shows the exact positions within the original text
        ↪   where the pattern was matched.
        indices := re.FindAllStringIndex(text, -1)
        fmt.Println("\nIndices of matched email addresses in the
        ↪   original text:")
        for _, pair := range indices {
                fmt.Printf("Start: %d, End: %d\n", pair[0], pair[1])
        }
}
```

289

Chapter 58

Tokenization and Parsing: String Scanning Techniques

Formal Foundations of Lexical Analysis

Tokenization constitutes the systematic decomposition of an unstructured character sequence into a finite sequence of atomic units, known as tokens. In mathematical terms, let Σ represent the input alphabet and let Σ^* denote the set of all finite strings over Σ. A token is defined as an element of a finite set T, and the process of tokenization can be formalized as a mapping function $f : \Sigma^* \to T^*$, where T^* is the set of token sequences. This formulation is grounded in the principles of formal language theory, wherein lexical elements correspond to equivalence classes determined by a specified grammar. Moreover, the delineation between tokens is implemented by employing techniques derived from finite automata theory. A deterministic finite automaton (DFA), defined by the quintuple $(Q, \Sigma, \delta, q_0, F)$, furnishes a rigorous framework for recognizing token patterns through state transitions. The tester of each input symbol against the transition function δ establishes token boundaries based on the principle of maximal munch, thereby ensuring that the longest lexeme consistent with the token's regular expression is selected. This theoretical foundation underpins the practical algorithms used in string scanning and lexical analysis.

Architecture and Mechanisms of String Scanning

The architecture for string scanning is predicated on the implementation of scanners that operate in a sequential and stateful manner. Within this framework, the input stream is processed one character at a time. Each character is evaluated in the context of a current state within an internal state machine. The transitions, dictated by the function δ, guide the scanner from one state to another until a token boundary is detected. The scanning process relies on precomputed transition tables and a well-defined set of accepting states, which collectively serve to identify the termination of a valid token. The operational efficiency of this method is evident in its linear time complexity relative to the length of the input string, typically expressed as $O(n)$, where n denotes the number of characters processed. A comprehensive design often incorporates lookahead mechanisms to resolve ambiguities and to ensure that tokens with overlapping patterns are accurately segmented. The integration of these techniques within the scanner's architecture facilitates a robust extraction of lexical units and lays the groundwork for subsequent syntactic analysis.

Custom Parsing Logic and Contextual Analysis

Beyond the initial phase of tokenization, custom parsing logic provides the methodological apparatus for constructing higher-level representations from the linear sequence of tokens. This stage involves the application of context-sensitive rules that are often formulated as a context-free grammar. The tokens produced by the scanner are assembled into structured constructs, such as abstract syntax trees, which encapsulate both the hierarchical and sequential relationships inherent in the input data. Custom parsing logic is frequently necessitated by domain-specific languages or specialized data formats that exhibit idiosyncratic syntactic rules. In these cases, the parser may combine recursive descent strategies, table-driven methodologies, or combinatorial parsing techniques to resolve ambiguities and to enforce contextual constraints. Error detection during parsing is achieved by identifying deviations from the prescribed grammar; this may include mismatches in expected token sequences or the presence of extraneous tokens, with such discrepancies being handled via recovery strategies that maintain the structural integrity of the resultant parse. The concerted use of custom parsing methodologies thus transforms raw token streams into semantically rich representations suitable for further computational analysis.

Go Code Snippet

```go
package main

import (
        "fmt"
        "unicode"
)

// TokenType represents the type of token identified by the scanner.
type TokenType string

const (
        // Special tokens
        ILLEGAL TokenType = "ILLEGAL"
        EOF     TokenType = "EOF"

        // Literals
        IDENT TokenType = "IDENT" // identifiers e.g., variable
        ↪   names
        INT   TokenType = "INT"   // integer literals

        // Operators
        PLUS     TokenType = "PLUS"     // +
        MINUS    TokenType = "MINUS"    // -
        ASTERISK TokenType = "ASTERISK" // *
        SLASH    TokenType = "SLASH"    // /

        // Delimiters
        LPAREN TokenType = "LPAREN" // (
        RPAREN TokenType = "RPAREN" // )
)

// Token structure encapsulates a token's type and its literal
↪   value.
type Token struct {
        Type    TokenType
        Literal string
}

// Lexer implements a simple deterministic finite automaton (DFA)
```

```go
// for tokenizing an input string. The DFA is defined conceptually
// ↪ as:
//    M = (Q, , , q0, F)
// where Q is a set of states,  the input alphabet,  the transition
// ↪ function,
// q0 the initial state, and F the set of accepting states.
type Lexer struct {
        input        string // The input character stream
        position     int    // Current position in input (points to
        ↪ current char)
        readPosition int    // Next reading position in input
        ch           rune   // Current character under examination
}

// NewLexer initializes the Lexer with the input string.
func NewLexer(input string) *Lexer {
        l := &Lexer{input: input}
        l.readChar() // Load the first character into the lexer
        return l
}

// readChar processes the next character in the input stream.
// It simulates the DFA's state transition delta: (current state,
// ↪ input symbol) -> new state.
func (l *Lexer) readChar() {
        if l.readPosition >= len(l.input) {
                // End-of-file marker; token with zero value
                // ↪ indicates EOF.
                l.ch = 0
        } else {
                l.ch = rune(l.input[l.readPosition])
        }
        l.position = l.readPosition
        l.readPosition++
}

// skipWhitespace advances the lexer past any whitespace characters
// ↪ (e.g. ' ', '\n', '\t', '\r').
func (l *Lexer) skipWhitespace() {
        for l.ch == ' ' || l.ch == '\t' || l.ch == '\n' || l.ch ==
        ↪ '\r' {
                l.readChar()
        }
}

// NextToken uses a stateful scanning mechanism (maximal munch) to
// ↪ identify the next token.
// It applies the DFA repeatedly to output a sequence of tokens
// ↪ (T*), implementing the mapping function:
//    f: * → T*
func (l *Lexer) NextToken() Token {
        var tok Token
```

293

```go
	// Ignore whitespace before tokenization.
	l.skipWhitespace()

	switch l.ch {
	case '+':
		tok = newToken(PLUS, l.ch)
	case '-':
		tok = newToken(MINUS, l.ch)
	case '*':
		tok = newToken(ASTERISK, l.ch)
	case '/':
		tok = newToken(SLASH, l.ch)
	case '(':
		tok = newToken(LPAREN, l.ch)
	case ')':
		tok = newToken(RPAREN, l.ch)
	case 0:
		// EOF encountered: no more tokens.
		tok.Literal = ""
		tok.Type = EOF
	default:
		// Check if the character is part of an identifier
		↪  (or keyword).
		if isLetter(l.ch) {
			// Maximal munch: Read the entire
			↪  identifier.
			literal := l.readIdentifier()
			tok.Literal = literal
			tok.Type = IDENT
			return tok
		} else if unicode.IsDigit(l.ch) {
			// Process number literal using maximal
			↪  munch.
			literal := l.readNumber()
			tok.Literal = literal
			tok.Type = INT
			return tok
		} else {
			tok = newToken(ILLEGAL, l.ch)
		}
	}

	l.readChar() // Transition to the next symbol
	return tok
}

// readIdentifier reads a sequence of characters that form an
↪  identifier.
// This function applies the maximal munch principle ensuring that
↪  the longest valid lexeme is captured.
func (l *Lexer) readIdentifier() string {
	position := l.position
	for isLetter(l.ch) {
```

294

```
                        l.readChar()
        }
        return l.input[position:l.position]
}

// readNumber reads a sequence of digit characters representing an
↪    integer literal.
func (l *Lexer) readNumber() string {
        position := l.position
        for unicode.IsDigit(l.ch) {
                l.readChar()
        }
        return l.input[position:l.position]
}

// isLetter returns true if the character is considered part of an
↪    identifier based on the input alphabet .
func isLetter(ch rune) bool {
        return unicode.IsLetter(ch) || ch == '_'
}

// newToken constructs a Token given a type and character literal.
func newToken(tokenType TokenType, ch rune) Token {
        return Token{Type: tokenType, Literal: string(ch)}
}

// main serves as an example driver for the lexer, demonstrating
↪    tokenization and the DFA algorithm in action.
func main() {
        // Example input string to be tokenized.
        input := "sum = a + 42 * (b - c) / 2"

        lexer := NewLexer(input)
        fmt.Println("Tokenizing input:", input)

        // Process and print tokens until the end of the file/input
        ↪    is reached.
        for {
                tok := lexer.NextToken()
                if tok.Type == EOF {
                        break
                }
                fmt.Printf("Token{Type:%q, Literal:%q}\n", tok.Type,
                ↪    tok.Literal)
        }
}
```

295

Chapter 59

Data Serialization: Using Gob Encoding

Fundamental Concepts and Theoretical Framework

The gob encoding mechanism constitutes a binary serialization format designed to transform complex Go data structures into a compact representation. The encoding process may be formalized by an encoding function

$$E : D \to \{0, 1\}^*,$$

where D denotes the set of Go data structures and $\{0, 1\}^*$ represents the set of finite binary strings. Central to this format is the self-descriptive inclusion of type metadata; the serialized stream commences with an explicit description of the data types that will follow, succeeded by the corresponding encoded values. Each data structure is analyzed to generate a type descriptor that encapsulates information about fields, composite types, and pointer relationships. The persistence of type consistency between serialization and deserialization is ensured through an internal registry that maps runtime types to their corresponding binary representations. In this manner, the gob encoding format leverages principles from formal language theory and finite automata to effectuate a systematic and deterministic translation of in-memory structures into an unambiguous binary stream.

Design Principles and Internal Architecture

The internal architecture of the gob encoding framework is built upon dynamic type introspection and reflective examination of composite data. During the serialization phase, each object is traversed and its layout is examined using reflection, resulting in the construction of a type graph that captures the relationships among fields and nested structures. For composite types, such as arrays, slices, and maps, the encoder performs a recursive analysis. Each distinct type is registered once and subsequently referred to via compact type indices, thereby eliminating redundancy in the encoded stream. The protocol is designed to ensure that the ordering of type definitions aligns with the order of occurrence in the data stream, which facilitates efficient decoding and guarantees type integrity. This architecture systematically differentiates between first-time type declarations and repeat occurrences, making use of reference mechanisms in lieu of re-emitting identical type information. Such an approach minimizes overhead and optimizes the binary size while maintaining a high degree of type fidelity.

Usage Advantages and Efficiency Considerations

The gob encoding format offers numerous advantages in the domain of data serialization. Foremost among these is the efficiency gained from its compact binary representation, which significantly reduces the volume of data transmitted or stored when compared to textual formats. The inclusion of comprehensive type metadata within the stream permits strict type checking during deserialization, thereby preserving the structural integrity and semantic correctness of the original data. Furthermore, by transmitting type information only once per unique type, the format minimizes repetitive overhead, especially in applications involving large or recursive data structures. The design also supports complex constructs inherent to Go, including nested composites and pointer indirections, ensuring that the serialized form retains an accurate mirror of the in-memory layout. Performance is enhanced by the strategic balancing of reflection-based introspection against the benefits of reduced redundancy, resulting in a serialization mechanism that is both robust and efficient in varied computational contexts.

Go Code Snippet

```go
package main

import (
    "bytes"
    "encoding/gob"
    "fmt"
    "log"
)

// Address represents a simple composite type with basic fields.
type Address struct {
    Street string
    City   string
    State  string
    ZipCode int
}

// Person represents a more complex data structure, including a
// ↪  pointer field,
// a slice, and embedded types to illustrate nested serialization.
type Person struct {
    Name    string
    Age     int
    Address *Address
    Friends []string
}

// init registers custom types with the gob package. This is crucial
// ↪  for ensuring
// that the type metadata is available during both encoding and
// ↪  decoding phases.
// Here, we register the types once so that subsequent references by
// ↪  their type indices
// avoid redundancy, echoing the internal design of type
// ↪  descriptors.
func init() {
    gob.Register(&Address{})
    gob.Register(&Person{})
}

// encodeData applies the core concept of gob encoding, mapping a Go
// ↪  data structure D
// to a binary stream {0,1}*. It leverages gob.NewEncoder to
// ↪  serialize the provided
// object along with its complete type metadata.
func encodeData(data interface{}) ([]byte, error) {
```

298

```go
    var buf bytes.Buffer
    encoder := gob.NewEncoder(&buf)
    if err := encoder.Encode(data); err != nil {
        return nil, err
    }
    return buf.Bytes(), nil
}

// decodeData reverses the encoding process. It decodes the binary
// ↪ stream into the
// provided data structure ensuring that the type information
// ↪ matches the one generated
// during the encoding phase.
func decodeData(data []byte, decoded interface{}) error {
    buf := bytes.NewBuffer(data)
    decoder := gob.NewDecoder(buf)
    return decoder.Decode(decoded)
}

func main() {
    // Construct a sample Person instance which includes nested and
    // ↪ composite data.
    original := &Person{
        Name: "John Doe",
        Age:  30,
        Address: &Address{
            Street:  "123 Main St",
            City:    "Anytown",
            State:   "CA",
            ZipCode: 12345,
        },
        Friends: []string{"Alice", "Bob", "Charlie"},
    }

    // The encoding function E : D -> {0,1}^* conceptually maps our
    // ↪ in-memory data
    // structure (D) to a compact binary form. The actual call below
    // ↪ performs the serialization.
    encodedData, err := encodeData(original)
    if err != nil {
        log.Fatalf("Error during gob encoding: %v", err)
    }
    fmt.Println("Encoded Gob Data:", encodedData)

    // Decode the binary data back into a Go data structure to
    // ↪ verify integrity.
    var decoded Person
    if err := decodeData(encodedData, &decoded); err != nil {
        log.Fatalf("Error during gob decoding: %v", err)
    }

    // Output the decoded data structure to demonstrate that the
    // ↪ original layout and data
```

```go
    // have been preserved through the serialization and
    ↪ deserialization process.
    fmt.Println("\nDecoded Data Structure:")
    fmt.Printf("Name: %s\n", decoded.Name)
    fmt.Printf("Age: %d\n", decoded.Age)
    if decoded.Address != nil {
        fmt.Printf("Address: %s, %s, %s, %d\n",
            decoded.Address.Street, decoded.Address.City,
            ↪ decoded.Address.State, decoded.Address.ZipCode)
    }
    fmt.Printf("Friends: %v\n", decoded.Friends)
}
```

Chapter 60

Network Programming: Basics with the net Package

Fundamental Concepts of Network Communication

Network communication is predicated on a layered paradigm that encapsulates both theoretical and practical constructs. At its core, the exchange of data between distributed processes is governed by protocols that operate over diverse transport mechanisms. These protocols, often abstracted by the operating system, follow established models such as the TCP/IP suite. The essence of this abstraction can be formulated as a mapping $N : S \to T$, where S represents a set of source inputs and T denotes the corresponding target endpoints. The architecture is inherently modular, emphasizing the separation of concerns by isolating connection management, error handling, and data segmentation. In this framework, both connection-oriented and connectionless paradigms are accommodated through distinct protocol behaviors, each with its own operational guarantees and trade-offs.

Protocol Abstractions in the net Package

The net package provides a cohesive interface that abstracts the low-level details of socket programming. By encapsulating system calls into a more manageable and type-safe API, the package enables the creation, manipulation, and management of network endpoints with minimal exposure to underlying operating system idiosyncrasies. Internally, the package leverages a uniform addressing scheme, where network addresses are represented by composite structures that amalgamate hostname and port information into a single entity. This abstraction facilitates operations that are agnostic to the particulars of the transport layer, thereby streamlining the development process. The design ensures that the conversion between human-readable addresses and their binary representations adheres strictly to the principles of robustness and error isolation.

TCP Communications: Stream-Oriented Mechanisms

Transmission Control Protocol (TCP) is characterized by its emphasis on reliable, ordered, and error-checked delivery of a continuous stream of bytes. The protocol establishes a virtual circuit through a three-way handshake that synchronizes sequence numbers and acknowledges connectivity parameters. Mathematically, a TCP connection may be conceptualized as a stateful function $C : I \times S \to O$, where I signifies the set of inputs, S the internal connection state, and O the output byte stream. The guarantees offered by TCP—such as congestion control, flow management, and packet reassembly—are accomplished through a combination of algorithmic state transitions and dynamic feedback mechanisms. The net package encapsulates these functionalities by providing interfaces that perform blocking or non-blocking operations without sacrificing the underlying protocol semantics. This approach ensures that the integrity of the data stream is maintained across disparate network conditions.

UDP Communications: Datagram-Oriented Interfacing

In contrast to TCP, the User Datagram Protocol (UDP) provides a connectionless communication paradigm that emphasizes reduced latency and minimal protocol overhead. UDP transmits discrete packets, known as datagrams, each forming an independent unit of data without any inherent guarantee of delivery or ordering. Formally, the operation of UDP can be represented as a relation $U \subseteq D \times D$, where D is the set of datagrams, and the relation does not enforce a bijective correspondence between transmitted and received packets. The net package addresses UDP's operational characteristics by offering a straightforward interface to create datagram sockets and to perform read/write operations that respect the message boundaries inherent in UDP communications. Although the protocol does not incorporate reliability mechanisms, its design is well suited to scenarios where timeliness supersedes assured delivery, such as real-time streaming and low-overhead signal messaging.

Integration with Concurrency Constructs and Error Handling

The interplay between network I/O operations and concurrent execution models is a critical consideration in the design of scalable applications. The net package integrates seamlessly with concurrency paradigms, allowing multiple network operations to be executed in parallel. This concurrency is achieved through the intrinsic properties of the Go runtime, which supports lightweight threads of execution that can be orchestrated to manage network events in a non-blocking fashion. Error detection in network communications is a multifaceted challenge, as it requires the identification and appropriate handling of both transient and persistent faults. Within the net package, error conditions are propagated via standard error types, facilitating the implementation of robust fault-tolerant designs. The abstraction layers ensure that error handling is proactive and that state transitions within network operations are conducted in a manner that preserves the consistency and integrity of the communication channel.

Go Code Snippet

```go
package main

import (
        "bufio"
        "fmt"
        "log"
        "net"
        "os"
        "sync"
        "time"
)

// Constants for server addresses.
const (
        tcpAddress = "localhost:9000"
        udpAddress = "localhost:9001"
)

// networkMap simulates the mapping function N: S -> T,
// where S represents a set of source inputs and T the corresponding
// ↪  target endpoints.
// For demonstration purposes, it appends a default port to a
// ↪  hostname.
func networkMap(source string) string {
        // Example: "localhost" -> "localhost:80"
        return source + ":80"
}

// startTCPServer sets up a TCP server that listens on tcpAddress,
// accepts one connection, processes it, and then shuts down.
// This is analogous to the stateful function C: I x S -> O
// ↪  described in the chapter,
// where I is the set of inputs received from the client, S is the
// ↪  connection state,
// and O is the resultant output byte stream.
func startTCPServer() error {
        listener, err := net.Listen("tcp", tcpAddress)
        if err != nil {
                return err
        }
        fmt.Println("TCP Server listening on", tcpAddress)

        // Accept a single connection for demonstration purposes.
        conn, err := listener.Accept()
        if err != nil {
                return err
        }
        fmt.Println("TCP Server accepted connection from",
        ↪  conn.RemoteAddr())
```

304

```go
        // Process the connection.
        if err := processTCPConnection(conn); err != nil {
                return err
        }

        conn.Close()
        listener.Close()
        return nil
}

// processTCPConnection handles the communication over a TCP
↪ connection.
// It reads a message from the client and echoes it back.
// This simulates the reliable, stream-oriented behavior of TCP.
func processTCPConnection(conn net.Conn) error {
        // In a TCP connection, we can think of the process as:
        // C: I x S -> O, where I is the input message and S is the
        ↪ connection state.
        reader := bufio.NewReader(conn)
        // Read input until a newline character (acts as a
        ↪ delimiter).
        msg, err := reader.ReadString('\n')
        if err != nil {
                return err
        }
        fmt.Printf("TCP Server received: %s", msg)

        // Echo the message back to the client.
        echoMsg := "TCP Server Echo: " + msg
        _, err = conn.Write([]byte(echoMsg))
        if err != nil {
                return err
        }
        return nil
}

// startTCPClient connects to the TCP server, sends a message, and
↪ waits for the echo.
func startTCPClient() error {
        conn, err := net.Dial("tcp", tcpAddress)
        if err != nil {
                return err
        }
        fmt.Println("TCP Client connected to", tcpAddress)

        message := "Hello from TCP client\n"
        // Send message to server.
        _, err = conn.Write([]byte(message))
        if err != nil {
                return err
        }

        // Read echo response from the server.
```

```go
        reader := bufio.NewReader(conn)
        reply, err := reader.ReadString('\n')
        if err != nil {
                return err
        }
        fmt.Printf("TCP Client received: %s", reply)
        conn.Close()
        return nil
}

// startUDPServer sets up a UDP server that listens on udpAddress,
// processes one incoming datagram, and sends an echo response.
// This reflects the datagram-oriented model of UDP, formally
// ↪ represented as:
// U  D × D, where each datagram in D is handled independently.
func startUDPServer() error {
        addr, err := net.ResolveUDPAddr("udp", udpAddress)
        if err != nil {
                return err
        }

        conn, err := net.ListenUDP("udp", addr)
        if err != nil {
                return err
        }
        fmt.Println("UDP Server listening on", udpAddress)

        // Allocate a buffer for the incoming datagram.
        buffer := make([]byte, 1024)
        n, clientAddr, err := conn.ReadFromUDP(buffer)
        if err != nil {
                return err
        }
        received := string(buffer[:n])
        fmt.Printf("UDP Server received from %v: %s\n", clientAddr,
        ↪ received)

        // Echo the received datagram back to the sender.
        echoMsg := "UDP Server Echo: " + received
        _, err = conn.WriteToUDP([]byte(echoMsg), clientAddr)
        if err != nil {
                return err
        }

        conn.Close()
        return nil
}

// startUDPClient sends a datagram message to the UDP server and
// ↪ prints out the reply.
func startUDPClient() error {
        conn, err := net.Dial("udp", udpAddress)
        if err != nil {
```

```go
                return err
        }
        fmt.Println("UDP Client connected to", udpAddress)

        message := "Hello from UDP client"
        _, err = conn.Write([]byte(message))
        if err != nil {
                return err
        }

        // Set a read deadline to avoid indefinite blocking.
        conn.SetReadDeadline(time.Now().Add(2 * time.Second))
        buffer := make([]byte, 1024)
        n, err := conn.Read(buffer)
        if err != nil {
                return err
        }
        reply := string(buffer[:n])
        fmt.Printf("UDP Client received: %s\n", reply)
        conn.Close()
        return nil
}

func main() {
        var wg sync.WaitGroup

        // Start the TCP server in a separate goroutine.
        wg.Add(1)
        go func() {
                defer wg.Done()
                if err := startTCPServer(); err != nil {
                        log.Printf("TCP Server error: %v", err)
                        os.Exit(1)
                }
        }()

        // Start the UDP server in a separate goroutine.
        wg.Add(1)
        go func() {
                defer wg.Done()
                if err := startUDPServer(); err != nil {
                        log.Printf("UDP Server error: %v", err)
                        os.Exit(1)
                }
        }()

        // Allow servers to start up, then initiate both TCP and UDP
        //   clients.
        wg.Add(1)
        go func() {
                defer wg.Done()
                time.Sleep(1 * time.Second)
                if err := startTCPClient(); err != nil {
```

307

```go
                log.Printf("TCP Client error: %v", err)
                os.Exit(1)
        }
        if err := startUDPClient(); err != nil {
                log.Printf("UDP Client error: %v", err)
                os.Exit(1)
        }
    }()

    wg.Wait()
}
```

Chapter 61

Network Requests: HTTP Client and Server

HTTP Protocol Architecture and Principles

The Hypertext Transfer Protocol (HTTP) constitutes a fundamental protocol within the realm of distributed computing, establishing a stateless request–response paradigm for client–server interactions. At its theoretical core, HTTP may be abstracted as a mapping $H : R \rightarrow S$, in which the set R corresponds to incoming request messages and the set S to the generated responses. Each HTTP message is composed of discrete components including a request or status line, header fields that encapsulate metadata, and an optional message body. The stateless design mandates that each interaction is self-contained, thereby necessitating that session persistence and state tracking be managed through ancillary mechanisms such as cookies or token-based authentication. This layered abstraction not only simplifies protocol implementation but also promotes interoperability across diverse network environments.

Implementation of HTTP Servers in the net/http Package

The construction of HTTP servers using the net/http package is underpinned by an architecture that abstracts the complexities of raw socket programming. The package orchestrates the conversion of low-level TCP connections into high-level HTTP requests by employing an integrated routine that accepts incoming connections, parses the byte streams, and decomposes them into structured request objects. Fundamental to this design is the modular approach to separating connection management, request parsing, and response synthesis. The processing of each request is allocated to a dedicated handler routine, thereby ensuring that protocol semantics are adhered to with precision and that concurrent connections are managed efficiently. The system enforces strict interface contracts between the layers, ensuring robustness in error propagation and the recovery of anomalous network conditions.

HTTP Client Implementation and Request Dispatching

In the context of outbound communications, the HTTP client within the net/http package is designed to seamlessly construct and dispatch requests to remote servers. Prior to transmission, an HTTP request is meticulously assembled to include an explicit method declaration, a target Uniform Resource Locator (URL), appropriate header fields, and an optional request body. The client is engineered to exploit connection pooling and automated keep-alive strategies, which serve to minimize overhead associated with TCP connection establishment. Concurrency is internal to the client design, as simultaneous requests can be managed in parallel without adversely impacting latency or throughput. Moreover, the client incorporates configurable timeouts and robust error-handling routines, all of which are essential to maintaining high-performance network communications and adherence to quality of service parameters.

Semantics of Handling Requests and Responses

A critical aspect of HTTP-based network communication lies in the rigorous handling of both requests and responses. On the server side, the conversion of a raw data stream into a structured request object involves parsing an array of elements such as the request line, HTTP method, Uniform Resource Identifier, protocol version, and associated headers. Subsequent processing necessitates the formulation of a response object that adheres to a structured format comprising a status code, a reason phrase, well-formed header collections, and an optional body payload. The client-side operation mirrors this process through the deconstruction of the response into its elemental parts, thereby facilitating precise interpretation of server feedback. Such meticulous parsing and serialization within the `net/http` framework guarantee that communication protocols are enforced with high fidelity, resulting in a reduction of ambiguities and promoting consistency across networked interactions.

Concurrency Considerations and Connection Management

The scalability and efficiency of HTTP servers and clients are closely linked to the effective management of concurrent network transactions. The `net/http` package leverages the concurrency primitives provided by the Go runtime, such as goroutines and channels, to allocate dedicated execution contexts for individual request-handling routines. This concurrent model enables the processing of multiple requests in parallel, thereby ensuring that high volumes of traffic can be accommodated with minimal performance degradation. Resource management is further optimized through strategies that dynamically allocate and recycle network connections based on real-time demands, while simultaneously enforcing timeouts and error isolation. The segregation of execution contexts minimizes the potential for shared state conflicts and contributes to a resilient, fault-tolerant operational paradigm.

Go Code Snippet

```go
package main

import (
        "fmt"
        "io/ioutil"
        "log"
        "net/http"
        "sync"
        "time"
)

// main starts the HTTP server and then demonstrates client
↪    requests.
func main() {
        // Register the default handler for all routes.
        http.HandleFunc("/", handler)

        // Start HTTP server in a new goroutine.
        go func() {
                log.Println("HTTP server is starting on :8080")
                if err := http.ListenAndServe(":8080", nil); err !=
↪    nil {
                        log.Fatalf("Server failed to start: %v",
↪    err)
                }
        }()

        // Allow some time for the server to be fully set up.
        time.Sleep(100 * time.Millisecond)

        // Prepare a set of concurrent client requests.
        var wg sync.WaitGroup
        requests := []struct {
                method string
                url    string
        }{
                {"GET", "http://localhost:8080/endpoint1"},
                {"GET", "http://localhost:8080/endpoint2"},
                {"POST", "http://localhost:8080/endpoint3"},
        }

        // Dispatch requests concurrently to demonstrate connection
↪    pooling,
        // concurrency, and the internal mapping of HTTP requests to
↪    responses.
        for _, reqInfo := range requests {
                wg.Add(1)
                go func(method, url string) {
                        defer wg.Done()
                        doRequest(method, url, nil)
```

```go
			}(reqInfo.method, reqInfo.url)
		}

		wg.Wait()
		log.Println("All client requests have been processed.")
}

// handler processes incoming HTTP requests.
// It utilizes the mapping function H which mimics an abstract
↪	equation H: R -> S,
// where R represents an HTTP request and S the corresponding
↪	response.
func handler(w http.ResponseWriter, r *http.Request) {
		// Process the request using the mapping function H.
		response := H(r)
		log.Printf("Handled %s request for %s", r.Method,
		↪	r.URL.Path)
		// Write the processed response back to the client.
		fmt.Fprintf(w, response)
}

// H is the mapping function representing the equation H: R -> S.
// It transforms an HTTP request (R) to a response string (S) by
↪	extracting
// and formatting key details such as the method and URL path.
func H(r *http.Request) string {
		return fmt.Sprintf("Processed %s request on %s", r.Method,
		↪	r.URL.Path)
}

// doRequest constructs and dispatches an HTTP request using the
↪	net/http package.
// It demonstrates client-side request configuration, header
↪	settings,
// connection pooling, and error handling.
func doRequest(method, url string, payload []byte) {
		client := &http.Client{
				Timeout: 5 * time.Second,
		}

		req, err := http.NewRequest(method, url, nil)
		if err != nil {
				log.Printf("Error creating %s request to %s: %v",
				↪	method, url, err)
				return
		}

		// Example header configuration.
		req.Header.Set("Content-Type", "application/json")

		// Dispatch the HTTP request.
		resp, err := client.Do(req)
		if err != nil {
```

313

```
                log.Printf("Error executing %s request to %s: %v",
                ↪ method, url, err)
                return
        }
        defer resp.Body.Close()

        // Read and log the response body.
        body, err := ioutil.ReadAll(resp.Body)
        if err != nil {
                log.Printf("Error reading response from %s: %v",
                ↪ url, err)
                return
        }

        log.Printf("Response from %s: %s", url, string(body))
}
```

Chapter 62

Context Package: Managing Request Lifecycles

Cancellation Semantics

The context package introduces a structured approach to managing cancellation across concurrent operations. Each context instance inherently possesses an associated cancellation signal that propagates through hierarchical derivations. In an abstract formulation, let $C : T \to \{0,1\}$ denote the cancellation function, where the value 1 indicates that a cancellation signal has been emitted for the given task. When a root context transitions to a canceled state, all contexts derived from it inherit this property, thereby enforcing a cascading termination protocol. This propagation mechanism is integral in scenarios where the cessation of one task necessitates the immediate interruption of all dependent computational routines. The rigor of this design is evident in its recursive nature, ensuring that no subordinate process continues execution in the presence of an overarching abort signal.

In concurrent systems that involve multiple interacting components, the timely detection and propagation of cancellation signals are essential. The cancellation protocol is encapsulated in a framework that periodically interrogates the state of a context via its internal signaling mechanism. When the condition $C(t) = 1$ is met for a given time instance t, the affected execution paths promptly transition to an interruption state. This formal model aids in minimizing computational overhead associated with abandoned operations and ensures the consistent deallocation of resources, thereby enhancing overall system resilience.

Deadline Enforcement and Temporal Constraints

The imposition of temporal boundaries on concurrent operations is facilitated through the specification of deadlines within a context. A derived context may incorporate a deadline parameter, denoted here as t_{deadline}, which serves as an upper bound for the permitted execution duration. By design, if the system time t satisfies the relation $t \geq t_{\text{deadline}}$, the context automatically transitions into a canceled state. This constraint mechanism not only prevents indefinite blocking but also assures that all operations complete within a finite temporal interval.

The enforcement of these deadlines is achieved via an internal monitoring process that compares the current time with t_{deadline}. Conceptually, the model can be viewed as mapping the continuous temporal domain onto a discrete decision function whereby the outcome switches from active computation to forced termination at the boundary. This approach imbues the system with determinism in the management of long-running or potentially stalled operations, thereby mitigating the risks associated with resource exhaustion in high-concurrency environments.

Contextual Storage of Request-Scoped Values

Beyond the management of cancellation and deadlines, the context package provides a facility for carrying request-scoped values throughout a chain of concurrent operations. This feature is underpinned by an immutable association mechanism that binds keys to specific data within the lifecycle of a context. Formally, let $V : K \to D$ represent the mapping function from a set of keys K to a domain D, where the values encapsulated by D are intended to persist for the duration of a particular request. The efficacy of this design lies in its immutability; once a value is associated with a key in a given context, it remains invariant across all derived contexts.

Such a structured approach to contextual storage ensures that critical metadata, be it for authentication, logging, or configuration purposes, is readily accessible to all concurrent tasks that share the same root context. By localizing these values within a confined scope, the system avoids the pitfalls of global state management and reduces the potential for unintended side effects. The encapsulation of request-specific data within a controlled context framework is, therefore, a pivotal aspect in designing scalable and maintainable concurrent architectures.

Go Code Snippet

```go
package main

import (
        "context"
        "fmt"
        "time"
)

// In our conceptual model, the cancellation function can be viewed
↪   as:
//   C: T -> {0, 1}
// where C(t) == 1 indicates a cancellation signal has been emitted
↪   at time t.
// Deadline enforcement is modeled via t_deadline such that if
↪   current time t >= t_deadline,
// the context is automatically cancelled. Additionally, we use the
↪   context to associate
// request-scoped values, represented as a mapping V: K -> D.

func main() {
        // Create a root context
        rootCtx := context.Background()

        // Derive a cancellable context from the root.
        // Cancellation semantics: when cancel() is invoked, then
        ↪   C(t) returns 1 for t >= t_cancel.
        ctx, cancel := context.WithCancel(rootCtx)
        defer cancel()

        // Define a deadline for the context: t_deadline = current
        ↪   time + 5 seconds.
        // If the current time t exceeds t_deadline, the context
        ↪   transitions to a cancelled state.
        deadlineCtx, deadlineCancel := context.WithDeadline(ctx,
        ↪   time.Now().Add(5*time.Second))
        defer deadlineCancel()
```

```go
    // Inject a request-scoped value into the context.
    // This mimics the mapping V: K -> D, with K as key type and
    ↪  D as the corresponding data.
    type key string
    const requestIDKey key = "requestID"
    valueCtx := context.WithValue(deadlineCtx, requestIDKey,
    ↪  "REQ-12345")

    // Launch a worker goroutine that simulates a long-running
    ↪  computation.
    go worker(valueCtx, "Worker-1")

    // Simulate concurrent activity in the main function.
    // Waiting for 3 seconds before optionally invoking manual
    ↪  cancellation.
    time.Sleep(3 * time.Second)
    // Uncomment the next line to manually cancel the context
    ↪  before the deadline.
    // cancel()

    // Block until the context is cancelled either by deadline
    ↪  or manual cancellation.
    <-valueCtx.Done()

    // Checking the error explains why the context was
    ↪  terminated.
    if err := valueCtx.Err(); err != nil {
            fmt.Println("Context finished with error:", err)
    }

    // Retrieve the request-scoped value.
    reqID := valueCtx.Value(requestIDKey)
    fmt.Println("Request ID retrieved from context:", reqID)

    fmt.Println("Main function completed.")
}

// worker simulates a task that periodically checks for cancellation
↪  signals.
// It also illustrates that when C(t)=1 (i.e., context is
↪  cancelled), the function exits immediately.
func worker(ctx context.Context, name string) {
        fmt.Printf("[%s] Started execution.\n", name)

        // Ticker simulates periodic computation at discrete time
        ↪  intervals.
        ticker := time.NewTicker(1 * time.Second)
        defer ticker.Stop()

        for {
                select {
```

318

```go
            // When the cancellation signal is detected via
            ↪  ctx.Done(), exit the loop.
            case <-ctx.Done():
                    // In our mathematical model, when C(t)==1,
                    ↪  we cease all computations.
                    fmt.Printf("[%s] Detected cancellation
                    ↪  signal. Terminating execution.\n", name)
                    return
            // Simulate computation at each tick.
            case t := <-ticker.C:
                    // If C(t)==0, continue processing.
                    fmt.Printf("[%s] Processing at time: %v\n",
                    ↪  name, t)
            }
    }
}
```

Chapter 63

Logging: Recording Runtime Events

Foundational Concepts in Logging

Logging in a contemporary Go runtime environment constitutes a systematic record of events that encapsulate operational states, error conditions, and noteworthy milestones during program execution. Intrinsic to this practice is the representation of a log entry as a structured tuple, typically denoted by $L = (t, s, m)$, where t signifies the precise timestamp at which the event is recorded, s represents the severity level assigned to the event, and m embodies the descriptive message that conveys contextual information. Such formalization is instrumental in enabling rigorous post hoc analysis and correlating distributed events across concurrent routines. Fundamentally, logging serves as a non-intrusive instrumentation mechanism that captures transient events and facilitates the subsequent reconstruction of execution traces for debugging and performance evaluation.

Standard Log Package in Go

The standard log package provided within the Go ecosystem establishes a minimalist framework that is both robust and efficient in its operation. This package is designed to output human-readable strings enriched with temporal markers and preformatted prefixes that delineate the context of each log entry. The inherent design of the package ensures that each output is imbued with a level of consistency, such that a log entry may be conceived as a text string whose formation adheres to predetermined formatting rules. In practice, these rules translate to the automatic inclusion of the current time, a customizable prefix, and the log message itself, all of which are orchestrated in a thread-safe manner. This design paradigm guarantees that, even in the presence of multiple concurrent executions, the sequential order of events determined by their associated t values remains both observable and coherent.

Architectural Considerations and Best Practices

The integration of logging within the architecture of a Go-based system necessitates careful deliberation regarding the placement, formatting, and subsequent processing of runtime events. A judicious logging strategy is characterized by the selective propagation of log messages based on defined severity thresholds and the precise categorization of log types in a hierarchical manner. One may model the hierarchy of severity levels as a partially ordered set, formally expressed as $(S, \leq)$, where S constitutes the finite set of defined log levels and the relation $\leq$ establishes their relative importance. In this manner, the logging framework supports the dynamic filtration of events, allowing only those entries whose severity surpasses a specified threshold to be recorded during phases of high operational demand.

Moreover, the architectural design of logging routines must account for the concurrent execution environment. The standard log package abstracts away the complexities associated with concurrent writes, mitigating risks of data interleaving and ensuring that the temporal integrity of log entries is maintained. Emphasis is placed on the deterministic ordering of events, a critical attribute when synthesizing logs across distributed components or replicating execution flows for forensic analyses. Additionally, the systematic aggregation of logging data facilitates the construction of a comprehensive timeline of system behavior, thereby enabling detailed performance metrics and diagnostic assessments to be conducted with mathematical precision.

Go Code Snippet

```go
package main

import (
        "log"
        "os"
        "sync"
        "time"
)

// Severity defines the level of a log entry. The hierarchy is
↪   defined as:
// DEBUG < INFO < WARN < ERROR, which can be modeled as a partially
↪   ordered set (S, ).
type Severity int

const (
        DEBUG Severity = iota
        INFO
        WARN
        ERROR
)

// String implements the Stringer interface for Severity.
func (s Severity) String() string {
        switch s {
        case DEBUG:
                return "DEBUG"
        case INFO:
                return "INFO"
        case WARN:
                return "WARN"
        case ERROR:
                return "ERROR"
        default:
                return "UNKNOWN"
        }
}

// LogEntry represents a structured log tuple, corresponding to the
↪   equation:
//   L = (t, s, m)
// where t is the timestamp of the event, s is the severity, and m
↪   is the descriptive message.
type LogEntry struct {
        Timestamp time.Time
        Severity  Severity
        Message   string
}
```

322

```go
// Logger is a custom concurrent logger that uses a buffered channel
↪   to sequence log entries.
// It guarantees that even with concurrent writes, the temporal
↪   ordering of log entries is maintained.
type Logger struct {
        severityThreshold Severity     // Only log entries with
        ↪   severity >= threshold will be recorded.
        logCh             chan LogEntry
        done              chan struct{}
        mu                sync.Mutex
}

// NewLogger initializes and returns a new Logger with the specified
↪   severity threshold.
func NewLogger(threshold Severity) *Logger {
        l := &Logger{
                severityThreshold: threshold,
                logCh:             make(chan LogEntry, 100), //
                ↪   Buffered channel for concurrency.
                done:              make(chan struct{}),
        }
        go l.processLogs()
        return l
}

// processLogs listens on the logCh and processes each log entry in
↪   a thread-safe manner.
// It simulates the deterministic ordering of log events even under
↪   concurrent operations.
func (l *Logger) processLogs() {
        // Create a standard logger that includes timestamps in its
        ↪   output.
        stdLogger := log.New(os.Stdout, "", log.LstdFlags)
        for entry := range l.logCh {
                // Format the log string to include timestamp,
                ↪   severity, and message.
                // This corresponds to constructing a formatted
                ↪   tuple (t, s, m).
                stdLogger.Printf("[%s] %-5s - %s",
                ↪   entry.Timestamp.Format(time.RFC3339Nano),
                ↪   entry.Severity, entry.Message)
        }
        close(l.done)
}

// Log adds a new log entry to the channel if its severity meets the
↪   defined threshold.
func (l *Logger) Log(sev Severity, message string) {
        // Dynamic filtration: only log if severity is greater than
        ↪   or equal to the threshold.
        if sev < l.severityThreshold {
                return
        }
```

323

```go
        entry := LogEntry{
                Timestamp: time.Now(),
                Severity:  sev,
                Message:   message,
        }
        l.logCh <- entry
}

// Close gracefully shuts down the logger by closing the log channel
↪   and waiting for processing to finish.
func (l *Logger) Close() {
        close(l.logCh)
        <-l.done
}

// simulateConcurrentLogging demonstrates the logging of multiple
↪   entries concurrently,
// highlighting the use of goroutines and ensuring that the
↪   underlying logger maintains order.
func simulateConcurrentLogging(logger *Logger) {
        var wg sync.WaitGroup
        // Sample log messages with varying severity.
        messages := []struct {
                severity Severity
                message  string
        }{
                {INFO, "Starting application."},
                {DEBUG, "Initializing modules."},
                {WARN, "Deprecated API usage detected."},
                {ERROR, "Failed to load configuration file."},
                {INFO, "Application terminated gracefully."},
        }

        for i := 0; i < len(messages); i++ {
                wg.Add(1)
                go func(i int) {
                        defer wg.Done()
                        // Simulate work delay.
                        time.Sleep(time.Millisecond *
                        ↪   time.Duration(100*i))
                        logger.Log(messages[i].severity,
                        ↪   messages[i].message)
                }(i)
        }
        wg.Wait()
}

func main() {
        // Initialize the logger with a threshold. Setting the
        ↪   threshold to DEBUG logs all messages.
        logger := NewLogger(DEBUG)

        // Log some concurrent events.
```

324

```
        simulateConcurrentLogging(logger)

        // Additional log entry demonstrating structured logging
        ↪  format.
        logger.Log(INFO, "Final log entry before shutdown.")

        // Close the logger to ensure all log entries are processed.
        logger.Close()
}
```

Chapter 64

Memory Management: Garbage Collection Overview

Foundations of Automatic Memory Management

Modern runtime environments employ automatic memory management to obviate the need for manual intervention in memory allocation and reclamation. In the Go runtime, memory management is predicated on the principle of reachability. Allocated objects reside on the heap, and an object is considered live if there exists at least one reference path from the set of root pointers. Formally, consider the directed graph $G = (V, E)$ where each vertex $v \in V$ represents a memory object and each edge in E denotes a pointer reference between objects. An object is preserved if there exists a path from some root $r \in R$ to v. This approach abstracts the reclamation process as the identification and recovery of objects that are unreachable from R, thereby ensuring that live objects are maintained and extraneous memory is reclaimed.

Automatic memory management in Go dispenses with explicit deallocation calls, relying instead on an intrinsic garbage collection mechanism. This automation minimizes common pitfalls such as memory leaks and dangling pointers. The system continuously monitors heap allocations and deallocates memory by traversing the object graph, thereby easing the cognitive burden on programmers and enhancing the overall reliability of large-scale applications.

Concurrent Mark-Sweep Collection Mechanism

The garbage collection strategy implemented in Go is fundamentally based on a concurrent mark-sweep algorithm that is designed to minimize pause durations and integrate efficiently with parallel execution contexts. During the marking phase, the collector identifies all reachable objects by initiating a graph traversal from the set of root pointers. As the traversal progresses, each object is assigned a color in the tri-color abstraction: white for unvisited objects, grey for those discovered but not yet fully processed, and black for objects that have been completely scanned. This process can be characterized by maintaining the invariant that if an object is reachable, it eventually transitions from white to grey and finally to black. Once the marking phase completes, the sweeping phase commences. In this phase, objects that remain white—that is, those that are unreachable from any root—are reclaimed and their memory is returned to the system.

The concurrent nature of the algorithm allows portions of the marking and sweeping phases to occur simultaneously with the execution of application threads. Although brief stop-the-world events are necessary to ensure the consistency of the heap at specific synchronization points, these pauses are minimized through careful scheduling and interleaving of garbage collection tasks. Parameters such as the cycle time T_{gc} and dynamic thresholds for object allocation are tuned to balance workload demands against the overhead introduced by the garbage collection process. The assurance that no live data is inadvertently reclaimed is formally encapsulated by the safety invariant I_{gc}, which stipulates that for every allocated object o, if o is reachable then o must remain intact following a garbage collection cycle.

Performance Implications and System Considerations

The automatic reclamation of memory via garbage collection has a significant impact on overall system performance. On one hand, it eliminates the risks associated with manual memory management, thereby enhancing system robustness and reducing the scope for programming errors. On the other hand, the continuous monitoring of allocations and the periodic execution of graph traversals introduce computational overhead that is directly related to the volume of live data and the frequency of allocation events. The trade-off is characterized by the parameter T_{gc}, which is a function of the allocation rate and the proportion of long-lived objects residing in the heap.

Optimization strategies within the Go runtime endeavor to minimize the impact of garbage collection on application throughput and latency. Techniques such as backfilling reclaimed memory into free lists and region-based reclamation are applied to counteract fragmentation and maintain a compact memory footprint. The system's adaptive tuning mechanisms adjust the frequency and duration of garbage collection cycles dynamically, based on real-time metrics of heap utilization and allocation patterns. Such adjustments ensure that the automatic memory management system operates in a homeostatic manner, balancing the competing demands of resource utilization and application responsiveness without direct programmer intervention.

This comprehensive approach to memory management, underpinned by robust theoretical models and practical optimizations, exemplifies the interplay between algorithmic rigor and system-level efficiency in the design of modern programming language runtimes.

Go Code Snippet

```
package main

import (
        "fmt"
        "sync"
        "time"
)
```

328

```go
// Tri-color constants for GC simulation
const (
        White = iota // Unvisited
        Grey         // Discovered but not fully processed
        Black        // Fully scanned
)

// Node represents a memory object (heap object).
// 'id' is a unique identifier, 'children' simulates pointers from
↪    this object to others,
// and 'color' holds the current state in the tri-color marking
↪    abstraction.
type Node struct {
        id       int
        children []*Node
        color    int
}

// markNode is a recursive function that simulates the marking phase
// of the concurrent mark-sweep garbage collection algorithm.
// When a node is processed, it is marked as Black. For each child,
// if it has not been visited (is White), it is set to Grey and
↪    processed concurrently.
func markNode(node *Node, wg *sync.WaitGroup) {
        defer wg.Done()

        // Process only if the node is marked Grey (ready to be
        ↪    scanned)
        if node.color != Grey {
                return
        }

        // Mark the current node as Black to indicate it has been
        ↪    fully scanned.
        fmt.Printf("Marking node %d as Black\n", node.id)
        node.color = Black

        // Process each child node concurrently.
        for _, child := range node.children {
                if child.color == White {
                        child.color = Grey
                        wg.Add(1)
                        go markNode(child, wg)
                }
        }
}

// concurrentMark initiates the concurrent marking phase starting
↪    from the root.
// It uses a WaitGroup to ensure that all goroutines complete before
↪    proceeding.
func concurrentMark(root *Node) {
        var wg sync.WaitGroup
```

329

```go
        // Mark the root as Grey to begin the process.
        root.color = Grey
        wg.Add(1)
        go markNode(root, &wg)
        wg.Wait()
}

// sweep simulates the sweeping phase.
// It iterates over all allocated objects and reclaims those that
// ↪   remain White (unreachable).
// Reachable objects (Black) are preserved and their color is reset
// ↪   to White for future GC cycles.
func sweep(allocated []*Node) []*Node {
        liveObjects := make([]*Node, 0)
        for _, obj := range allocated {
                if obj.color == Black {
                        // Reset for next cycle and preserve the
                        // ↪   object.
                        obj.color = White
                        liveObjects = append(liveObjects, obj)
                } else {
                        // The object is unreachable and is
                        // ↪   reclaimed.
                        fmt.Printf("Sweeping unreachable node:
                        // ↪   %d\n", obj.id)
                }
        }
        return liveObjects
}

func main() {
        // Simulate a heap by creating nodes (memory objects)
        n1 := &Node{id: 1}
        n2 := &Node{id: 2}
        n3 := &Node{id: 3}
        n4 := &Node{id: 4}
        n5 := &Node{id: 5} // n5 will remain unreachable

        // Establish pointer relationships:
        // n1 is the root and points to n2 and n3.
        // n2 further points to n4.
        n1.children = []*Node{n2, n3}
        n2.children = []*Node{n4}
        // n3 and n4 have no children.
        // n5 is not linked and simulates an object that is not
        // ↪   reachable.

        // All allocated objects on our simulated heap.
        allocated := []*Node{n1, n2, n3, n4, n5}

        // Display initial state.
        fmt.Println("Before Garbage Collection:")
        for _, obj := range allocated {
```

330

```go
        fmt.Printf("Node %d, initial color: White\n",
        ↪    obj.id)
}

// Simulate a garbage collection cycle.
gcStart := time.Now()

fmt.Println("\nStarting concurrent mark phase...")
concurrentMark(n1)
fmt.Println("Mark phase completed.")

fmt.Println("\nStarting sweep phase...")
allocated = sweep(allocated)
gcDuration := time.Since(gcStart)

// Display post-GC live objects.
fmt.Println("\nAfter Garbage Collection, reachable nodes:")
for _, obj := range allocated {
        fmt.Printf("Node %d remains in memory.\n", obj.id)
}
fmt.Printf("\nGC cycle completed in %v\n", gcDuration)

// Safety Invariant Check (I_gc): Every reachable object
↪    must be preserved.
// In our simulation, the reachable nodes are n1, n2, n3,
↪    and n4.
// If the invariant is violated, it means some reachable
↪    node was erroneously reclaimed.
fmt.Println("\nPerforming safety invariant check...")
if len(allocated) != 4 {
        fmt.Println("Invariant I_gc violated: Some reachable
        ↪    objects were not preserved!")
} else {
        fmt.Println("Invariant I_gc validated: All reachable
        ↪    objects are intact.")
}
}
```

Chapter 65

Custom Data Structures: Stacks and Queues

Abstract Data Types and Theoretical Underpinnings

Stacks and queues are canonical abstract data types that underpin a wealth of algorithmic frameworks. A stack is defined through its two primary operations: insertion at one end, commonly referred to as "push," and removal from the same end, or "pop," thereby adhering to Last-In-First-Out (LIFO) semantics. In contrast, a queue operates under a First-In-First-Out (FIFO) discipline, where elements are enqueued at the rear and dequeued from the front. Fundamental to both structures is the requirement that operations be efficient, ideally requiring constant time $O(1)$ on average for insertion and deletion, while accommodating variability in operation sequences as the size of the data structure, denoted by n, changes dynamically.

The translation from abstract specification to practical implementation mandates rigorous attention to memory organization and operational efficiency. In particular, the examination of fixed-size versus dynamically allocated storage has implications for both time complexity and memory overhead. The discourse here encapsulates a formal treatment of these concepts, establishing a bridge between theoretical performance bounds and the practical considerations intrinsic to the Go programming language.

Stacks: Conceptual Framework and Implementation Considerations

In Go, the implementation of a stack can be realized via either arrays or slices. Arrays in Go represent fixed-size, contiguous memory allocations that require the programmer to determine the maximum capacity in advance. This fixed allocation ensures that elements reside in contiguous memory locations, a property that can be beneficial for cache performance. However, the inherent limitation of arrays is their inflexibility; a capacity defined as K imposes a hard ceiling on the number of elements, necessitating alternative mechanisms if the stack exceeds its predetermined bounds.

Slices, conversely, are dynamic constructs that encapsulate a pointer to an underlying array, an explicit length, and a capacity parameter. The dynamic nature of slices aligns naturally with the operational requirements of a stack, where push and pop operations are expected to occur frequently. When elements are appended to a slice and the current capacity is exceeded, Go automatically reallocates memory—typically following geometric growth patterns—to ensure that the amortized time complexity of operations remains $O(1)$. The interplay between fixed arrays and dynamically resizing slices illustrates a rich trade-off between predictability of resource usage and operational flexibility. This paradigm exemplifies how abstract data type design can be reconciled with concrete memory management strategies in modern programming languages.

Queues: Conceptual Framework and Implementation Considerations

Queues, adhering to FIFO behavior, present an alternative set of challenges that are elegantly addressed in Go by leveraging arrays and slices. A queue must efficiently manage additions at one end and removals from the opposite end. When implementing a queue with a fixed-size array, a circular buffer is frequently employed to optimize space utilization. In this configuration, indices representing the front and rear of the queue are maintained, allowing for wraparound once the end of the array is reached. This strategy

333

guarantees that enqueue and dequeue operations maintain a constant time complexity of $O(1)$, without necessitating costly data shifts.

When implementing queues with slices, the dynamic resizing feature of slices offers significant flexibility; however, it introduces additional considerations regarding memory overhead and operational efficiency. Specifically, removing an element from the front of a slice may result in the retention of unused space if the underlying array is not re-sliced appropriately. Consequently, careful management of the slice's start index and potential reallocation is required to ensure that the effective complexity remains within acceptable bounds. The comparative analysis of fixed arrays versus dynamic slices in queue implementations underscores the importance of selecting an underlying data structure that aligns with the targeted performance characteristics and resource constraints.

Methodological Considerations and Complexity Analysis

The computation of time complexity for stack and queue operations reveals that the majority of operations—push, pop, enqueue, and dequeue—can be performed in amortized constant time, $O(1)$, under ideal conditions. This conclusion holds provided that the underlying data structure, whether an array or a slice, is managed with an eye toward minimizing expensive reallocations. In instances where reallocation is necessary, the worst-case time complexity may transiently escalate to $O(n)$; however, with appropriate growth factor strategies, such as a doubling mechanism, the amortized cost per operation remains tightly bounded.

Furthermore, the choice of data structure impacts both spatial locality and cache behavior. Arrays, by virtue of their contiguous memory allocation, exhibit favorable cache performance. In contrast, slices, though imposing minimal additional overhead, require meticulous consideration of the reallocation process and the preservation of contiguous memory regions during expansion. Consequently, the decision between employing arrays or slices is not solely an exercise in selecting the appropriate abstraction, but also one of aligning the implementation with broader system-level goals, such as memory efficiency and throughput. The rigorous analysis of these trade-offs is essential for developing high-performance, custom data structures that are both theoretically sound and practically effective in real-world applications.

Go Code Snippet

```go
package main

import (
        "errors"
        "fmt"
)

// Stack implements a Last-In-First-Out (LIFO) data structure using
↪    a slice.
// The push operation appends an element to the slice,
// while the pop operation removes the last element.
// The amortized time complexity for both push and pop is O(1),
// despite occasional O(n) cost during slice reallocation.
type Stack struct {
        data []int
}

// Push adds an element to the top of the stack.
func (s *Stack) Push(val int) {
        // The append function may trigger reallocation if capacity
        ↪    is exceeded.
        s.data = append(s.data, val)
}

// Pop removes and returns the element from the top of the stack.
// Returns an error if the stack is empty.
func (s *Stack) Pop() (int, error) {
        if len(s.data) == 0 {
                return 0, errors.New("stack is empty")
        }
        // Retrieve the last element.
        val := s.data[len(s.data)-1]
        // Slice off the last element.
        s.data = s.data[:len(s.data)-1]
        return val, nil
}

// IsEmpty returns true if the stack is empty.
func (s *Stack) IsEmpty() bool {
        return len(s.data) == 0
}

// Queue implements a First-In-First-Out (FIFO) data structure using
↪    a circular buffer.
// It uses a slice to hold data, with indices to track the front and
↪    rear.
```

```go
// Enqueue and Dequeue operations are designed to run in amortized
↪   O(1) time.
type Queue struct {
        data   []int  // Underlying slice to store queue elements.
        front  int    // Index of the front element.
        rear   int    // Index at which the next element will be
        ↪   inserted.
        size   int    // Current number of elements in the queue.
}


// Enqueue adds an element to the rear of the queue.
// When the underlying slice is full, the capacity is doubled.
// This reallocation follows the geometric growth pattern that
↪   guarantees
// an amortized O(1) cost per operation.
func (q *Queue) Enqueue(val int) {
        // Check if resizing is required.
        if q.size == len(q.data) {
                newCapacity := 2 * len(q.data)
                if newCapacity == 0 {
                        newCapacity = 1
                }
                newData := make([]int, newCapacity)
                // Copy elements to the new slice preserving their
                ↪   order.
                for i := 0; i < q.size; i++ {
                        newData[i] = q.data[(q.front+i)%len(q.data)]
                }
                q.data = newData
                q.front = 0
                q.rear = q.size
        }
        q.data[q.rear] = val
        q.rear = (q.rear + 1) % len(q.data)
        q.size++
}


// Dequeue removes and returns the front element of the queue.
// Utilizes modular arithmetic to manage the circular buffer.
// Returns an error if the queue is empty.
func (q *Queue) Dequeue() (int, error) {
        if q.size == 0 {
                return 0, errors.New("queue is empty")
        }
        val := q.data[q.front]
        q.front = (q.front + 1) % len(q.data)
        q.size--
        return val, nil
}


// IsEmpty returns true if the queue has no elements.
func (q *Queue) IsEmpty() bool {
        return q.size == 0
```

```go
}

func main() {
    // Demonstrate Stack operations.
    fmt.Println("=== Stack Demonstration ===")
    stack := &Stack{}
    // Push elements 1 through 5.
    for i := 1; i <= 5; i++ {
        fmt.Printf("Pushing %d onto the stack\n", i)
        stack.Push(i)
    }
    // Pop all elements, demonstrating LIFO behavior.
    for !stack.IsEmpty() {
        val, err := stack.Pop()
        if err == nil {
            fmt.Printf("Popped: %d\n", val)
        } else {
            fmt.Println(err)
        }
    }

    // Demonstrate Queue operations.
    fmt.Println("\n=== Queue Demonstration ===")
    queue := &Queue{}
    // Enqueue elements 1 through 5.
    for i := 1; i <= 5; i++ {
        fmt.Printf("Enqueuing %d into the queue\n", i)
        queue.Enqueue(i)
    }
    // Dequeue all elements, demonstrating FIFO behavior.
    for !queue.IsEmpty() {
        val, err := queue.Dequeue()
        if err == nil {
            fmt.Printf("Dequeued: %d\n", val)
        } else {
            fmt.Println(err)
        }
    }

    // ------------------------------------------------
    // Conceptual Algorithm and Equation Commentary:
    //
    // For Stack operations:
    //   - Push: The operation is defined as
    //         s.data = append(s.data, x)
    //     which, in the worst-case when reallocation occurs,
    //     takes O(n) time.
    //     However, using geometric growth (e.g., doubling
    //     capacity), the amortized
    //     time per push remains O(1).
    //
    //   - Pop: Removing the last element via slicing:
    //         s.data = s.data[:len(s.data)-1]
```

337

```
//      also executes in O(1) time.
//
// For Queue operations implemented with a circular buffer:
//    - Enqueue: Involves inserting an element at the rear
↪   index and updating the
//      index modulo the current capacity. When resizing is
↪   necessary, elements are
//      copied with a loop such that:
//          for i = 0 to size-1: newData[i] = data[(front+i)
↪   mod capacity]
//      The resizing has worst-case O(n) complexity, but
↪   amortized analysis yields O(1)
//      per operation.
//
//    - Dequeue: Removes the element at the front index and
↪   updates it similarly:
//          front = (front + 1) mod capacity
//      This also runs in O(1) time.
//
// These implementations encapsulate the theoretical
↪   performance bounds and
// practical considerations discussed in the chapter,
↪   connecting abstract data types
// to real-world application in Go.
// ----------------------------------------------
}
```

Chapter 66

Concurrency Patterns: Worker Pools and Pipeline

Conceptual Framework

Concurrency patterns in modern software engineering provide a formal mechanism for decomposing computational problems into concurrently executable units. This approach facilitates efficient resource management by leveraging the capabilities inherent in the Go runtime environment. In the study of concurrent systems, abstraction is achieved by partitioning tasks into discrete units that can be scheduled independently, with the overall system performance often characterized by amortized complexities such as $O(1)$ for routine operations and, in exceptional cases, up to $O(n)$ under peak load circumstances. The patterns discussed herein serve as fundamental constructs in the orchestration of parallel task execution, ensuring that processing is both scalable and predictably efficient under variable demand.

Worker Pools: Architectural Design and Mechanisms

The worker pool pattern is predicated upon the creation of a fixed set of worker entities that collectively execute incoming tasks. Each worker, instantiated as a lightweight concurrent unit, extracts tasks from a shared job queue, thereby decoupling task submission from task execution. The mathematical underpinnings of this design rest on queuing theory, where system stability is achieved if the average service rate meets or exceeds the average arrival rate. By maintaining a pool with a predetermined number of workers, the architecture achieves significant reductions in scheduling overhead and resource contention. The design philosophy emphasizes resource reutilization and minimizes context switching, with the Go scheduler efficiently managing underlying goroutines. In effect, the worker pool pattern ensures that the dispatching of tasks adheres to predictable performance bounds, thereby facilitating high-throughput concurrent processing even in environments characterized by intensive computational demands.

Pipeline Architectures: Data Flow and Stage Chaining

Pipeline architectures offer a sequential approach to data processing, wherein the output of one stage becomes the input for the next through well-defined channels. Each stage within a pipeline is responsible for a distinct transformation or filtering operation, collectively contributing to the resolution of a complex computational task. The design of a pipeline necessitates meticulous attention to inter-stage communication, as the overall system performance is contingent upon the efficient handoff of data between stages. The theoretical framework supporting pipelines involves computations of propagation delays and the aggregation of stage-specific processing times, with overall latency represented as the sum of individual stage delays. By structuring complex operations into a series of homogenous processing units, pipelines facilitate modularity and scalable parallelism. The orchestration of channels, combined with synchronization mechanisms, ensures that the data flow remains continuous and that backpressure is managed systematically, thereby optimizing throughput and minimizing resource underutilization.

Complexity and Performance Considerations

The performance analysis of both worker pools and pipeline architectures reveals a nuanced landscape of computational complexities and resource allocation efficiencies. In the context of worker pools, each task dispatch operation attains an amortized time complexity of $O(1)$ under optimal conditions, although transient spikes in operational complexity may occur during periods of extensive task redistribution. Similarly, pipeline architectures must account for inter-stage communication delays and synchronization overhead, which collectively influence the effective latency of the entire system. The strategic partitioning of operations across multiple stages is critical to mitigating bottlenecks and ensuring that the aggregate performance aligns with theoretical predictions. Advanced concurrency primitives, such as channels for inter-process communication and synchronization constructs for critical section management, underpin these architectures, providing robust performance even under high-load scenarios. Detailed analysis of these patterns reinforces the importance of aligning algorithmic strategies with system-level constraints, thereby ensuring that the architectural design adheres to both theoretical and practical performance metrics.

Go Code Snippet

```go
package main

import (
        "fmt"
        "sync"
        "time"
)

// Job represents a task to be processed by the worker pool.
// It includes an ID and an integer Value that might be mapped to a
↪    formula.
// For instance, the processing function applies a simple operation:
//    Processed = (Value * 2) + workerID
// which, under optimal conditions, runs in O(1) time.
type Job struct {
        ID    int
        Value int
}
```

```go
// Result holds the outcome of processing a Job.
// It contains the original value and the result after applying the
//     transformation.
type Result struct {
        JobID     int
        Original  int
        Processed int
}


// worker is a function that represents a worker in the pool.
// Each worker continuously reads from the jobs channel, processes
//     the job,
// and sends the result into the results channel.
// The processing here simulates a mathematical transformation with
//     constant time complexity.
func worker(workerID int, jobs <-chan Job, results chan<- Result, wg
//     *sync.WaitGroup) {
        defer wg.Done()
        for job := range jobs {
                // Simulated processing based on an arithmetic
                //     formula.
                processed := (job.Value * 2) + workerID
                // Simulate computational delay to emulate realistic
                //     workload.
                time.Sleep(100 * time.Millisecond)
                results <- Result{
                        JobID:     job.ID,
                        Original:  job.Value,
                        Processed: processed,
                }
        }
}

// pipelineStage represents a single stage in a pipeline
//     architecture.
// It reads integer values from its input channel, transforms them
//     by adding a stage-specific constant,
// and then sends the transformed values to the output channel.
// This transformation is analogous to an algebraic function f(x) =
//     x + constant.
func pipelineStage(in <-chan int, out chan<- int, stageID int,
//     stageWG *sync.WaitGroup) {
        defer stageWG.Done()
        for val := range in {
                // Apply transformation: f(x) = x + stageID
                transformed := val + stageID
                // Forward the transformed value to the next stage.
                out <- transformed
        }
        // Close the output channel once all data has been
        //     processed.
        close(out)
```

342

```
}

func main() {
        // ==========================
        // Worker Pool Demonstration
        // ==========================
        numWorkers := 4
        numJobs := 10

        // Create buffered channels for jobs and results.
        jobs := make(chan Job, numJobs)
        results := make(chan Result, numJobs)
        var poolWG sync.WaitGroup

        // Launch worker goroutines forming the worker pool.
        for i := 1; i <= numWorkers; i++ {
                poolWG.Add(1)
                go worker(i, jobs, results, &poolWG)
        }

        // Submit jobs to the job queue.
        // Here, each job's Value is computed as a multiple of its
        ↪   job ID, simulating input for transformation.
        for j := 1; j <= numJobs; j++ {
                jobs <- Job{
                        ID:    j,
                        Value: j * 3, // Example payload, could
                        ↪   reflect a function f(j) = 3*j
                }
        }
        // Close the jobs channel after dispatching all tasks.
        close(jobs)

        // Wait for workers to finish processing in a separate
        ↪   routine.
        go func() {
                poolWG.Wait()
                close(results)
        }()

        // Collect and display results from the worker pool.
        fmt.Println("Worker Pool Results:")
        for res := range results {
                fmt.Printf("Job ID: %d, Original: %d, Processed:
                ↪   %d\n", res.JobID, res.Original, res.Processed)
        }

        // ==========================
        // Pipeline Architecture Demo
        // ==========================
        // The pipeline is composed of sequential stages where each
        ↪   stage applies a transformation.
```

```go
// Total latency in a pipeline is theoretically the sum of
↪   the delays of individual stages:
//    TotalDelay = Delay(Stage1) + Delay(Stage2) + ...
// providing a modular way to analyze performance.

// Stage 0: Generator that produces a stream of integers.
gen := make(chan int)
go func() {
        for i := 1; i <= 5; i++ {
                gen <- i
                // Simulate a short delay between emissions.
                time.Sleep(50 * time.Millisecond)
        }
        close(gen)
}()

// Create channels for each pipeline stage.
stage1 := make(chan int)
stage2 := make(chan int)
var stageWG sync.WaitGroup

// Launch pipeline stages:
// Stage 1: Add 10 to each input integer.
// Stage 2: Add 20 to the result of Stage 1.
stageWG.Add(2)
go pipelineStage(gen, stage1, 10, &stageWG)
go pipelineStage(stage1, stage2, 20, &stageWG)

// Output final results from the last stage of the pipeline.
fmt.Println("Pipeline Results:")
for v := range stage2 {
        // Each output follows the transformation: v =
        ↪   original + 10 + 20.
        fmt.Printf("Final Value: %d\n", v)
}

// Ensure all pipeline stages have completed.
stageWG.Wait()

// Summary:
// The above code illustrates two core concurrency patterns.
// 1. The Worker Pool Pattern:
//    - Achieves constant time task dispatching (O(1)) under
↪   optimal conditions.
//    - Effectively balances workload across a fixed pool of
↪   goroutines.
// 2. The Pipeline Pattern:
//    - Enables modular data processing by chaining
↪   transformation stages.
//    - Total processing latency is the sum of individual
↪   stage delays,
//      adhering to the theoretical model of stage-wise
↪   propagation delays.
```

344

}